OECD
Economic Surveys

Netherlands

2008

OECD

ORGANISATION FOR ECONOMIC CO-OPERATION AND DEVELOPMENT

The OECD is a unique forum where the governments of 30 democracies work together to address the economic, social and environmental challenges of globalisation. The OECD is also at the forefront of efforts to understand and to help governments respond to new developments and concerns, such as corporate governance, the information economy and the challenges of an ageing population. The Organisation provides a setting where governments can compare policy experiences, seek answers to common problems, identify good practice and work to co-ordinate domestic and international policies.

The OECD member countries are: Australia, Austria, Belgium, Canada, the Czech Republic, Denmark, Finland, France, Germany, Greece, Hungary, Iceland, Ireland, Italy, Japan, Korea, Luxembourg, Mexico, the Netherlands, New Zealand, Norway, Poland, Portugal, the Slovak Republic, Spain, Sweden, Switzerland, Turkey, the United Kingdom and the United States. The Commission of the European Communities takes part in the work of the OECD.

OECD Publishing disseminates widely the results of the Organisation's statistics gathering and research on economic, social and environmental issues, as well as the conventions, guidelines and standards agreed by its members.

Also available in French

Table of contents

Figures

This Survey is published on the responsibility of the Economic and Development Review Committee of the OECD, which is charged with the examination of the economic situation of member countries.

The economic situation and policies of the Netherlands were reviewed by the Committee on 6 November 2007. The draft report was then revised in the light of the discussions and given final approval as the agreed report of the whole Committee on 21 November 2007.

The Secretariat's draft report was prepared for the Committee by Jens Høj, Ekkehard Ernst and Jasper Kieft under the supervision of Patrick Lenain.

The previous Survey of the Netherlands was issued in December 2005.

This book has...

StatLinks

A service that delivers Excel® files from the printed page!

Look for the *StatLinks* at the bottom right-hand corner of the tables or graphs in this book. To download the matching Excel® spreadsheet, just type the link into your Internet browser, starting with the ***http://dx.doi.org*** prefix.
If you're reading the PDF e-book edition, and your PC is connected to the Internet, simply click on the link. You'll find *StatLinks* appearing in more OECD books.

BASIC STATISTICS OF THE NETHERLANDS, 2006

THE LAND

Area (1 000 km^2)	42	Major cities (thousand inhabitants), 2006	
Agricultural area (1 000 km^2)	23	Amsterdam	741
Woodland	4	Rotterdam	583
		The Hague	476

THE PEOPLE

Population (thousands)	16 358	Employment (thousands, full-time equivalents):	7 200
Inhabitants per km^2	485	Agriculture	3%
Net natural increase (thousands)	24	Industry and construction	21%
		Other	76%

PRODUCTION

Gross domestic product (billion euro)	534	Gross fixed investment	
Gross domestic product per head	33	Per cent of GDP	19.7
		Per head (euro)	6 436

THE PUBLIC SECTOR

Per cent of GDP:		Composition of Parliament	
Public consumption	25.4	(number of seats):	
Current receipts	46.3	Christian democratic appeal	41
Current disbursements	45.3	Labour Party (PvdA)	32
		Socialist Party	26
		Popular Party for freedom and democracy	22
		Others	29
		Total	150
		Last election: February 2007	

FOREIGN TRADE

Exports of goods and services (per cent of GDP)	73.2	Imports of goods and services (per cent of GDP)	65.8

THE CURRENCY

Monetary unit: Euro		
	Currency units of euro per USD, average of daily figures:	
	Year 2007	1.37
	December 2007	1.46

Executive Summary

After a long stagnation during the first half of the decade, the Dutch economy has made a successful comeback. Growth has strengthened, unemployment has fallen back and the fiscal position has been brought into balance. Though the current recovery is partly cyclical, it is also built on a robust medium-term performance, which has helped to maintain living standards among the highest in the OECD.

Increases in labour utilisation have been the main source of growth, but the economy is now facing labour shortages, related to the greying of the population and the continued weak labour market-participation of several groups. In addition, part-time work remains widespread and net migration flows have turned negative in recent years. If the policy setting remains unchanged, medium-term growth is likely to be impaired by insufficient labour resources and demographic ageing will be a burden for the public finances. While the previous Economic Survey focused on raising productivity growth, the present one focuses on the following challenges:

- **The ageing of population and its effects on fiscal sustainability.** *Public spending on health care and pensions is projected to increase sharply in the next four decades, despite second pillar pension funds being well funded. These trends should improve thereafter, but not by enough to avoid a spiral of debt accumulation. Policy solutions to restore sustainability should focus on containing ageing-related costs, including a reform of the state pension scheme and later retirement. Additional measures should include an expansion of the funding base through increased labour participation and a certain degree of prefunding.*

- **The need to increase labour-market participation further and lengthen working time.** *Dutch participation rates are high, but there are a number of groups who remain less active on the labour market, notably lone parents, low-skilled women, partially disabled persons and inactive migrants. For those people, reforms in the tax-and-benefit system are needed and activation strategies should be enhanced. Their job-search activities would also be facilitated by an easing of employment protection legislation, which currently reduces the fluidity of the labour market. For parents with young children, the provision of pre-school child care continues to be lacking despite recent progress, contributing to a high incidence of part-time work. Recent reforms requiring primary schools to offer before- and after-school care go in the right direction, but more could be done to facilitate full-time careers for mothers.*

- **The scope for opening borders more widely to labour flows and to enhance the integration of immigrants into the labour market.** *The Netherlands has tightened rules for non-work migration, partially reflecting the unsuccessful integration of non-OECD migrants into the labour market and their dependence on social benefits. As well, the entry of non-European workers is subject to a strict labour market test that hampers cross-border labour flows. To ease labour market shortages, it could be envisaged to open new entry routes, such as a skill-based visa system. In order to improve the prospects for a successful integration of the migrant population, the likely adverse impact of early streaming on the educational attainment of immigrants' children should be evaluated.*

ISBN 978-92-64-04076-2
OECD Economic Surveys: Netherlands
© OECD 2008

Assessment and recommendations

Recent economic performance has been strong...

After the stagnation in the first half of the decade, the Netherlands is once again in good shape. The pace of real GDP growth has strengthened since 2005, unemployment has fallen back to a low level and the fiscal position has been brought back into balance. Though the current recovery is partly cyclical, it is also built on an impressive underlying performance, which has helped to maintain income *per capita* among the highest in the OECD. While the Dutch economy displays a high level of productivity, the trend growth of productivity has been lower than in many other countries during the past decade, which may in part reflect the continued reliance on traditional industries. The government has taken measures to foster innovation, facilitate entrepreneurship and stimulate competition so as to spur productivity growth. These policy goals were discussed at length in the previous *Economic Survey* and are not addressed in detail here.

... but labour shortages could impair further strong growth

The present *Survey* focuses on labour utilisation, which has been the main source of growth in the past decade, but is likely to slow sharply with the greying of the Dutch population. Improving work incentives is therefore a key imperative. Although labour-market participation rates are high, there are several groups who continue to be less active. Labour utilisation is also being held back by the relatively short working week and the high incidence of part-time employment. In addition, net migration flows have turned negative, as fewer foreign migrants are entering the country and more natives are leaving it, a rare occurrence in a high-income nation. Accordingly, the following challenges are the central focus of this *Survey*:

- Addressing the effects of population ageing on the sustainability of the public finances (Chapter 2).
- Boosting the labour market involvement of under-participating groups, notably recipients of out-of-work benefits (Chapter 3).
- Helping parents reconcile work and family responsibilities, so as to facilitate fuller participation and promote female careers (Chapter 4).
- Improving immigration policy and the integration of immigrants (Chapter 5).

*The economy should continue expanding
relatively fast, but there is a large degree
of uncertainty...*

Real GDP growth quickened in 2006-07, reaching an average annual rate close to 3%, reflecting buoyant business investment and exports. The economy is projected to continue expanding slightly above trend in 2008, eliminating the slack in productive capacity and raising output above potential. At the same time, the unemployment rate is projected to decrease further and fall below the Secretariat's estimate of the structural unemployment rate (3½ per cent), indicating labour market tightness. As the job vacancy rate is already at an historical high, there is a risk that real wages will accelerate, repeating events at the turn of the century when labour costs reacted strongly to labour shortages, hurting competitiveness and corporate profitability. However, high uncertainty prevails in these short-term prospects, magnified by the financial market turbulence during the summer of 2007. Like other countries, the Netherlands is exposed to the prospect of a bank credit squeeze. Dutch households have highly-leveraged balance sheets, hold a large part of their assets in the form of housing and have a high marginal propensity to consume out of housing wealth. Even though OECD estimates suggest that the risk of a house price correction is not particularly high, there is evidence that house prices have diverged from fundamentals. A stagnation of house prices would imply a less dynamic growth of private consumption and a decline in house prices could exert a significant drag.

*... and automatic stabilisers should be allowed
to play freely if growth falters*

This high degree of uncertainty calls for a cautious fiscal policy stance. The government plans to achieve a budget surplus of 0.5% in 2008, reflecting cyclical increases in tax receipts and a rebound in natural gas revenues. The cyclically-adjusted balance is expected to become positive again and to gradually improve further over the cabinet term, which is a desirable development given the foreseeable increase in ageing-related spending. Fiscal policy needs to address both short-term downside risks and long-term ageing-related challenges. *In these circumstances, a sensible fiscal strategy would be to let automatic stabilisers operate freely, while keeping the structural balance on a medium-term path of consolidation, so as to progress towards sustainability.* Starting from the current fiscal position, the risk of running an excessive deficit is limited. Moreover, in case of unexpected adverse economic events, the revised Stability and Growth Pact allows some flexibility with respect to the 3% of GDP budget deficit reference value.

*While the fiscal framework seeks to promote
expenditure control, the budget tends to have
pro-cyclical effects*

In the Netherlands, the fiscal framework is an important tool of macroeconomic management. The framework comprises: i) a set of multi-annual expenditure ceilings established for the term of each coalition government ii) a requirement that new tax measures are off-set by compensating revenue measures, so as to have a neutral impact on the budget balance; iii) a "signal value" of 2% of GDP for the budget deficit that, if exceeded, triggers fiscal consolidation measures; and iv) a medium-term goal of preparing the public finances for the effects of demographic ageing. This framework did not prevent the budget deficit from breaching the 3% Maastricht limit in 2003, which forced the government to put in place a strict consolidation package, with most of budget restraint unfolding during the period of output stagnation. Nor did the framework prevent the budget from turning expansionary in 2007, when the economy was running close to full capacity and overheating risks were looming large. This pro-cyclical pattern of fiscal policy has been a recurrent feature over the past decade. In order to address this issue, the government has strengthened the fiscal framework. The efficacy of the multi-annual spending ceiling has been improved by removing from its definition several items over which the government has no direct control, such as interest payments. *To improve budgetary control further, the government should consider excluding all counter-cyclical items from the expenditure ceilings, such as unemployment benefits. As well, including certain revenue items in the expenditure ceilings (such as dividends and central bank profit) is questionable, as this allows greater spending in good times.*

Tax expenditures should be kept under review

Significant deductions from income taxes are allowed, which represent a costly and growing form of government intervention. The level and purpose of these expenditures are not clearly established and contribute to higher marginal tax rates than otherwise would be necessary. *The reporting of tax expenditures should be improved, as was announced in the government's budget memorandum. Furthermore, their periodical assessment should be strengthened, so as to evaluate whether they achieve their purposes and whether they do so in a cost-effective manner, following the existing practice in some OECD countries. In addition, the government could consider including some of the tax expenditures under the expenditure ceilings when they are close substitutes to government spending.*

Public spending on pension and health care is projected to increase sharply

The Netherlands is better prepared than many other countries to cope with the challenge of ageing, thanks to its second pillar pension scheme. Recent health-care reforms also aim at containing the increase in health care spending. In addition, the government has decided to raise the structural budget surplus to 1% of GDP by 2011, so as to pre-fund some of the future expenditure burdens. This nonetheless leaves a fiscal sustainability gap. This gap has been revised upwards recently as a result of lower interest rates reducing future revenue streams (second pillar pension plans are mostly on a defined-benefit basis) revisions in life expectancy and delays in securing sustainability, only partially offset by government measures to increase participation. All in all, measures equivalent to more than 2% of GDP would be necessary to achieve sustainability. The government could run large surpluses for a long period of time to close this gap, but this would be hard to achieve for political economy reasons, as experienced in other countries. *Therefore, in addition to building up surpluses further after 2011, policy solutions to restore sustainability should address the core of the problem, namely to further control ageing-related costs, by cutting back public pension entitlements and by encouraging later retirement. Expanding the funding base through higher participation is also an important objective in this regard.*

*The first-pillar pension scheme is largely
unreformed*

Health care and first-pillar state pensions (AOW) are the two largest sources of ageing-related spending pressures. The health care insurance system has been subject to a comprehensive restructuring and the government plans to make further adjustments as needed. State pensions, by contrast, are largely unreformed. Under this (post-war Beveridgian) scheme, the government pays the same pensions to all residents having lived sufficiently long in the country, irrespective of past contributions. The age of eligibility to a state pension (65 years) has been kept unchanged since the establishment of the scheme in 1957, even though life expectancy has increased by more than 6 years. *Hence, although the current government has decided not to do so, eligibility to state pensions should be postponed in several pre-announced steps (for instance to 67 years) over a reasonable transition period and then be kept in line with developments in life expectancy.* Model simulations of increasing the pension age suggest that this would have favourable effects not only on fiscal sustainability but also on labour market participation. Moreover, first-pillar pensions are relatively high in relation to average income (about 31% of average earnings) in comparison to neighbouring countries (about 22% of average earnings) which makes the state pension a relatively costly scheme to combat old-age poverty (annual spending of 4½ per cent of GDP and rising). Indeed, simulations by the Secretariat suggest that lowering the level of first pillar pensions would have a favourable effect on labour participation and would improve public finances substantially, although this would score low in terms of equity as some people would be worse off.

*Labour market participation is high; even so,
there are pockets of under-participation among
various groups of the population*

Dutch governments have successfully sought to encourage labour market participation. Recent measures include the closing of early-retirement routes and greater emphasis on activating (long-term) unemployed, the partially disabled and social assistance recipients. Nonetheless, labour supply is still restrained by comprehensive social entitlements for those out of work, which benefit almost 17% of the working-age population. In addition, the tax-and-benefit system and labour-market policies continue to discourage participation of several groups and to incite working short hours.

*Further measures are needed to stimulate
continued work at older ages*

Labour market participation of older workers remains low, although it has increased in recent years following the removal of tax incentives for early retirement and pre-pension schemes. The government plans to increase the work-related tax credit for workers older than 57 years. In addition, the government plans to introduce a new levy for pensioners who stopped working before the age of 65. However, this measure is only being phased in gradually and affects only people born after 1945 and with pension income above a certain threshold. *Thus, a more encompassing and rapid implementation of this measure would further strengthen incentives to participate.* Continued work is also discouraged by the possibility of using the unemployment benefit system in combination with generous severance payment as a transition into (early) retirement, indicating a need for reform in these areas (see below). Moreover, tax favoured saving schemes such as the life course scheme can be used for retiring early, pointing to *the need for phasing out such schemes*. In addition, firms that employ workers aged 65 and over must pay their wages during sickness absence (as for their other workers) for a period of up to two years, even though they cannot insure against this risk. Thus, to strengthen labour demand for older workers, *the government should consider easing the obligation to pay wages during periods of sickness leave for workers older than 65 years.*

Women work mostly part-time

About two-thirds of Dutch working women opt for part-time jobs, bringing down the country's average working time to one of the lowest levels in the OECD. While individual preferences may play a role, international evidence strongly links the incidence of part-time work to taxation and childcare. In the Netherlands, full-time female participation is hampered by a high marginal effective tax burden on second earners, reflecting the withdrawal of social benefits conditioned on family income. *The government should continue to reduce the marginal effective tax rate faced by second earners by reducing further the rate at which housing and child benefits are tapering off. Moreover, certain work-related entitlements and tax credits could be conditioned on the number of hours worked, as in some other OECD countries.* Recent government decisions have stimulated the provision of childcare services and helped reduce their cost, making it easier for parents to work longer hours. But not all obstacles to the supply of childcare services have been removed. *The government should consider designating childcare as an essential facility in the zoning law in order to facilitate the deployment of services.* A new law requires schools to arrange the provision of care before and after school hours, by either supplying care themselves or by acting as a matchmaker between external providers and parents. *In addition, the government should require that schools take responsibility for the provision of childcare services during agreed opening hours, at least as providers of last resort. As well, school premises should be available to external childcare providers outside normal school hours.*

Tax measures continue to discourage low-skilled women from working

The aggregate female participation rate is relatively high, but low-skilled married females tend to remain at the margin of the labour market. This group is often willing to work and the service sector has a strong demand for their labour, but the tax system discourages their participation. Each family member is taxed separately, independently of the income of other household members, making the tax system in principle neutral with respect to marriage. Nonetheless, the tax system contains elements based on joint taxation, in particular the right for non-working partners in single-earner couples to transfer their general tax credit (about € 2 000) to the primary earner. Such an element of joint taxation scores high in terms of equity, because it takes into account the fact that the family is the consumption unit and applies the progressivity of the tax system to family incomes. But it scores low in terms of efficiency because it discourages the labour market participation of the secondary earner. On balance, the government has decided to phase out the transferability of the tax credit (completing the individualisation of the tax system) starting in 2009, but over 15 years and with exemptions for mothers with children aged five and under and those born before 1972. Estimates by the Netherlands Bureau for Economic Policy Analysis indicate that the full phase-out would have a significant impact on female participation. To get this benefit at an early stage, *the transferability could be eliminated more rapidly and without exemptions.*

Activation of social assistance beneficiaries can be improved

The number of social assistance recipients has declined over recent decades, but their share of the labour force remains high internationally. Various tools have been used to enhance job-search incentives and facilitate labour market reintegration. As well, activation has been well served by transferring the budgetary and implementation responsibilities of the social assistance scheme (WWB) to the municipalities and allowing them to use budget surpluses in this area for other purposes, thus providing strong incentives to monitor and activate benefit recipients. *To ensure continued success, existing availability for work requirements should be strictly enforced and the envisaged exemptions from these requirements should be reconsidered.*

Successful reform of disability benefits should be continued

Several reforms since the 1990s have reduced the inflow of new recipients into the disability benefit scheme, notably by introducing more restrictive entry requirements and expanding the sickness period paid by the employer from one to two years. Nevertheless, the number of disability benefit beneficiaries remains high internationally. A sensible strategy in these circumstances is to conduct regular assessments of work capacity and encourage individuals, when possible, to resume labour market participation. *In this respect, the government should reconsider its decision to apply lighter testing criteria to current beneficiaries in the age group 45 to 50.* Moreover, the reduction of inflows has been concentrated on the age group 25-45, with less progress achieved in partially reintegrating older and younger benefit recipients into the labour market. A worrying development is the increasing inflow (often for unspecified psychological disorders) of young people into the special *Wajong* scheme for young disabled, which offers limited reintegration services. This creates a risk of excluding an increasing number of young people permanently from the labour market. *To avert this risk, those registering in the Wajong scheme should be requested to first apply for social assistance and receive disability benefits only as a top-up after some waiting period.* This would allow case managers in appropriate cases to apply the full range of activation measures associated with social assistance.

Further reform of the unemployment benefit system is needed

Although unemployment is low, the incidence of long-term unemployment is relatively high in comparison to countries with similarly low unemployment rates reflecting, among other factors, the generosity of unemployment benefits. The duration of unemployment benefits has been reduced from 5 years to a maximum of 38 months, which is a welcome move, but benefit duration remains long by international standards, especially for workers with long seniority. In combination with non-decreasing benefits, this is likely to dampen job-search incentives and create paths into early retirement. *Thus, the government should further reduce the duration of unemployment benefits. Alternatively, the replacement rate could be reduced with the length of the unemployment spell. As well, the use of sanctions penalising insufficient job-search activities could set in earlier.*

Employment protection legislation should be eased

The incidence of long-term unemployment may be raised by strict employment protection legislation, which tends to reduce labour market fluidity and prolong unemployment spells for those at the margin of the labour market. A reform of the dismissal system is therefore under consideration. At present, layoffs can occur through two channels: employers can address their request to the individual employment service (CWI), but the procedure is bureaucratic, involves long notice periods and comes with unpredictable results; alternatively, employers can request a local court to dissolve the individual employment contract, which is faster but also more expensive, as firms face much higher severance pay obligations. *The system should be reformed to become simpler, more predictable and less time-consuming for both employers and workers; accordingly, the rules governing layoffs should be clearly specified in law, making dismissals a more predictable process, with appeal to local courts only possible as an ex post option, in case one of the parties feels unfairly treated.* In addition, severance payments are currently quite costly by international comparison. Dismissed workers can be entitled to payments equivalent to one month of salary per year of service, which may result in costly redundancy costs for workers with long job tenure. This can also contribute to lower mobility incentives for workers concerned about losing severance pay rights. A funded severance payment system, like in Austria, could be used to preserve severance payment rights during job transfers, thus helping to increase the fluidity of the job market. Under the present system, workers see their severance pay rights increase to two months of salary for years worked after the age of 50. This is likely to be harmful to the hiring of older workers and therefore have the perverse effect of encouraging earlier retirement. *Hence, the accumulation of severance payment rights of older workers should be aligned with that of other workers.*

Immigration policies should be adapted further to respond to labour market needs

Immigrants have traditionally made an important contribution to increasing the labour supply, as first-generation immigrants and their children constitute about 19% of the labour force. In recent years, however, the net flows of migration turned negative, as emigration increased while inward migration dropped, in part reflecting adverse cyclical developments. The drop in inward migration was partly caused by the tightening of age and income requirements for family-related migration and the introduction of language and cultural tests. Also, the introduction of the Alien Act of 2000, which considerably changed asylum policy, seems to have reduced inflows. On the other hand, entry procedures for high-skilled workers from outside the European Economic Area (EEA) have been simplified by abolishing the work permit requirement for employees with an income above € 45 000 (€ 33 600 for employees younger than 30 years). *To increase the attractiveness of the Netherlands for high-skilled migrants, the current scheme, which is largely demand-driven, should be supplemented by a supply-driven immigration system, under which workers with desired characteristics would be granted a work permit without the ex ante requirement of holding a job contract.* The number of temporary work permits granted to workers from the countries that joined the EU in 2004, mainly for low-skilled employment, rose to almost 60 000 in 2006 (0.6% of the working-age population) under a sector-based transition arrangement. All remaining restrictions were abolished for this group in May 2007. People coming from Bulgaria and Romania remain subject to the strict labour market test applicable to all workers from outside the EEA. In many cases, this test entails a bureaucratic process to prove that no job seeker is available within the EEA. *If labour shortages persist, the government should consider implementing a transition scheme for Bulgaria and Romania similar to the earlier scheme for the other new EU member states. Furthermore, to allow a smoother adjustment of migration flows to labour market needs, the authorities should consider reducing the overall length and administrative complexity of the general labour market test.*

The economic integration of immigrants could be improved

The contribution of immigrants to the economy depends on their labour market performance, which is significantly lagging behind that of natives, notably for immigrants of non-OECD origin. Several labour market institutions seem to pose barriers to immigrants as outsiders on the Dutch labour market. *Strict employment protection legislation for regular contracts hampers opportunities for outsiders, of which immigrants are an important group and should therefore also for this reason, be eased. Also administrative and regulatory burdens should be further reduced, as they can be particularly discouraging to immigrant entrepreneurship.* Two specific groups with lagging labour market performance are women who enter for family-formation or reunification reasons and former asylum seekers; *encouraging an early entry into the labour market seems particularly relevant for these groups.* Another problem behind the poor labour market integration is the educational attainment of immigrants, which lags behind that of natives. A negative factor in the Dutch educational system seems to be the early streaming taking place at the start in secondary education (age 12). *The authorities should postpone the age at which children are placed into different streams during secondary education. It is also important to introduce greater flexibility between streams thereafter, which would improve the educational performance of immigrants and facilitate their integration.* To enable immigrants to better reap economic opportunities, geographical and social mobility should be improved, *notably by changing regulations in the rental housing market that hamper mobility.*

ISBN 978-92-64-04076-2
OECD Economic Surveys: Netherlands
© OECD 2008

Chapter 1

Challenges facing the Dutch economy

The Netherlands is well out of its economic stagnation in the first half of the 2000s and is now once again in good shape. The recovery of the past years has been robust, helping to maintain GDP per capita in the OECD's top league. The very open Dutch economy has benefited from the supportive international environment and investors have continued to be attracted by its business-friendly environment. The country has also benefitted from past structural reforms, notably reforms of pension systems, health care and disability benefits, which have contributed to putting public finances on a sounder footing and have encouraged labour market participation. Productivity growth, however, has remained sluggish, which may be partly due to the relatively high weight of traditional industries in the economy and a lack of innovation activity. Labour utilisation has therefore contributed to growth more than in most other countries. So far, this has been made possible by the availability of under-utilised labour resources, but employers are running into increasing difficulties in hiring workers. This is largely because the working-age population has virtually stopped growing. Large groups of baby-boomers are reaching retirement ages, a trend that will accelerate from 2010 onwards and persist for the following three decades. In addition, net migration flows have turned negative, as less foreign migrants are entering the country and more natives are leaving it, a rare occurrence in a high-income nation. Furthermore, labour utilisation is being reduced by the relatively short working week and the high incidence of part-time employment. If unaddressed, these hurdles will impose a constraint on growth in the medium-term. Hence, the present coalition government has decided to encourage labour market participation. The 2008 budget introduces several welcome measures in the tax-and-benefit system for this purpose. Nevertheless, more ambitious and broad-based reforms will be needed to keep growth on a strong trend in the medium-term.

After a difficult phase after the turn of the century, the Dutch economy is once again performing well by international comparison:

- Real GDP growth has been strong throughout the recovery (around 3% annually in 2006-07).

- The level of *per capita* GDP remains among the highest in the OECD (Figure 1.1).

- The income gap *vis-à-vis* the United States has remained roughly (abstracting from cyclically variations) at about 15% since the early-1990s, in contrast to the widening gap observed in the larger euro area countries (Figure 1.2).

- Unemployment has fallen to one of the lowest levels in the OECD area (standardised rate of about 3½ per cent).

- After breaching the Maastricht budget deficit limit in 2003, the fiscal position has been strengthened rapidly and the budget is projected to generate a surplus in 2008 (0.7% of GDP) while the debt ratio should fall to 45% of GDP.

The strong performance owns a lot to both the open economy and business-friendly environment, placing the Netherlands well for attracting investors and benefiting from

Figure 1.1. **The sources of real income differences, 2006**

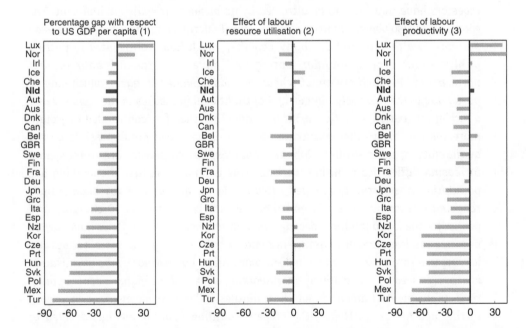

StatLink ᵐᵢₛₗ http://dx.doi.org/10.1787/185702343547

1. Based on 2006 purchasing power parities (PPPs). In the case of Luxembourg, the population is augmented by the number of cross-border workers in order to take into account their contribution to GDP.
2. Labour resource utilisation is measured as total number of hours worked divided by the population.
3. Labour productivity is measured as GDP per hour worked.

Source: OCDE, Going for Growth, 2008 (forthcoming).

Figure 1.2. **GDP per capita, 1991-2006**

Relative to USA, in PPP 2006 terms

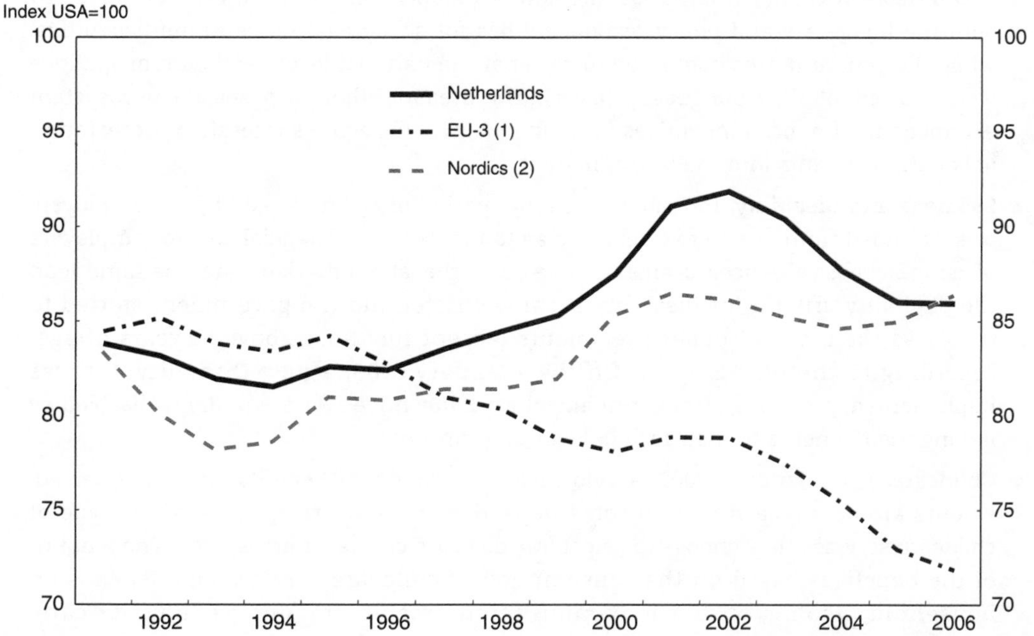

Index USA=100

StatLink ᴍᴤ᷒ http://dx.doi.org/10.1787/185716088624

1. France, Germany and Italy.
2. Nordic countries: Denmark, Finland, Mainland Norway, Sweden.

Source: OECD National Accounts Database, OECD Economic Outlook 82 database.

globalisation in the past decade (Cotis, 2006) as well as to the ongoing reforms to improve the fiscal framework, the tax-and-benefit system and the welfare state and to encourage social partners to modernise their collective agreements (Box 1.1).

The Dutch economy is nonetheless facing important challenges, which may soon impair trend growth if they are not addressed. Productivity levels are high by international standards, although this is partly related to special factors (Box 1.2), but the trend growth in productivity has been sub-par and GDP growth has thus relied heavily on increases in labour utilisation. As a result, the economy is running out of available labour resources at an early stage of the recovery and employers are facing growing labour shortages, as shown by the record-high number of unfilled job vacancies. This may cause upward pressures on labour costs and hurt the profitability and competitiveness of Dutch firms, with the risk of a new, long period of stagnation to re-establish macroeconomic balance, as experienced during the boom-and-bust episode at the turn of the century. There are also other downward risks related to the consequences of the international financial turmoil. Like other countries, the Netherlands is exposed to the prospect of a bank credit squeeze. Balance sheets of Dutch households tend to be highly leveraged, although this mostly reflects mortgage loans with long term fixed interest rates, which reduces the direct effect a global squeeze on bank credits would have. Moreover, households are exposed to the risk of housing price falls, which could trigger a downturn because of the high propensity to consume out of housing wealth. A cautious fiscal policy together with ambitious reforms would go a long way towards mitigating these risks.

Box 1.1. **Recent structural reforms**

- **Social Assistance.** In January 2004, the new Work and Social Assistance Act transferred both the budgetary and policy responsibilities for social assistance to municipalities, while the benefit norms continued to be set at the national level. As the municipalities were allowed to utilise budget surpluses in this area for other purposes, the new system enhanced the financial incentives for municipalities to secure successful re-integration of benefit recipients into the labour market.

- **Sickness and disability.** In January 2004, the period of sickness paid by the employers was extended from one to two years, so as to increase the financial cost for employers of using sickness absences as an exit route out of the labour market. Later the same year, the eligibility criteria for disability became stricter and the government started to re-assess the stock of benefit recipients (except for those above 50 years of age) according to the new criteria. On the 1 January 2006, a new Disability Act was implemented, providing stronger financial work incentives for the partially disabled by linking their benefits to their residual working capacity.

- **Childcare.** On 1 January 2005, a reform of the Childcare Benefits Act was enacted. Parents are now receiving an income-dependent benefit, irrespective of the type of childcare services they choose to select (*e.g.* day care centres, nurses, etc.). The amount of the benefit is based on the consumption of childcare services and depends on household income, with a maximum reimbursable amount per hour of care. Since January 2007, employers also contribute to financing childcare, financing one third of the overall burden through higher contributions to unemployment insurance.

- **Unemployment benefits.** In 2006, the entitlement conditions to unemployment benefit became stricter and their maximum duration was reduced from five years to three years and two months. The general benefit level was increased for the first two months from a replacement rate of 70% to 75%.

- **Employment protection.** In 2006, reforms were introduced to lower the cost of dismissal. The Last-In-First-Out principle was replaced by the "reflection" principle, whereby workers are selected to mirror the age composition of the firm's employees. In addition, the scope of the culpability test was narrowed to specific cases, reducing legal and bureaucracy costs of dismissal.

- **Early retirement.** In 2006, tax incentives for early retirement and pre-pension were abolished. Income tax must now be paid on all contributions to the early and pre-pension schemes. A transition scheme has been put in place for those who turned 55 before 1 January 2005.

- **Health reforms.** On 1 January 2006, a new Health Insurance Act was introduced with the aim of increasing competition. Under the new system, the government determines a mandatory minimum health package and insurers are obliged to accept all applications, but are compensated through a risk equalisation scheme that is funded by an income-dependent employer contribution. Insurance is mandatory and the insured pay a premium on which insurers compete. A system of income-dependent health allowances secures affordability of health care for low-income earners.

> ### Box 1.2. **The Netherlands' high productivity level – a qualifier**
>
> The level of productivity is probably boosted by the short Dutch working time, which implies less fatigue effects (Bourles and Cette, 2005). Empirical work suggests that if the Netherlands had the same duration of working time as in the United States, then the Dutch hourly productivity level would be about 12% lower than the observed level (Cette, 2005). An implication is that the Netherlands can still harvest productivity gains by reaching the technical efficiency frontier through the implementation of structural reform. Moreover, the main factor behind the relatively low average hours worked is a high prevalence of part-time work among the relatively well-educated women, suggesting that increasing labour utilisation through expanding hours worked for this group would only lead to a minor transitional reduction in productivity growth. Moreover, the high Dutch employment rate of low-skilled workers means that the Netherlands is faced with to a lesser extent, than other countries with the prospect of a temporary slowdown of labour productivity growth if policies are successful in enhancing employment among low-skilled workers.

Recent trends

The economic expansion remained strong in 2007 as real GDP is estimated to have increased by around 3% for the second year in a row (Table 1.1). Exports have continued to benefit from the recovery in world trade, with the Netherlands enjoying smaller losses in export market shares than many other OECD countries. This is mainly related to the strong growth of re-exports, but also to the stabilisation of cost competitiveness since 2003, as measured by unit labour costs in manufacturing (Figure 1.3).[1] Private consumption

Table 1.1. **Short-term outlook**

Percentage change from previous period, at constant prices

	2004	2005	2006	2007	2008	2009
	Current prices € billion	Percentage changes, volume (2000 prices)				
Private consumption	242.8	0.7	−0.8	2.0	2.3	2.2
Government consumption	118.9	0.0	9.4	2.4	1.0	0.8
Gross fixed capital formation	92.4	3.0	7.2	3.0	3.5	4.0
Final domestic demand	454.1	1.0	3.5	2.3	2.2	2.2
Change in stockbuilding[1]	0.8	−0.1	−0.1	−0.2	0.1	0.0
Total domestic demand	455.0	0.9	3.4	2.2	2.3	2.2
Exports of goods and services	326.1	5.9	7.0	6.0	5.6	6.0
Imports of goods and services	289.9	5.5	8.1	5.7	6.0	6.4
Change in net exports[1]	36.2	0.7	−0.1	0.6	0.2	0.1
GDP at market prices	491.2	1.5	3.0	2.6	2.4	2.2
GDP deflator	...	2.1	1.9	1.5	1.9	2.5
Memorandum items						
Harmonised index of consumer prices	...	1.5	1.7	1.5	1.7	2.4
Private consumption deflator	...	2.1	2.3	1.6	1.6	2.4
Unemployment rate	...	4.9	4.1	3.4	3.0	2.8
Household saving ratio[2]	...	6.3	6.4	5.5	5.1	5.2
General government financial balance[3]	...	−0.3	0.5	−0.3	0.5	1.0
Current account balance[3]	...	7.7	8.6	6.8	6.6	6.4

1. Contribution to GDP growth.
2. As a percentage of disposable income.
3. As a percentage of GDP.
Source: OECD, Economic Outlook No. 82 database.

Figure 1.3. **Export performance and relative unit labour cost**[1]
In selected OECD countries

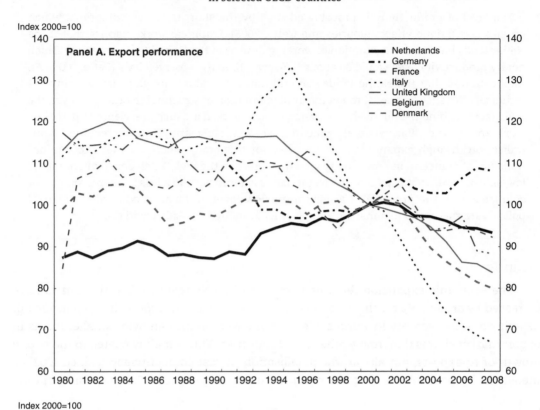

StatLink ⟦⟧ http://dx.doi.org/10.1787/185818563312

1. Export performance is calculated as the difference between growth of Dutch exports of goods and services and the weighted growth of goods and services imports of its trading partners.

Source: OECD Economic Outlook No. 82 database.

expanded for the second consecutive year by about 2% on the back of growing employment and real wages.[2] A contributing factor in this respect has been the increase in household wealth due to higher house prices (Box 1.3). Business investment began to expand strongly in 2006 and continued to do so in 2007, as capacity utilisation approached levels similar to those prevailing at the peak of the previous cycle, leading to an increasing pace of capital deepening in 2007. Residential construction is only partially benefiting from stronger house prices, as continued demand for owner-occupied housing is difficult to satisfy rapidly with the current strict zoning regulation.[3] Finally, growth also benefited from an easing of the fiscal stance following the fiscal consolidation in 2003-06.

Employment gains have been significant for the second year running. Job creation accelerated in 2007 on the back of buoyant labour demand from private sector employers. As the expansion of the workforce has been much less dynamic, the unemployment rate has continued to decline and almost reached the Secretariat's estimate of its structural level of 3¼ per cent by the end of 2007. The favourable labour market developments have notably benefited some of the unemployed with difficult transition paths into employment, such as the long-term unemployed and workers with immigrant backgrounds. Moreover, the employment rate of older workers (particularly in the age cohort 55-59 years) has increased significantly following the removal of tax exemptions for early retirement. However, signs of labour market tightness are emerging with a historically high vacancy rate and increasing labour market mismatches as measured by an outward movement of the Beveridge curve (Figure 1.4). So far, wage developments have remained relatively subdued; real wages have expanded in 2007 at a rate below that of productivity. This might appear somewhat surprising given the relatively decentralised wage negotiation system, where contracts in different sectors are concluded continuously over the year, but the relatively large number of long lasting collective wage agreements that was agreed in 2005 provides part of the explanation. Moreover, there is a high degree of coordination taking place within the Labour Foundation (*Stichting van de Arbeid*), which sets (indicative) norms for wage increases that correspond with macroeconomic stability. This institutional set-up has in the past been able to control wage growth for an extended period of time, but has been unable to avoid labour market tensions ultimately producing a strong (delayed) wage reaction, as witnessed in the previous cycle. This delayed reaction has, in the past, caused real wages to continue accelerating after the economy has started to slow, thus requiring a prolonged period of below-trend growth to re-establish macroeconomic balance.[4]

The economy is projected to slow somewhat, but nevertheless continues to grow above its potential rate in 2008-09, under the influences of higher private consumption, exports and business sector investment. With only a small annual improvement in the structural government balance from 2008, the positive output gap is set to widen further. The labour market is projected to continue its tightening as employment creation continues to outpace labour supply. As a result, wages could start to accelerate as early as from the second half of 2008 onwards as more and more wage agreements are renegotiated.

Although both CPB and OECD projections foresee continued growth at a healthy pace, there are substantial downside risks to the short-term outlook. OECD economies are vulnerable to a tightening of bank credit conditions, as the full effects of delinquencies in the US subprime mortgage markets and the global re-pricing of credit risks are yet unknown. Being very open, the Dutch economy is particularly exposed to a downturn in world trade. Moreover, the household sector is highly leveraged by international

Box 1.3. **House prices and the business cycle**

During the 1990s, real house prices increased on average by 9% a year. The long-term propensity to consume out of housing wealth is estimated to be higher than in most other countries, although the 2004 abolition of tax deductibility of interest on loans arising from housing equity withdrawal (and second homes) is likely to have reduced this propensity (Catte *et al.*, 2004). The main factors behind the house price increases were increasing household income and falling real interest rates. When the economy slowed, real disposable incomes started to decline and the real interest rates began to drift upwards. Nevertheless, real house prices continued to increase by around 3% a year. This raises the issue of whether house prices have developed in line with fundamentals, particularly in view of the fact that both the price-to-income and the price-to-rent ratios have increased continuously since the early 1990s. Available evidence is not conclusive in this area. OECD model estimations indicate that the probability of reaching a turning point in 2005 was lower than around the turn of the century (van der Noord, 2006), confirming other empirical findings of no deviation from fundamentals (Hofman, 2005). On the other hand, Verbruggen *et al.* (2005) did find indications of a 10% overvaluation in 2003 with respect to what fundamentals would indicate. An update of the study indicates that nearly half of the increase in real house prices in 2004-2006 represents a further increase in the deviation from fundamentals (Table 1.2).

Table 1.2. **Determinants of real house price developments in the Netherlands**

	1980-1990	1991-2003	2004-2006
Real disposable income	13.1	45.9	3.3
Real interest rate	−17.0	26.3	−4.1
Other financial wealth households	17.0	17.2	10.5
Housing stock	−28.4	−21.4	−3.5
Unexplained	−0.4	12.4	4.5
Total (real)	−15.6	80.5	10.7
Inflation	24.6	34.6	4.0
Total (nominal)	8.9	115.1	14.7

Source: Verbruggen *et al.* (2005).

An important factor behind this development is the inability of the housing supply to match demand, reflecting strict zoning regulations and other government interventions (Vermeulen and Rouwendal, 2007). Indeed, estimates of the price elasticity of housing supply in the Netherlands are much lower than in neighbouring countries (Swank *et al.* 2002). Nonetheless, the housing supply expanded by 1.1 million houses between 1991 and 2006 (with a dampening effect of about 25% on house prices). Following the economic slowdown, construction slowed and the government's objectives in this area have rarely been achieved. In addition, the spatial mismatch is substantial with most of the increase in the housing stock having taken place outside the economic growth centres, leading to large geographical differences in house price development (Renes *et al.*, 2006). Only in 2004 was the restrictive zoning regulation eased by introducing opportunities for municipalities to allow the housing stock to expand in line with their natural population increases. However, the overall problem in this area seems to be insufficient land set aside for residential development (Segeren, 2007). To sum up, there are some indications that house prices have moved further away from fundamentals since the peak of the previous cycle. Moreover, it appears unlikely that the market can return to equilibrium through an adjustment on the supply side.

Figure 1.4. **The labour market**

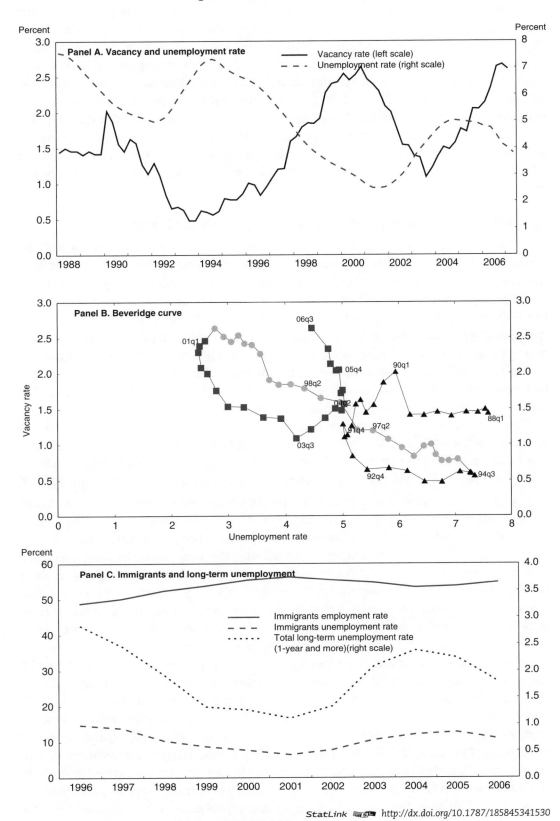

StatLink ⟨ᵐⁱˢ⟩ http://dx.doi.org/10.1787/185845341530

Source: OECD, *Main Economic indicators*, 2006, Statistics Netherlands.

comparison: household indebtedness is unusually high because homebuyers tend to contract mortgage loans with high loan-to-value ratios and very long maturities, thus depressing the ratio of household net wealth to disposable income (Girouard *et al.*, 2006). However, most mortgage loans carry fixed interest rates, which protect existing debt-holders from interest rate increases. The adoption of a new mortgage lending code of conduct in January 2007 was intended to avoid the deterioration in the quality of loans, as has happened in the United States. So far, the historic experience with mortgage delinquency is therefore limited. Nonetheless, falling house prices and deteriorating real incomes could put some categories of households under pressure, notably younger groups who tend to have the most elevated debt-to-income ratios (DNB, 2007). Declines in house prices would also severely reduce the extraction of home equity, cutting back an important driver of private consumption.

Strong growth has kept living standards in the top OECD league

Thanks to its underlying strength, the Dutch economy has performed well by international comparison. The Netherlands has avoided the income gap widening *vis-à-vis* the United States as experienced by large euro area countries. Indeed, *the trend growth rate of GDP per capita* has remained close to that of the United States, both in the second half of the 1990s and the first half of the present decade (Figure 1.5). However, *productivity growth* has been sluggish and, relative to other OECD countries, the Dutch performance has relied more on expanding labour utilisation. Despite this, most of the remaining income gap can be explained by lower labour utilisation in the Netherlands (van Ark, 2005). The principal factor behind the *low labour utilisation* is the low average hours worked (OECD, 2007a). Indeed, the other elements in the labour utilisation rate compare favourably with other OECD countries: the participation rates are relatively high and only about 5 percentage points below the high participation countries in Scandinavia; and the unemployment rate has fallen to among the lowest levels in the OECD (Figure 1.6). This suggests that an important source of growth resides in a potential lengthening of the average hours worked.

Despite some recovery in overall trend labour productivity growth, it remains lower than in other countries (Figure 1.7). Moreover, hourly productivity growth has been trending downwards since the mid-1990s, unlike the revival observed in the United States. Nor is the Dutch hourly productivity growth exhibiting the same dynamism as in countries that have undergone prolonged restructuring, such as Japan, or in the high-technology Nordic countries, such as Sweden. On the other hand, Dutch productivity growth has surpassed the sluggish performance of Italy and Spain; nevertheless, these countries have benefited from important increases in labour utilisation, whereas the current recovery in Dutch employment – apart from the higher employment rate among older workers – appears to be mostly a cyclical phenomenon. But employment growth may be held back by the lack of readily available labour resources, as reflected in the low unemployment rate, the increasing mismatch problems and increasing inflows of workers from the new EU member states to fill (mostly) low-skilled vacancies. Thus, improving the medium- to long-term growth perspectives hinges on both improving productivity and expanding labour utilisation. The main drivers behind improving productivity are competition and innovation, where the framework conditions in the Netherlands were described in detail in the 2005 *Survey* and with progress on the main recommendations presented in Annex 1.A1. The need for further improving innovative activity has induced the new government to make innovation one of its main pillars (Box 1.4).

Figure 1.5. **Accounting for GDP per capita growth**[1]

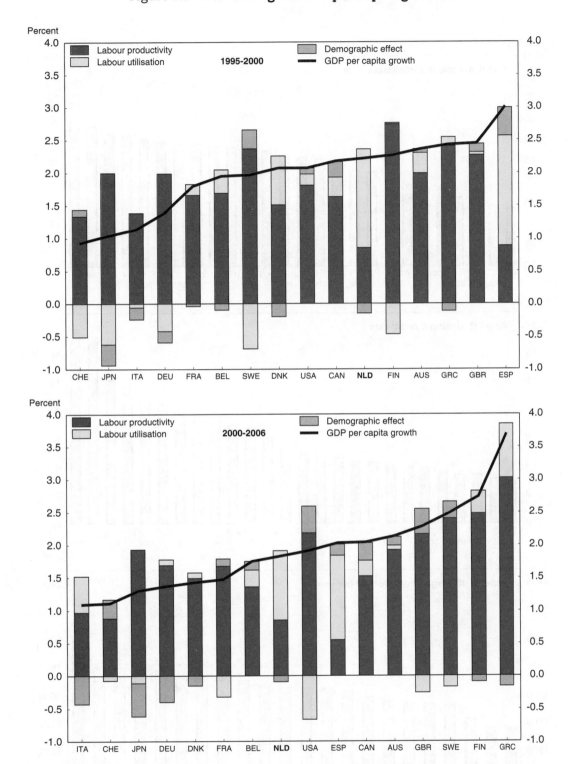

StatLink ⫘ http://dx.doi.org/10.1787/185853170052

1. The figures show the decomposition of GDP *per capita* growth over the periods 1995-2000 and 2001-06 into contributions from labour productivity per hour worked, total hours worked (labour utilisation) and changes in the working age population.

Source: OECD, Labour Productivity database.

Figure 1.6. **Labour participation in the OECD countries**
2006

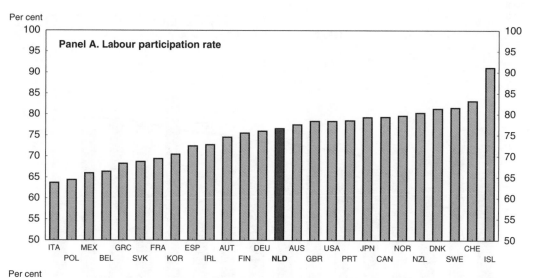

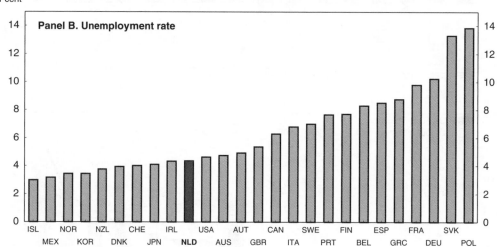

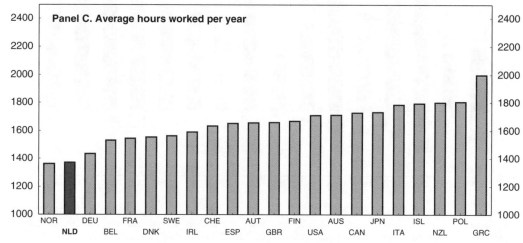

StatLink ᴍꜱ᷅ᴸ *http://dx.doi.org/10.1787/185886228501*

Source: OECD Labour Force Statistics, OECD Economic Outlook 82 database.

OECD ECONOMIC SURVEYS: NETHERLANDS – ISBN 978-92-64-04076-2 – © OECD 2008

Figure 1.7. **Productivity growth**

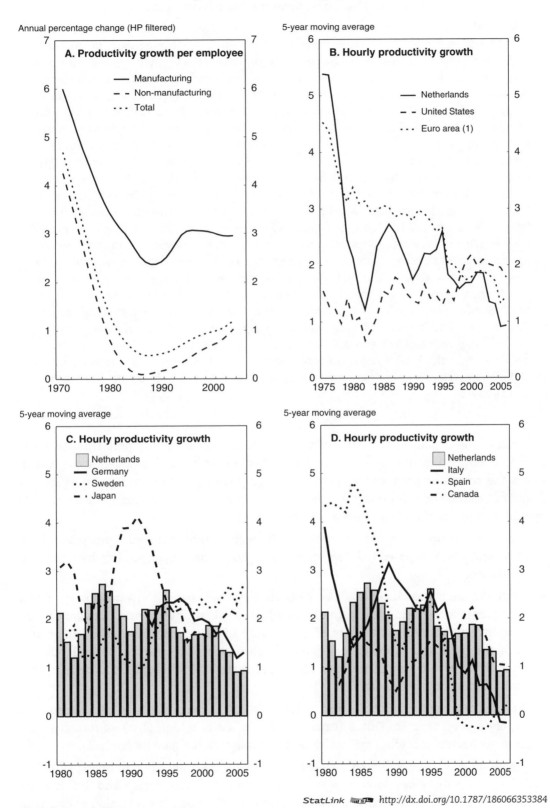

1. Excluding Belgium, Austria and Portugal.

Source: OECD, KLEMS.

StatLink ⓡ http://dx.doi.org/10.1787/186066353384

Box 1.4. **The Government's Innovation pillar**

Innovation is a complex process and the government has accordingly created a broad-based innovation pillar by including, among other elements, entrepreneurship, research, and clustering of knowledge and education. The funding of the entire pillar amounts to an additional € 2.9 billion during this government's term in office. To foster entrepreneurship the government has allocated an additional € 450 million for spending on, among other things, expanding the innovation voucher system for SME to purchase R&D from knowledge centres and to create micro-credits for entrepreneurs who otherwise would have no access to finance. The vouchers were introduced in 2004 and two years later, funding comprised € 22½ million to finance 6 000 vouchers (European Commission, 2006). First experiences were that the vouchers were successful since about 80% of the granted vouchers led to research orders that otherwise, would not have been placed (Cornet et al., 2006). Subsequent investigations indicate, however, that the positive effects are mostly on improvements in production processes, while it is more difficult to find evidence of positive effects either on process innovation or on product innovation and improvement (Cornet et al., 2007). Recognising the positive effects of clustering on innovative activity, the government has allocated € 250 million to strengthen regional cluster programmes. Finally, the government will provide additional direct financial support to R&D amounting to € 375 million over the legislative period. Within this pillar, additional funding has also been allocated to improve educational outcomes across the education system. On the other hand, private financing of SMEs is very reliant on credit from the highly concentrated (particularly at the local level) retail bank sector, which follows pricing strategies where SME related activities are cross-subsidising services directed at household consumers (OECD, 2007b).

Part of the explanation for the relatively lacklustre productivity performance is the high level of productivity as compared with other countries as mentioned above, which limits the scope for productivity gains by moving closer to the production efficiency frontier. A particular feature of the economy that contributes to its high efficiency is its openness in terms of trade and investments:

- The large openness to international trade means that domestic producers have traditionally been exposed to international competitive pressures, forcing them to strive for efficiency.

- The Netherlands has one of the least restrictive regimes towards inwards foreign direct investment, contributing to internationally high levels of inward and outward foreign direct investment (FDI) as a share of GDP (Figure 1.8) (Koyama and Golub, 2006).[5] As a result, there is a strong presence of foreign multinational firms in the Netherlands and Dutch firms have a strong presence abroad, allowing the Netherlands to benefit from intra-firm technology transfers.

- The large degree of openness is also reflected in the increasingly open and transparent corporate governance of Dutch firms, which has led to a high share of foreigners on company boards, providing for international management expertise (Box 1.5).

More broadly, the productivity slowdown over the past decade can be explained by negative productivity developments in the non-market service sector and decelerating productivity growth in the manufacturing sector (with the notable exemption of electrical machinery) (van Ark et al., 2007). The latter may be partly explained by the orientation of the

Figure 1.8. **Stocks of foreign direct investment and FDI restrictions**
2006

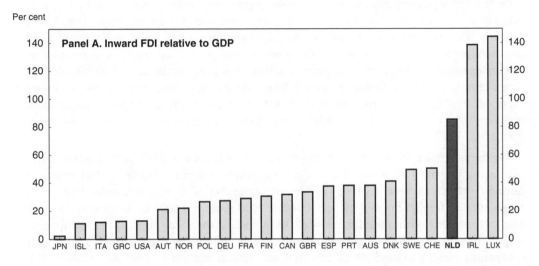

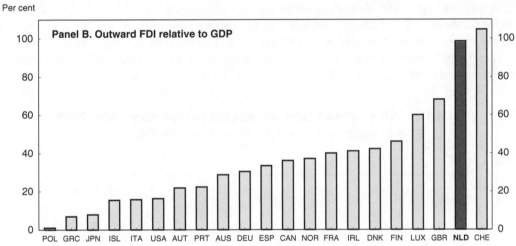

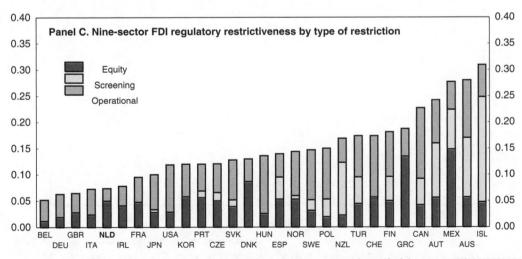

StatLink ᴍᴸᴸ http://dx.doi.org/10.1787/186107337543

Source: OECD, Foreign Direct Investment Database and Koyama and Golub (2006).

Box 1.5. **Corporate governance in the Netherlands**

On the 1st of January 2004 a new corporate governance code ("Code Tabaksblat") came into force. The new code includes many recommendations based on international best practices with respect to strengthening the independence of the supervisory board from the managerial board and increasing the power of the general assembly of shareholders. The independence of external financial reporting has been strengthened by introducing direct reporting to the supervisory board. The code has been anchored in the law by an "apply or explain" rule; corporations that seek to deviate from the code are required to motivate their reasons, leading to a high compliance rate (*Commissie corporate governance*, 2006).

The more active role of international private equity firms has been instrumental in the increasing inward and outward flows of foreign direct investment (FDI) that emerged during the 1990s. In recent years, an increasing number of Dutch companies have been taken over by foreign ones; between 2004 and 2006 around 3 000 Dutch companies were sold to foreigners with a total value of € 188 billion. At the same time, Dutch companies acquired about 1 000 foreign companies worth € 140 billion. In total, affiliates of foreign companies employ around 7% of the total and 10% of market sector employment. The substantial involvement of Dutch firms in mergers and acquisitions (M&A) has made the Netherlands one of the largest mergers and acquisition countries in the OECD, both in terms of outward and inward M&As (Figure 1.9). The internationalisation of Dutch corporations has also affected their corporate governance as the share of foreign board members has increased from 16% in 1998 to 25% in 2006.

Figure 1.9. **Value of M&A in international perspective, 1996-2005**
Nine largest outward M&A countries, values as % of GDP

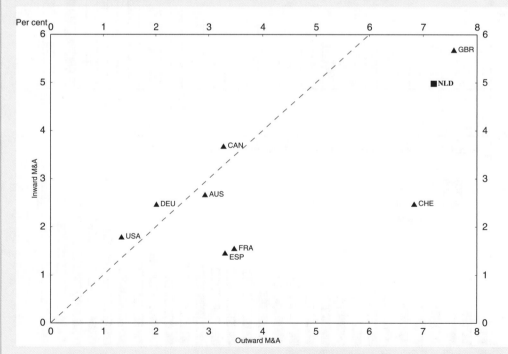

StatLink http://dx.doi.org/10.1787/186117622221

Source: OECD calculations based on Cross-border mergers and acquisitions, *CESifo working paper No. 1823*.

Dutch manufacturing industry towards low-technology industries, which tends to hamper faster productivity growth (Table 1.3).[6] By contrast, productivity growth has been relatively strong in some of the market-based services, such as the wholesale, transportation, and communication sectors, which has mostly been driven by greater use of information and communication technology than can be observed in other European countries (van Ark et al., 2007). In addition, the communication sector has benefited from intense competition, particularly in the mobile segment, where service prices are among the lowest in the OECD area (OECD, 2007b). Even so, the performance of other network industries has been held back by a lack of competition. Legal barriers to entry remain considerable, which, together with exemptions from the competition law and local government ownership in public transportation and the energy sectors, have hindered third-party access. In the distribution sector, good productivity performance is being held back by the mediocre performance of the retail sector, arising from strict zoning regulations and some restrictions on shop opening hours (especially on Sundays).[7] Another aspect that has hampered stronger productivity growth is the export orientation towards relatively slow growing European economies, which creates fewer opportunities for a rapid introduction of new technologies and products (Bernard e.a., 2003). Indeed, there are indications that the benefits of globalisation have mostly materialised through lower prices (Box 1.6).[8]

Table 1.3. **Sectoral specialisation and productivity growth in manufacturing**

	1995			Employment shares (2003)			Average productivity growth (1995-2003)		
	Low-tech industries	Medium-tech industries	High-tech industries	Low-tech industries	Medium-tech industries	High-tech industries	Low-tech industries	Medium-tech industries	High-tech industries
Austria	43.5	44.7	11.9	39.7	49.0	11.3	4.4	3.6	4.5
Belgium	40.0	51.5	8.5	38.2	53.1	8.6	3.3	3.3	5.5
Canada	50.1	43.2	6.8	48.5	44.9	6.7	3.0	2.2	3.3
Denmark	44.4	46.5	9.2	41.7	47.3	10.9	2.2	2.2	4.7
Germany	30.6	55.4	14.0	28.4	57.6	13.9	0.6	1.4	3.5
Spain	48.5	45.4	6.2	46.1	48.1	5.8	0.5	0.8	0.9
Finland	45.4	42.3	12.3	40.3	45.4	14.3	2.8	0.8	14.3
France	40.3	49.0	10.8	39.2	49.7	11.1	1.4	2.8	9.0
Greece	66.4	31.4	2.2	64.7	32.5	2.8	2.8	4.8	4.2
Italy	46.3	44.8	9.0	42.8	47.7	9.5	0.6	−0.2	−0.6
Japan	42.5	40.2	17.4	40.2	42.7	17.0	0.6	1.6	12.0
Korea	37.0	46.4	16.5	32.6	48.4	19.1	5.8	7.4	18.0
Netherlands	**49.6**	**40.8**	**9.6**	**48.0**	**42.3**	**9.7**	**1.4**	**1.8**	**0.0**
Norway	48.0	44.4	7.5	47.0	44.9	8.1	1.7	1.4	0.6
Portugal	68.5	25.5	6.0	66.1	26.2	7.7	1.0	3.0	3.6
Sweden	37.7	50.1	12.3	34.6	54.2	11.2	3.1	3.3	23.8
Switzerland				31.1	48.3	20.6	3.7	1.8	5.1
United Kingdom	40.4	48.1	11.5	39.6	49.3	11.1	1.4	2.4	4.9
United States	43.1	44.5	12.4	42.7	45.8	11.5	2.5	2.9	24.0
OECD average[1]	45.9	44.1	10.0	42.7	46.2	11.1	1.9	2.4	13.8

Note: The technological classification of sectors into low-tech, medium-tech and high-tech industries is based on the OECD Science, Technology and Industry Scoreboard 2003.
1. OECD average based on GDP weights.
Source: OECD STAN database and Secretariat's calculations.

A manifestation of laudable framework conditions is the continued modernisation of the capital stock. For example, spending on ICT in the first half of the 2000s increased about twice as fast as in the OECD area despite the business cycle related contraction of

Box 1.6. **Globalisation and the Dutch economy**

The impact of globalisation on the Dutch economy is mainly taking place through three main channels: increased trade with emerging economies; lower import prices; and the benefits of global competition for productivity growth.

Emerging dynamic markets present new market opportunities and production locations, although proximity remains an important determinant in geographical specialisation (Brakman and van Marrewijk, 2007). In this respect, it appears that the Netherlands has not fully benefited from globalisation as its trade is concentrated on European countries and is less present in some of the high growth countries, such as China and the United States; an experience that it shares with many European countries (ECB, Occasional Paper, 2006).

Sectors that offer services particularly relevant for trade, such as wholesale trade, transportation and financial services, have benefited from globalisation as well. However whereas the financial sector has increased its importance in terms of employment and value added, the importance of transport services has declined. The latter is in line with many other countries, but tends to be more pronounced (Table 1.4).

Table 1.4. **Sectoral specialisation in trade-related services sectors (1993 vs. 2003)**
Share of value added

	Wholesale trade		Transportation		Financial sector	
	1993 (%)	2003 (%)	1993 (%)	2003 (%)	1993 (%)	2003 (%)
Australia	4.6	4.5	2.6	2.5	4.5	5.9
Austria	6.2	6.5	4.3	3.9	6.4	5.1
Belgium	7.4	7.2	3.6	3.4	6.1	5.7
Canada	4.4	4.9	2.9	2.8	4.3	4.6
Czech Republic	5.2	7.2	5.4	3.3	4.2	3.1
Germany	5.2	4.8	2.1	1.8	4.4	4.2
Denmark	6.8	6.6	3.8	4.0	4.7	5.0
Finland	5.1	5.6	4.6	4.4	4.1	2.7
France	4.4	4.5	2.3	2.2	4.7	4.0
Greece	3.6	3.4	2.8	4.3	4.0	4.4
Hungary	4.3	4.6	4.2	3.5	4.5	3.5
Ireland	4.4	3.5	1.1	0.8	3.8	4.4
Italy	5.0	4.9	3.7	2.9	5.8	5.0
Japan	8.1	7.9	4.2	3.7	5.5	7.2
Korea	4.4		3.7		5.1	
Luxembourg	5.7	4.5	3.0	2.8	13.4	28.2
Netherlands	**7.2**	**7.4**	**3.1**	**2.6**	**4.7**	**6.8**
Norway	5.9		6.5		5.1	
Poland	6.6	11.3	3.8	4.4	0.6	1.8
Portugal	7.3	6.2	2.1	1.7	6.2	5.7
Slovak Republic	8.8	7.3	5.6	3.6	4.4	5.1
Spain	3.5	3.4	3.4	3.9	5.5	4.8
Sweden	5.5	5.2	3.7	3.4	4.7	3.4
United Kingdom	4.8	4.6	2.8	2.0	6.0	5.8
United States	4.6	4.5	1.7	1.6	6.3	7.5

Source: Groningen Growth and Development Centre, 2007.

> Box 1.6. **Globalisation and the Dutch economy** (cont.)
>
> The low consumer price inflation over the past two decades can partly be ascribed to an increase in imports from low-cost countries. This has reduced inflation directly through lower import prices and indirectly through substitution to cheaper imported goods and increased competitive pressures on domestic markets. More recently, a countervailing force has been the increase in commodity prices. Eventually, the downward pressure will disappear as the price levels in emerging countries, converge with those in developed economies. For the Netherlands, Pain *et al.* (2006) estimates that the effects of globalisation may have reduced inflation by over 0.3 percentage point *per annum* over the 2000-05 period, which is more than in most other OECD countries.
>
> The large inflows and outflows of FDI should in principle, help Dutch firms to re-allocate their production in the most efficient manner and thus boost productivity growth. However, at the aggregate level other OECD counties have experienced higher productivity growth alongside increasing FDI outflows as such outflows reflect the off-shoring of low productivity activities. However, as seen above, the Netherlands has had a relatively low rate of labour productivity growth despite the economy's openness in terms of outwards FDI.

business investment (OECD, 2006). However, capital deepening (*i.e.* capital services per hour worked) has taken place at a slower pace than in other countries because of weak non-ICT business investment. There is likely to be an important factor behind the relatively weak growth of productivity (both in terms of labour and multi-factor productivity) (OECD, 2007c). Thus, despite an investor-friendly framework, business investment seems to be lower than necessary to maintain growth prospects. This may reflect the fact that the required rate of return on investments is increasingly set internationally in a world with free movement of capital. Moreover, globalisation has undoubtedly raised this required rate of return, and it may be that fewer investment projects in the Netherlands can provide such returns. Even so, there should be scope for making both labour and product markets more investment-friendly so as to raise the expected return from investment.

Looking ahead, the ageing of the workforce may weigh on the trend growth of productivity, although to what extent this will happen is difficult to predict (Box 1.7). However, labour market interventions may have an impact on older workers' productivity, as recently empirically demonstrated (OECD, 2007d).[9] For the Netherlands, the main labour market interventions tend to have both positive and negative effects. The strict EPL for workers with permanent contracts tends to hamper productivity-enhancing reallocation of labour resources.[10] But, strict EPL also tends to strengthen incentives to invest in firm-specific human capital (Bassanini and Ernst, 2002). The relatively high minimum wage tends to push up the level of productivity, but mainly because low-productivity workers are priced out of work. In addition, more dynamic effects on productivity may arise from the improved incentives for firms to invest in training. The relatively generous unemployment benefit may have a positive effect on productivity through improved allocation of labour resources as generous benefits allow the unemployed sufficient time to find a well-matched job vacancy and create incentives for workers to accept high-risk, high-productivity jobs. These positive effects are, however, offset by the long duration of benefits, which tend to erode the work capacity of the unemployed. Parental leave has a

---

Box 1.7. **Does an ageing population entail lower productivity growth?**

Among the many factors affecting labour productivity is the age of workers. A recurrent concern is whether an ageing population entails lower trend productivity growth as the productivity of older workers is negatively affected by declines in physical strength and cognitive skills, although these may be off-set by experience based productivity increases. These factors are likely to be less important than in the past as today's older workers are better educated and healthier as witnessed by their higher life expectancy (Ekamper, 2005). A number of empirical studies have suggested a hump-shaped relation between job performance and age, although omitted variables (such as capital stock and firm organisation) may bias such findings. Indeed, a higher share of younger workers within a firm may be the result and not the reason for a firm's success, reflecting that successful firms hire more and that new employees tend to be younger.

Newer empirical research, however, reveals a more complex and multidimensional situation (Ilmakunnas *et al.*, 2007). Productivity is found to be decreasing with age, but that decline is partly endogenous and sensitive to labour market behaviour, which again can be affected by policies. The decline tends to be compensated by workers with long tenures, allowing them to accumulate job-specific experience. Likewise, human capital investments are found to be an important factor to maintain productivity. This suggests that the relatively strict employment protection legislation (EPL) in the Netherlands would have a positive effect on ageing related productivity as strict EPL tend to increase tenures. On the other hand, investment in human capital after termination of the formal education is relatively limited in the Netherlands and tends to be concentrated on higher educated and younger workers, implying a negative effect on ageing-related productivity (OECD, 2007d). Indeed, the Netherlands' fixed retirement age is likely to have a negative effect on productivity as both firms and employees tend to stop or reduce training efforts at a relatively early stage. Two additional factors may contribute positively to age-related effects on productivity: the changing sectoral composition of the economy away from manufacturing and towards services is likely to reduce age-related effects on productivity; and better health at a higher age should improve both cognitive and physical skills.

A more indirect effect that may have a potential negative effect on productivity in an ageing society is that ageing tends to depress the rate of savings, which reduces the volume of productivity-enhancing investment (Feldstein, 2006). This will in itself reduce productivity growth, but an additional effect is that the lower growth in investment is also reducing the rate of introducing new technologies, further slowing productivity growth. Moreover, the seniority based elements in the Dutch wage system mean that wage costs increase with age with negative consequences for the competitive position of firms as well as of the older workers within the organisation (Ekemper, 2005). This could point to possible substitution effects between labour and capital as well as between the Netherlands and alternative places of production.

positive effect on productivity as this measure allows workers with family responsibilities to maintain links with their workplace, and can thus capitalise on prior (firm-specific) human capital investments.[11] Many of these labour market interventions have negative effects on the employment prospects of groups with weak labour market attachment. In addition, the beneficial effects on older workers` productivity are to a large extent offset by the low effective retirement age, which strongly reduces firms` incentives to invest in training of older workers.

The objectives of improving productivity growth and expanding labour utilisation can be difficult to achieve simultaneously, as higher employment of less-productive workers tends to weigh on overall productivity growth (OECD, 2007a). Although some studies find a longer-term negative impact of the employment rate on labour productivity, like Cette (2005), others find that such effects tend to be of a more temporary nature and relatively small as the productivity of new hires catches up over time as their experience-based human capital expands. On average in the OECD, a 1 percentage point rise in the employment rate reduces labour productivity growth by less than 0.3%, an effect that peters-out in less than 5 years (McGuckin and van Ark, 2005). The effects for the Netherlands are likely to be smaller if higher labour utilisation involves expanding hours worked for the many relatively high-skilled female part-time workers. Thus, over the medium-term, there are few conflicts between policies to boost trend growth in productivity and policies to augment labour utilisation.

Key challenges are related to ageing

The Dutch economy is faced with the short-term challenge of avoiding overheating of the economy and the long-term challenge of addressing both the fiscal and labour market consequences of population ageing. With respect to the short-term challenge, the coalition agreement contains policy measures that in many aspects can be seen as supplementing and continuing the reforms already implemented, particularly with respect to increasing labour market participation (Box 1.8).[12] Concrete proposals were made in the context of the 2008 budget to adjust the tax-and-benefit system in this direction (Chapter 2). However, more could be done.

The Netherlands is in many ways in an enviable situation to meet the economic challenges of ageing with its relatively healthy public finances and extensive fully-funded and actuarially-neutral pension system. These, however, cannot address the problems arising from the profound effects that ageing is having on the labour force. These effects are already feeding through in the form of an increase in the average age of the labour force, a change in the age composition of the labour force and a deceleration in the expansion of the labour force (Figure 1.10). An additional factor in this respect has been the recent and unusual (among OECD countries) experience of net outflows of migrants. The impact of ageing on the labour supply will accelerate from 2010 onwards, when the large post-war cohorts reach retirement age, and continue for the following three decades, before the effects start to peter-out (Ekemper, 2005). As a consequence, the effective labour supply is set to shrink unless participation is increased or hours worked expanded. If such a fall in the effective labour supply materialises, then estimations by the Secretariat show that the trend growth rate of GDP per capita can only be sustained if labour productivity grows on average by about 2¼ per cent per year over the next quarter of a century. Offsetting the negative labour supply effects of ageing by higher immigration would not be a solution since it would require unprecedented and steadily rising levels of immigrants each year, especially as immigrant workers eventually become pensioners and thus requiring additional and larger migration inflows to offset associated ageing effects. On the other hand, the poor labour market performance of immigrants that have entered in the past indicates that they constitute an important source for expanding the effective labour supply.

Box 1.8. **The main economic measures in the Coalition Agreement**

The coalition government's programme consists of six pillars with the following headings: 1) an active international and European role; 2) an innovative, competitive and enterprising economy; 3) a sustainable living environment; 4) social cohesion; 5) safety, stability and respect; and 6) government and public service. The pillars comprise 74 government goals and 10 projects.

In the second pillar, the government aims at stimulating research, innovation and entrepreneurship. The direct innovation measures include increasing the number of innovation vouchers (for small and medium-sized companies to purchase research), extending wage subsidies for research and development activities for small companies, and introducing a micro-credit arrangement for start-up entrepreneurs. Entrepreneurship is to be stimulated by further reducing the regulatory burden for companies and by allocating extra resources to stimulate regional clusters.

Within the environmental pillar, the government also reserves additional money for small scale projects aimed at reducing the most severe bottlenecks in water and road infrastructure. The first phase towards a comprehensive system of road pricing (differentiated with respect to time, place and environmental impact) is planned to be introduced during the cabinet period.

The largest additional funding is reserved for the fourth pillar. The government aims at increasing labour participation by extending the existing work-related tax credit and increasing financial incentives to work until 65. Moreover, special measures to enhance female participation will be introduced, including an additional income-dependent tax credit for parents aimed at the second earner and extending the paternity leave from 13 to 26 weeks. More resources will be allocated to education, among other things, to attract more teachers and reduce the number of drop-outs. In addition, school books in secondary education will be free from 2009 onwards. Furthermore, special funds will be earmarked for urban renewal, education, job support and other social measures to the 40 most deprived neighbourhoods. Extra money will be spend on child care, *e.g.* to harmonise the different forms of pre-school care and to extend pre-school language education for children with language deficiencies. An additional objective for the government is to reinsert into the labour market 200 000 people with very weak labour market attachment.

In relation to the fourth pillar, the government initiated a Participation Summit with employer organisations, unions and municipalities. This summit took place on 27 July 2007 and the agenda included, in particular, a reform of employment protection legislation (EPL). The parties involved broadly agreed on the overall necessity to increase labour participation. However, no agreement could be reached on reforming the EPL system and the government presented its own proposal to social partners. These, however, have failed to endorse the proposal unanimously. Subsequently, the government decided not to pursue the reform for now, but to install a commission to advice on how to raise participation.

Returning public finances to a sustainable path

In 2006, the public finances recorded a surplus of 0.6% of GDP, completing an impressive turnaround from a deficit of 3.1% three years earlier. However, despite strong growth in 2007 a deficit of around 0.3% of GDP is expected to re-emerge as the result of fiscal loosening, in particular higher-than-expected spending (particularly on health), and lower-than-expected natural gas revenues. Looking ahead, fiscal policy has to balance the

Figure 1.10. **The demographic effects on the labour force**

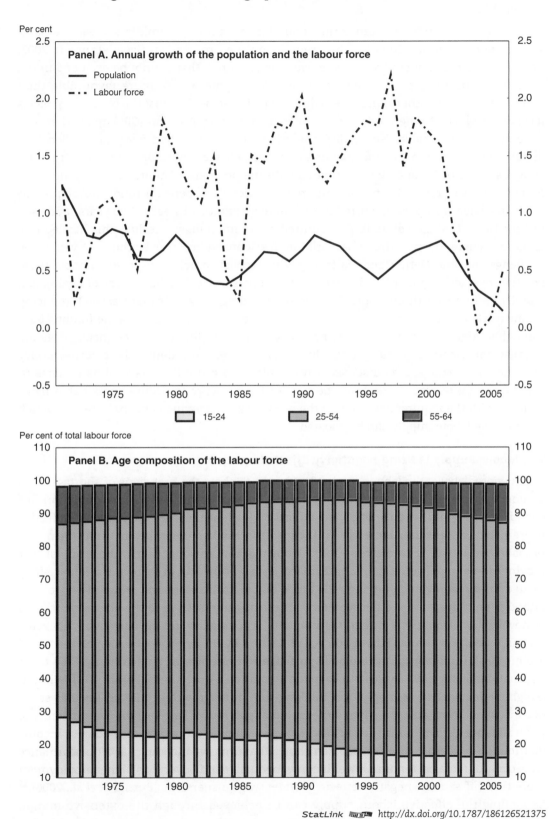

StatLink http://dx.doi.org/10.1787/186126521375

Source: OECD Labour Force Statistics.

needs for accommodating the uncertain macroeconomic outlook and for improving fiscal sustainability.

The government's medium-term fiscal objectives imply a mildly contractive fiscal stance over the period 2008-11, thus remedying the pro-cyclical fiscal stance in 2007. However, this may not suffice to avoid overheating, a risk that cannot be excluded in the short-term, particularly if macroeconomic developments are more favourable than anticipated. On the other hand, the requirement for achieving sustainable fiscal policies has increased. The Netherlands Bureau for Economic Policy Analysis (CPB) updated in 2006 its long-term sustainable fiscal policy analysis that was published five years earlier. This update revealed that achieving sustainable fiscal policy now requires a larger structural budget surplus of 3% of GDP as compared with the previous estimate of 1.2%, principally because of lower interest rates and the reduced wealth of pension funds. Subsequently, there has been an upwards correction in life-expectancy of nearly two years, adding a further 1¼ percentage points to the required structural budget surplus. This has led to a situation where, despite the substantial budget consolidation over the past years, the challenge that the Netherlands is facing with respect to achieving a sustainable fiscal position has actually increased since the previous survey. The fiscal cost of ageing can broadly be financed through pre-funding (i.e. building up government assets), reducing ageing related costs (such as controlling health care costs), or expanding the funding base through a larger labour supply. Relying solely on pre-funding can be politically difficult, because sustained large budget surpluses tend to generate demands for other policy priorities. Nevertheless as discussed in Chapter 2, pre-funding, as well as policies to control ageing related costs, must be part of the strategy to secure sustainable fiscal policies, with the requirements put on these policies being reduced by the extent to which the effective labour supply can be boosted.

The labour supply is being negatively affected by ageing

As noted above, the labour market has begun to show the first signs of shortages and demographics are already weighing on labour supply. Labour market participation has been increasing and because of cohort effects and recent measures to boost the effective retirement age, another increase is likely to materialise over the medium-term, but probably too late to relieve the current labour market tensions. Lastly, there are (slower moving) demographic effects arising from the ageing of the labour force and a cohort effect related to younger women having a 2½ times higher participation rate than older women, although participation for older women is increasing in response to the above-mentioned removal of tax exemptions for early retirement.[13] Looking beyond the current cycle, ageing means that the potential labour force will decline by an average of 0.3% per year until around 2040, implying that the labour participation rate has to gradually increase to an internationally high 86% by 2040 to keep the labour force unchanged (Figure 1.11). Without a higher effective labour supply over the long-run, trend growth in GDP *per capita* is set to decline. In addition, an expansion of the labour supply would improve the sustainability of public finances by widening the tax base. Moreover, higher utilisation may address income distribution concerns as OECD research shows that improved labour market performance (especially of females) tends to lower income inequality and poverty as higher employment more than off-sets the negative effects of wider wage dispersions (Burniaux *et al.*, 2006).[14] Expanding the effective labour supply can be achieved through the extensive margin (*i.e.* increasing labour market participation) or through the intensive margins

Figure 1.11. **Projected development in the working age population and the dependency ratio**[1]

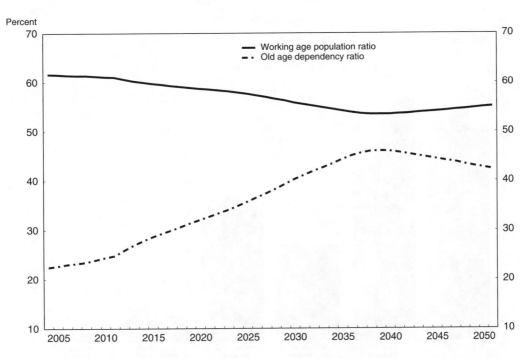

StatLink ⬛ᵐˢ▱ http://dx.doi.org/10.1787/186134224522

1. Working age population is measured as the share of the population between 20-64 years relative to the total population; the dependency ratio is the share of the population 65 years and more relative to the working age population.

Source: Statistics Netherlands.

(*i.e.* expanding average hours worked). The challenges associated with expanding the effective labour supply are discussed in Chapters 3 and 4.

Increasing effective participation

The overall participation rate is relatively high, but there is considerable scope for expanding the effective labour supply through the activation of groups with weak labour market attachment, such as long-term unemployed, social assistance recipients, inactive spouses, the partially disabled and older workers. The current economic upswing has not had an equal impact on the employment outlook for these groups (Figure 1.12). Despite the substantial fall in unemployment, the incidence of long-term unemployment remains high, probably reflecting that the deterioration in their human capital means that the long-term unemployed are among the last to benefit from the improved labour market situation. The female participation rate increased strongly in the 1990s, before decelerating in the 2000s as the rate reached a level equal to the OECD average. Currently, female participation is mostly increasing for older workers. The latter has increased even faster than for older male workers, although from a lower level. The higher participation of older workers is directly related to recent measures to increase the effective retirement age, and the effect on the age cohort 55-59 has been stronger than on the age cohort 60-64. Another positive development is the reduction in the stock of disabled, which reflects a tightening of (partial) disability criteria and improved reassessment procedures. These measures have reduced the inflow into the disability scheme and increased outflows. With respect to the

Figure 1.12. **Inactivity rates**

In per cent of total working age population

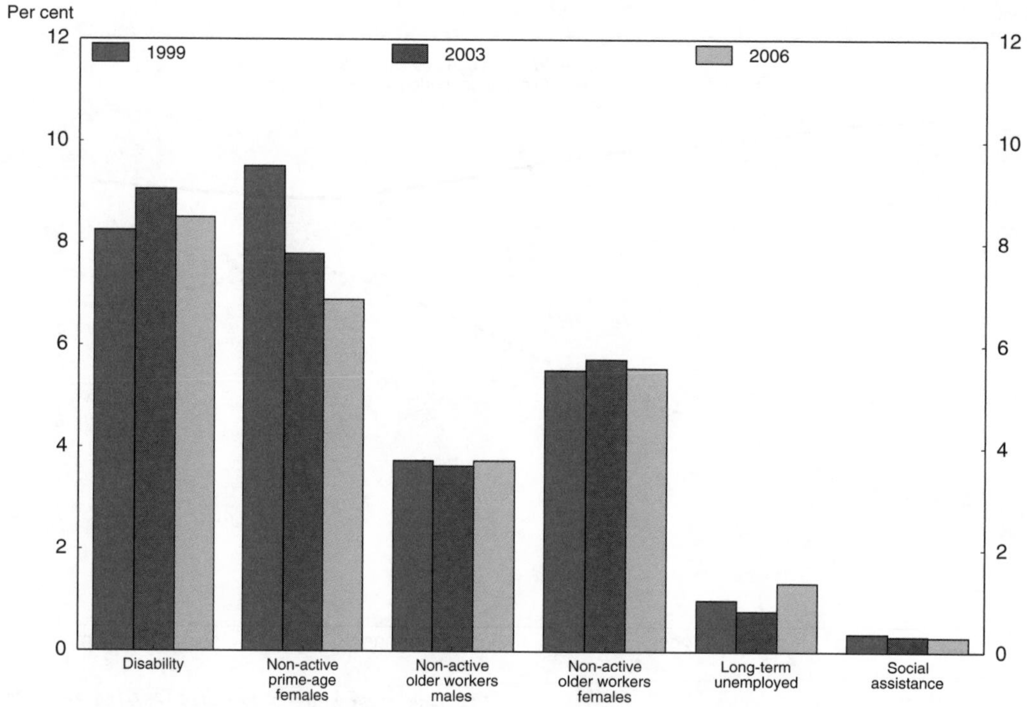

StatLink ≋⫸ http://dx.doi.org/10.1787/186140344153

Source: OECD Labour Force Survey and Carcillo and Grubb (2006)

latter, available evidence is not conclusive about subsequent status, although some are thought to enter other benefit schemes. Despite this emphasis on activation policies, the inactivity rate of the disabled remains relatively high.

Overall, first experiences with the new activation measures are positive and all the effects have probably not yet materialised. However, those activated, were often close to the labour market. For example, the financial incentives for municipalities for activating social assistance recipients are based on the number of activated recipients, implying that activation efforts initially were concentrated on the relatively easy cases. In a similar vein, those partially disabled that have been successfully activated are likely to be those with disabilities that are most easily reintegrated into the labour market. Also the phasing-out of tax benefits for early retirement will probably not suffice to align the effective and the official retirement age as alternative exit routes are still in place. The challenge of improving activation of these groups with weak labour market attachment is discussed in Chapter 3.

Extending average working hours has the largest potential to boost the effective labour supply

Average hours worked are among the lowest in the OECD. This is mostly related to the very high incidence of female part-time work with relatively few hours. Moreover, the persistence of part-time work is very high, reflecting that most women reduce their hours worked after becoming mothers and thereafter only few of them ever return to full-time work (Figure 1.13). Although recent measures, such as more generous childcare benefits, have been implemented to facilitate combining work and family life, there are still strong

Figure 1.13. **Female part- and full-time employment**

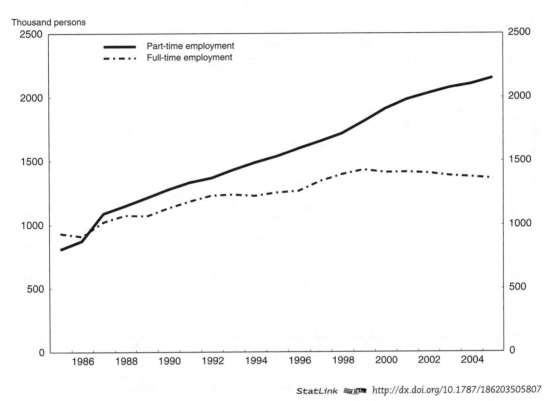

StatLink ⟨▤▥⟩ http://dx.doi.org/10.1787/186203505807

Source: OECD Labour Force Statistics.

disincentives in place for spouses to expand their hours worked. Marginal effective tax rates are relatively high and the supply of childcare is still being developed from a historically low base. In addition, there are strong incentive mechanisms in place to work part-time. Employees have a large degree of freedom to ask for reduced working time conditioned on the implied financial burden for the employer, but in practice very few requests have been rejected. An additional factor behind the short average hours worked is the relatively short full-time working week, which reflects that collective agreements in many instances contain a short collectively agreed working time, generous holiday and non-holiday leave, as well as relatively little use of overtime. The latter is related to strict working time regulation and high negotiated over-time pay. Short working hours are in many respects a reflection of high income levels. However, extending hours worked constitutes the single largest source of readily available supply of potential labour. The challenges associated with enhancing incentives for expanding working time are discussed in Chapter 4.

Enhancing the economic benefits of immigration

Immigrants have traditionally been an important source of labour supply. However, since the start of this decade immigration has decreased and emigration has increased, leading to the unusual situation of more people leaving the Netherlands than entering. Moreover, the labour market performance of (non-Western) immigrants is relative poor compared with natives (Figure 1.14). This is partly related to the fact that migration over the past decades has reflected less labour market needs and has become more oriented towards family (both reunification and formation) and humanitarian reasons. Thus, their

Figure 1.14. **Relative labour market performance of immigrants, 2003-2005**[1]

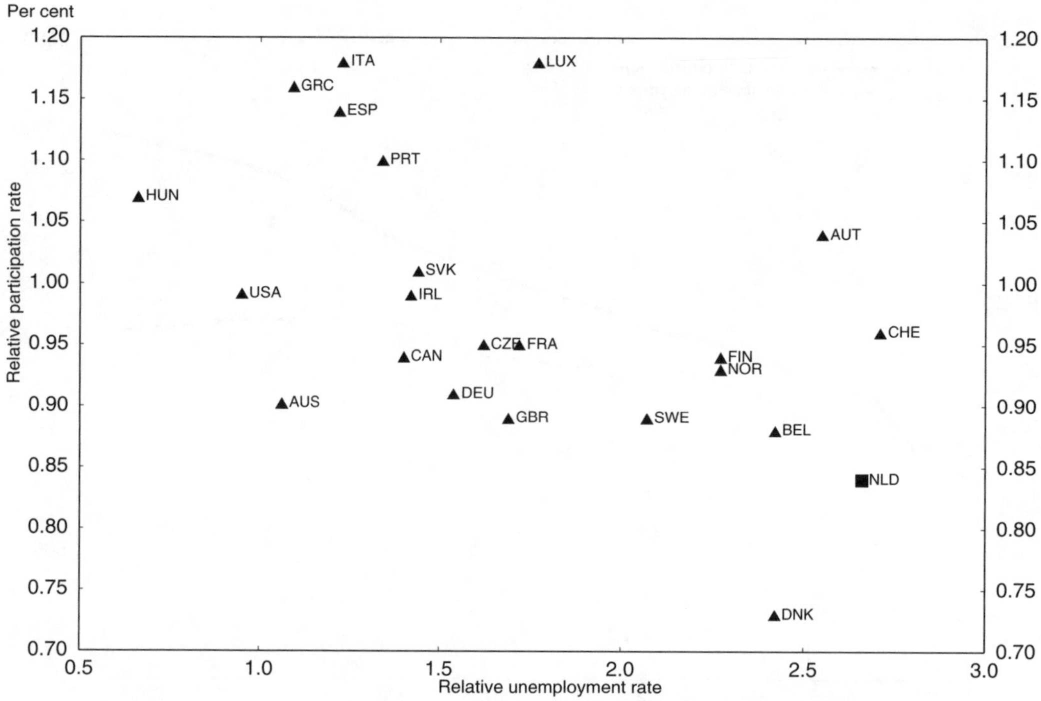

1. Numbers are shown as the participation/unemployment rate of immigrants as a share of that of natives.
Source: OECD, *International Migration Outlook.*

average fiscal contribution to society is relatively low. In response, immigration policies have been increasingly focussed on immigrants with greater potential to integrate and contribute to the society. The measures introduced include stricter visa rules and procedures for immigrants entering for family formation reasons as well as special schemes for facilitating entry for high-skilled workers. A recent initiative has been to abolish the work permit requirement for workers from the new EU members (except Bulgaria and Romania). A labour market test (covering the European Economic Area) is in place for workers from outside the EU that do not qualify for the special schemes for high skilled worker. Despite these changes to immigration policy, it remains unclear whether the immigration of high-skilled workers has increased and whether there is a sufficient supply of workers from the new EU members to ease labour market tensions. The poor labour market performance of first and second generation immigrants seems to be related to their relatively poor educational attainment and integration problems created by the insider-oriented organisation of the labour market. The challenges of aligning immigration to the requirements of the labour market and of improving immigrants' labour market integration are discussed in Chapter 5.

Notes

1. The international trend towards increasing re-exports is likely to boost recorded world trade; with the implication that Dutch export market losses (proxied by the difference in domestically produced exports growth and world trade growth) may be over-estimated. For the Netherlands itself, the relatively strong growth in re-exports since the mid-1980s means that re-exports now

account for more than half of Dutch manufacturing exports. Over the past decade, the expansion of re-exports is estimated to have on average contributed nearly 0.3 percentage points per year to overall economic growth (Mellens *et al.*, 2007).

2. The introduction of a new health insurance system on 1 January 2006 led to a statistical shift of health care expenditure from the private to the government sector, explaining the 2006 contraction of 1.2% in the national accounts' concept of private consumption.

3. Narrowly defined monetary conditions, on the other hand, are not underpinning private investments as Taylor rules indicate a somewhat tight stance due to the low levels of inflation. Although, broadly defined (*i.e.* including stock market developments) the same rules tend to reverse this assessment of monetary conditions.

4. The previous *Survey* provided some econometric evidence of a kinked shaped Phillips curve (the relationship between unemployment and wages) (OECD, 2005).

5. A majority of outwards FDI is undertaken by large multinational companies, particularly in the financial and oil sectors (Gorter *et al.*, 2005).

6. Although within its industries, the Netherlands enjoy an internationally high degree of efficiency in two of its largest sectors – food industry and chemicals and petroleum refining.

7. In addition, collective labour agreements often stipulate high surcharges for working outside normal business hours, discouraging some retailers from expanding opening hours in the evening. Also separate agreements governing retailing and other services (*e.g.* cooking) have been quoted as factors making it difficult for retailers to broaden their range of services (McKinsey, 1997).

8. Goods export has increasingly been concentrated on European countries and since the turn of the century the Netherlands has not benefited much from globalisation's impact on transit trade as the export of services has remained roughly constant as a share of GDP. Another indication in this direction is that the road and water transport sector's share of total value added and total employment is lower in the 2000s than in the 1990s.

9. The channels through which labour market interventions affect productivity are somewhat more complex than described above and may even have opposite effects. For example, overly long duration of relatively high unemployment benefits may prolong unemployment spells with negative consequences for the human capital of the unemployed. In this sense, the reported effects are those that have been found to dominate in the empirical investigation.

10. Albeit the direct effect on labour productivity is relatively small, the total effect is larger when including the effect on multi-factor productivity growth. There is some evidence that the effect of EPL on growth is U-shaped, as increasing the strictness of EPL at low levels of EPL enhances growth through stronger incentives for accumulating firm-specific human capital. At the same time, increasing the strictness of already strict EPL will have negative growth effects because increasing reallocation cost of labour resources (Belot *et al.*, 2007).

11. There seem to be a larger effect on productivity if leave is paid. On the other, there are also strong signs that extending paid leave to beyond 10 weeks has little effect and too long leave periods has negative effects on female career and income prospects.

12. Following the general election in November 2006, a new coalition government was formed the beginning of 2007 by the Labour, Christian Democrats and the Christian Union Parties. In contrast with earlier detailed coalition agreements, the current coalition agreement presented the government's general plans and objectives. In a subsequent step, the government used its first 100 days in office for an extensive social dialogue with the aim of collecting ideas and further develop those already embodied in the coalition agreement. The resulting more detailed policy programme was presented in mid-2007.

13. The ageing is also affecting the age structure of the employment. Over the past decade, the share of 55-64 years employed has increased between 3 and 5 percentage points for nearly all sectors, with the exceptions of Agriculture and Fishing sector (Ekamper, 2005).

14. Interestingly, the same research could not detect any role of the unemployment benefit system in affecting inequality or poverty, pointing to the need for using such systems to provide newly unemployed with incentives for searching for a good job match rather than as a means of long-term income support.

Bibliography

Bassanini, A. and E. Ernst (2002), "Labour Market Regulation, Industrial Relations, and Technological Regimes: A Tale of Comparative Advantage", Industrial and Corporate Change, 2002, 11/3.

Belot, M., J. Boone and J. van Ours (2007) "Welfare Improving Employment Protection", Economica, No. 74.

Bernard, A., J. Eaton, J. Jenson and S. Kortum (2003), "Plants and Productivity in International Trade", Amsterican Economic Review, 93(4).

Bourlés, R. and G. Cette (2005) "A Comparison of Structural Levels of Productivity in the Major Industrialised Countries" OECD Economic Studies, No. 41, 2005/2.

Burniaux, J-M., F. Padrini and N. Brandt (2006) "Labour Market Performance, Income Inequality and Poverty in OECD Countries", OECD Economics Department Working Paper, No. 500.

Carcillo, S. and D. Grubb (2006), "From Inactivity to Work: The Role of Active Labour Market Policies", OECD Social Employment and Migration Working Papers, No. 36.

Catte, P., N. Girouard, R. Price and C. André (2004) "Housing Markets, Wealth and the Business Cycle", OECD Economics Department Working Papers, No. 394.

Cette, G. (2005), "Are Productivity Levels Higher in Some European Countries than in the United States?", International Productivity Monitor, No. 10, Spring 2005.

Commissie corporate governance (2006), Monitoring Commissie Corporate Governance Code – tweede rapport over de naleving van de Nederlandse corporate governance code, december 2006, Den Haag.

Cornet, M., F. Huizinga, B. Minne and D. Webbink (2006) "Successful knowledge policies", CPB memorandum 158.

Cornet, M., F., M.W. van der Steeg, B.L.K. Vroomen (2007) De effectiviteit van de innovatievoucher 2004 en 2005; effect op innovatieve input en innovatieve output van bedrijven. CPB Document 140.

Cotis, J-P (2006), Globalisation and the Dutch economy, Speech delivered at the Symposium on Globalisation, Den Haag, 11 December 2006.

DNB (2007), Will the mortgage crisis in the US affect financial stability?, Quarterly Bulletin, June 2007.

Ekamper, P. (2005), "Ageing of the Labor Market in the Netherlands: An Overview", in Rocca, T.S. and J.G.L. Thijssen (eds) (2005), Older Workers, New Directions; Employment and Development in an Ageing Labor Market. Miami Center for Labour Research and Studies, Florida International University.

European Commission (2006), Annual Innovation Policy Trends and Appraisal Report – The Netherlands, 2006. Bruxelles.

Feldstein, M. (2006), "The Effects of the Ageing European Population on Economic Growth and Budgets: Implications for Immigration and Other Policies", NBER Working Paper No. W12736.

Girourard, N., M. Kennedy, P. van den Noord and C. André (2006), "Recent House Price Developments: The Role of Fundamentals", OECD Economics department working Papers, No. 475, OECD Publishing.

Gorter, J., P. Tang and M. Toet (2005), "Verplaatsing vanuit Nederland", CPB Document, No. 76.

Ilmakunnas, P., V. Skirbekk, J. van Ours and M. Weiss (2007), "Ageing and Productivity", paper presented at the Fondazione Rodolfo Debennedetti conference, Limone – 26 May 2007.

Koyama, T. and S. Golub (2006), "OECD's FDI Regulatory Restrictiveness Index: Revision and Extension to more Economies", OECD Economics Department Working Papers No. 525.

McGuckin, R. and B. van Ark (2005), "Productivity and Participation: An International Comparison", Research Memorandum GD-78, Groningen Growth and Development Centre, University of Groningen.

Mellens, M.C., H.G.A. Noordman and J. P. Verbruggen (2007), Re-exports: international comparison and implications for performance indicators, CPB Document No. 149.

OECD (2005), Economic Survey of the Netherlands, Paris.

OECD (2006), Information Technology Outlook, Paris.

OECD (2007a), Going for Growth, Paris.

OECD (2007b), Communication Outlook.

OECD (2007c), *Review of Competition in the Dutch Retail Banking Sector*, Paris.

OECD (2007d), *OECD Employment Outlook*, Paris.

Pain, N., I. Koske and M. Sollie (2006), "Globalisation and Inflation in the OECD economies", *OECD Economics Department Working Paper No. 524*.

Renes, G., M. Thissen and A. Segeren (2006), Betaalbaarheid van koopwoningen en het ruimtelijk beleid, Ruimtelijk Planbureau, The Hague.

Segeren, A. (2007), De grondmarkt voor woningbouwlocaties. Belangen, strategien van grondeigenaren, Ruimtelijk Planbureau, The Hague.

Swank J., J. Kakes and A.F. Tieman (2002), "The Housing Ladder, Taxation, and Borrowing Constraints", WO *Research Memoranda* 688, Netherlands Central Bank, Amsterdam.

Van Ark, B. (2005), "Does the European Union Need to Revive Productivity Growth?", Research memorandum GD-75, Groningen Growth and Development Centre, University of Groningen.

Van Ark, B., M. O'Mahony and G. Ypma (2007), The EU KLEMS Productivity Report, Issue No. 1. March 2007.

Van der Noord, P. (2006), *Are house prices nearing a peak?* "A probit analysis for 17 OECD countries", *OECD Economics Department Working Paper No. 488*.

Vendrik, M. and Cörvers, F (2007), "Male and female labour force participation: the role of dynamic adjustments to changes in labour demand and autonomous trends", Mimeo, Maastricht University.

Verbruggen, J., H. Kranendonk, M. van Leuvenstijn and M. Toet (2005), *Welke factoren bepalen de ontwikkeling van de huizenprijs in Nederland?*, CPB Document No. 81, The Hague.

Vermeulen, W. and J. Rouwendal (2007), "Housing Supply in the Netherlands", *CPB Discussion Paper No. 87*.

ANNEX 1.A1

Progress in structural reform

This annex reviews actions taken to follow policy recommendations made in the *2006 OECD Economic Survey of the Netherlands* and, where indicated, still outstanding from earlier *Surveys*. Recommendations that are new in this Survey are shown in the boxes at the end of each relevant chapter.

Recommendations in previous Survey	Actions taken and current assessment
A. Public finances	
Lending coherence to the fiscal framework	
Return close to budget balance and aim for a medium-term surplus. Following the impressive fiscal consolidation in 2004-05, the authorities should resist emerging pressures for renewed spending programmes and tax relief. Revenue windfalls should be used to reduce the deficit, rather than increase spending.	After a further improvement of the budget balance in 2006 fiscal policy was loosened substantially in 2007, Over the medium term the balance is expected to improve again as the new government targets a structural surplus of 1% of GDP by 2011.
Strengthen the fiscal rule. Even though the "trend-budgeting framework" has well served the purpose of spending restraint, it can be circumvented by creative gimmicks. The authorities should record more comprehensively all tax expenditures and deductions, including for owner-occupied housing and pension plans.	Several changes have been made to the fiscal rule: 1) Interest payments are excluded from the ceilings. 2) A realistic, rather than a cautious, scenario is used as the budget basis. 3) to break the link between the *volatility* in natural gas revenues and FES investments through a fixed funding level over the cabinet's term (see below). No action has been taken on improving the reporting of tax expenditures.
Promote an integrated decision making process. The strong and sudden increase of available resources for investment that results from higher gas revenues should not erode the quality of the investments or the selection process of eligible projects. Therefore, the earmarking of natural gas revenues to special programmes should be subject to close examination.	The government has decoupled the funding of the Economic Structure Enhancing Fund (FES) from the volatile developments in natural gas revenues to avoid "spending urge" in case of revenue windfalls by a fixed funding level over the cabinet's term.
Pensions: combining strategies to re-establish sustainability	
Pre-fund pension liabilities. The budget path has deviated from the pre-funding strategy described in 2000, which called for achieving budget surpluses of 1% of GDP. Given past slippages, and weaker financial performance of pension fund investments, re-establishing a general government surplus is important.	The government targets a structural surplus of 1% of GDP by 2011 (and an improvement of the budget balance in each single year). This will be achieved through budgetary measures and supported by the strengthened fiscal framework.
Encourage later retirement. The government should continue to encourage later retirement by closing early retirement routes, such as the misuse of disability and unemployment insurance, and reducing the scope of fiscal instruments subsidising early individual retirement strategies. The government should also index the age of eligibility for first-pillar pensions to life expectancy.	Several measures were taken to close early retirement routes. The criteria for becoming entitled to the disability insurance scheme were sharpened, the maximum duration of unemployment benefits was shortened, the obligation of older workers to apply for a job was reintroduced and the tax-favoured treatment of early retirement schemes was abandoned. No action taken to tackle the high severance pay, tax financed saving schemes or the retirement age.

Recommendations in previous Survey	Actions taken and current assessment
B. Labour market	

Ease EPL

The government should ease strict EPL on regular contracts to increase macroeconomic resilience and raise employment among groups with low participation rates.	No action taken.
Further simplifying dismissal procedures.	No action taken
Widening the circumstances in which a dismissal is justified.	No action taken
Reducing severance pay obligations for dismissed employees with long tenure.	No action taken

Lengthen working hours

Consider further reducing the taper rate for withdrawing childcare subsidies as household income rises, subject to findings of the evaluation in 2006 of the child care financing system.	Starting January 2007 the levels of childcare benefits have been adjusted in a way that the marginal pressure or taper rate is reduced for higher incomes.
Increase subsidies for out-of-school hours care.	Since the Childcare Act came into force (January 2005) the costs for parents have been reduced by the allocation of additional resources.
Require schools to make arrangements so that children are not sent home when teachers are absent.	Starting August 2007 schools are obliged to make arrangements with day care providers concerning out-of school hours care for children in primary education (4-12 years). This does not include obligations in case of absence of teachers.
Go further in reducing high marginal effective tax rates associated with the withdrawal of household income related benefits by withdrawing individual rent subsidies more slowly.	The government has proposed to abolish the transferability of the general tax credit (in 15 years), to introduce a means-tested supplementary combination credit (IAACK) and an Earned Income Tax Credit (EITC) to reduce marginal effective tax rate for second earners and for people at the margins of the labour market.
Encourage the social partners to reduce overtime wage premiums.	In a growing number of collective labour agreements, social partners have made agreements about overtime wage premiums. In certain collective agreements overtime has been more narrowly defined. In addition, several collective agreements have diminished or abolished wage premiums for weekend hours.

Raise older workers participation

Closely monitor the impact of the reform of the UB-scheme on its use as an exit-route to early retirement. Even after the reform, the maximum duration of the benefit is relatively long compared with other countries, where duration of 1-2 years is more usual.	The government is currently monitoring the effect of the unemployment benefit scheme as an exit route to early retirement.
Monitor the use of the new individual life course savings scheme and prevent it from becoming an alternative route to early retirement.	The government has decided to extend use of the life course saving scheme to better facilitate flexibility over the entire life cycle and investigates how it can be adjusted to stimulate part-time early retirement instead of full-time early retirement.
Index the future official retirement age to life expectancy and encourage social partners to make concomitant adjustments to the age at which (actuarially fair) early retirement can be taken in occupational pension schemes.	Fiscal rules for occupational pensions were changed to increase the statutory retirement ages in these schemes to 65. No action has been taken to increase the official retirement age.
Promote the employability of older workers by encouraging greater participation in lifelong learning, especially at mid-career ages (35-50).	No actions taken

C. Product markets	

Reform of product market regulation

Implement a "silence is consent" rule for issuing licenses in cases where there are no severe (dangerous) consequences for society, the rights and duties of companies are clear and third party interests are not harmed.	In the first few months of 2006 all licenses were scrutinized on the possibility of abolishment and/or replacement by general rules. For those licenses deemed necessary, the possibility of the "silence is consent" rule was examined. This resulted in 22 cases where this rule will be (or has been) implemented.
Introduce single contact points ("one-stop shops") for issuing licenses.	In 2006 a single contact point for companies was introduced on the internet. It gives companies direct and easy access to government information, for instance on how to get a license.
Relinquish golden shares in the incumbent telecoms and postal operators.	In December 2005, the State disposed the special share in KPN; in November 2006 it disposed the special share in TNT.
Introduce rules of conduct for public bodies to prevent competitive neutrality problems.	Legislation on this subject is pending.

Recommendations in previous Survey	Actions taken and current assessment
Retail and financial sectors	
Abolish restrictions on the development of large stores.	In early 2006 the National Spatial Strategy has been adopted in which local authorities have been given more decision-making power on the establishment of large scale retail-facilities.
Monitor local governments to ensure that they are not unduly responsive to incumbent interests.	No action has been taken.
Consider increasing the financial incentive for municipalities to attract large out-of-town stores, *e.g.*, through a share in retail trade related taxes.	No action has been taken.
Consider further liberalisation of shop opening hours.	No action has been taken.
Foster the European integration of retail financial markets.	A Financial Markets Office has been set up, creating a single point of contact for financial institutions wanting to operate in the Netherlands and should lead to easier access to the Dutch markets. On 1st January 2007 the Act on financial supervision entered into force. This act unites the former sector-oriented laws on supervision of financial markets. It will enable foreign financial institutions to find out more easily which regulatory requirements are applicable within the Netherlands.
Introduce portability of bank accounts.	The government perceives it impossible to introduce portability of bank account numbers in the Netherlands, due to the high implementation costs associated. As an alternative, an 'interbank switching service' has been introduced in retail banking to reduce switching costs.
D. Innovation policy	
Boost business R&D	
Continue to strengthen the linkages between firms and knowledge institutes to enhance the use of (scientific) knowledge in new products, processes and services.	These linkages have been targeted in 2006 by an additional investment of € 300 million from the gas revenue fund (FES) to strengthen the research infrastructure through public-private partnerships like technological top institutes. The Technopartner Action Programme, innovation vouchers and stimulation of public-private initiatives through the programme package are continued.
Make university funding partly dependent on performance in diffusion of knowledge to firms to strengthen linkages between public research organisations and firms, as the government is considering doing.	In 2006 € 50 million of the basic funding of universities was redistributed dependent on scientific performance and valorisation of knowledge gains. From 2007 this will grow to € 100 million.
Rationalise financial support for R&D activities, which is presently dispersed among a variety of agencies, so as to improve co-ordination.	The renewal of financial support schemes has resulted in two coherent schemes: a basic package and a programme package.
Make greater use of evaluations of arrangements offering financial support to business R&D in policy development.	Financial support schemes are evaluated on average every 4 years on their efficiency and effectiveness. These evaluations are used for adjusting the instruments and for future policy development.
Take recent reforms to facilitate immigration of knowledge workers further by introducing a points system for immigrants, as in Canada, Australia and New Zealand, and by relaxing work permit rules for certain groups of non-employees, as is being considered.	The minimum income level to qualify for the Knowledge Migrant scheme has been abolished for knowledge migrants that accept a job in scientific research. A points-based system for self-employed was introduced.
Compete more aggressively for foreign PhD students in science and engineering and relax work permit rules to make it easier for them to stay in the Netherlands after graduation.	The time that graduated foreign students may take to find a job will be extended from 3 months to 1 year and the minimum income level to qualify for the Knowledge Migrants Scheme for this group is lowered to € 25 000. PhD students are exempt from the minimum income level.
Reduce the corporate tax rate to attract more FDI inflows, as planned.	In 2006 the corporate tax rate on profits up to € 22 689 has been reduced from 25.5% in 2005 to 20% in 2006 and the base has been broadened to € 25000. For profits from € 25 000 up to € 60 000, a rate of 23.5% has been introduced. The rate on profits higher than € 60 000 has been lowered from 29.6% to 25.5%. Further, in 2006 a royalty box has been introduced where income derived from patents is taxed at a rate of 10%.
Increase tertiary education	
Provide funding for universities to offer short (two-year) courses, as in most other countries and as is being considered.	In 2006 the government introduced Associate degree (Ad)-programmes in the higher education system, hoping to attract more employees and more students with upper vocational education to higher education. In 2010 the introduction of Ad-programmes will be evaluated.

Recommendations in previous Survey	Actions taken and current assessment
Increase the share of higher education funding based on performance in terms of inputs and outputs, as planned.	No action taken.
Differentiate tuition fees, as this will provide universities with an incentive to offer courses that are more attractive to students.	Currently there are experiments with differentiation in tuition fees. The results of the evaluation will be published later this year.
Continue experiments with opening access to public funds for education services by allowing more private education suppliers to compete for public education funds so as to enhance the quality and diversity of courses offered.	These experiments have been started and students will enter these courses in September 2007, 2008 and 2009. The effects of the experiments on students and institutions (public and private) will be scientifically monitored until 2015.
Enhance the diffusion of innovation	
Continue education programmes in favour of entrepreneurship.	Education programmes in favour of entrepreneurship have been intensified from November 2005 onwards.
Reform bankruptcy law to reduce the personal costs of bankruptcy and increase options for a quick re-start of non-fraudulent bankrupts, as planned.	While new legislation is pending temporary legislative measures have been taken to clarify the admission criteria of debt-relief procedures and thus reduce the burden on the courts and the delays in starting individual procedures.
Ease EPL on regular contracts to facilitate workplace re-organisation in industries undertaking radical innovation.	No action taken.

ISBN 978-92-64-04076-2
OECD Economic Surveys: Netherlands
© OECD 2008

Chapter 2

Securing fiscal sustainability

The Dutch public finances are generally in a good condition. Following the breach of the 3% limit in 2003, an impressive fiscal consolidation programme brought the budget successfully back into surplus in 2006. The fiscal stance was, however, eased somewhat in 2007 at a time when the economy was already running out of available capacity. The draft budget for 2008 shows an improvement in the structural balance, reflecting a projected rise in natural gas revenues. A gradual further improvement is planned for later years. Given the high uncertainty surrounding short-term prospects in the international economy, the authorities should be prepared to allow a flexible operation of automatic stabilisers. Over the medium-term, the challenge of ageing looms large, but less so than in other countries, thanks to the well-funded second pillar pension system. Since the last Survey, the required consolidation for achieving fiscal sustainability has increased, reflecting both a re-assessment of future cost and revenue developments, but also an increase in life expectancy. A possible strategy to cope with the "sustainability gap" would be to run large budgetary surpluses for a long period of time, but this is likely to prove politically challenging. An alternative strategy is the adoption of incentives to increase participation in the labour market, including at older ages, so as to widen the revenue basis. It would also be important to enact measures containing age-related spending. Various proposals to reform the first pillar pension scheme, which besides health care expenditures accounts for the bulk of future deficits, are discussed in this chapter.

Short-term budget developments

After a tense period at the start of the decade, Dutch public finances are once again balanced. The general government deficit crossed the Maastricht threshold of 3% of GDP in 2003, but was then rapidly restrained. Fiscal consolidation measures were introduced and a surplus of 0.6% of GDP was achieved in 2006, making the turnaround of public finances one of the most impressive in the euro area. While part of the improvement resulted from the operation of automatic stabilisers, the budget has also improved in structural terms, reflecting the combined effects of expenditure cuts (lower transfers and wage payments) and revenue measures (social security contribution rates were raised and excise duties were increased). With fiscal consolidation well on target and strong revenue windfall gains, the authorities have allowed a slight easing in the fiscal policy stance in 2006, so as to make up for the rise in the tax burden in previous years and support household real incomes (amounting to about € 2½ billion, some 0.5% of GDP).[1]

Table 2.1. **Key figures for the general government, 2004-11**
In per cent of GDP

	2004	2005	2006[1]	2007	2008	2011
Government expenditure	**46.1**	**45.2**	**46.2**	**46.4**	**46.5**	**46.5**
Direct expenditure	28.5	28.3	29.5	29.8	29.6	30.3
compensation of employees	10.0	9.7	9.4	9.4	9.4	9.6
purchase of goods and services (excl. capital formation)	7.2	7.1	7.1	7.0	6.9	6.8
fixed capital formation	3.2	3.3	3.3	3.3	3.2	3.1
social benefits in kind	8.2	8.1	9.8	10.1	10.0	10.8
Transfers in cash	15.1	14.5	14.5	14.4	14.6	14.3
subsidies (incl. EU)	1.7	1.5	1.4	1.5	1.5	1.5
other transfers in cash	13.4	13.0	13.0	12.9	13.2	12.8
Households	10.7	10.3	10.4	10.2	10.2	10.2
Corporations	0.4	0.3	0.2	0.4	0.4	0.4
Rest of the world	2.2	2.4	2.4	2.3	2.3	2.2
Interest	2.5	2.4	2.2	2.2	2.2	1.9
Government revenues	**44.3**	**44.9**	**46.9**	**46.1**	**47.1**	**47.5**
Taxes	23.6	24.8	25.3	25.9	26.3	27.0
Social security contributions	13.9	13.1	14.2	13.6	13.7	13.9
Non-tax revenue	6.8	7.0	7.4	6.6	7.1	6.6
material sales	3.3	3.4	3.2	3.2	3.1	3.1
revenues from natural gas	1.0	1.1	1.5	1.2	1.8	1.3
other revenue	2.5	2.6	2.7	2.3	2.2	2.2
EMU-balance	*-1.7*	*-0.3*	*0.6*	*-0.3*	*0.7*	*1.1*
Memorandum items (% change on previous year):[2]						
Real gross government expenditure	0.4	-0.4	5.3	3.0	2¾	2.0
Employment general government	-1.8	0.1	0.6	½	¾	¼
Employment health sector	3.6	1.5	2.2	2½	2½	2¼

1. The introduction of the new healthcare system increases both revenue and expenditure by 1.25% of GDP in 2006.
2. Numbers for 2011 are the average percentage change over the 2008-11 period.
Source: CPB Netherlands Bureau for Economic Policy Analysis.

A deficit of about 0.3% of GDP is expected to have re-emerged in 2007. This reflects, to some extent, the reduced contributions from volatile budgetary items, which had added positively to the budget in 2005-06 (such as natural gas revenues) but, by contrast, were lower than expected in 2007. The re-emergence of a budget deficit also reflects measures incorporated in the government budget for 2007, such as tax reductions,[2] additional spending on education and security as well as higher investment spending in infrastructure and health care (Ministry of Finance, 2006a). Finally, as in the past, the transition period between the general election in late 2006 and the forming of the new government in spring 2007 was not fortuitous for fiscal consolidation because no annual expenditure ceilings were adopted for that year, although expenditures were controlled by not allowing new spending initiatives. Notwithstanding the reasons explaining the fiscal deterioration, it came at the time when the economy was growing rapidly and running out of available capacity at a relatively fast speed, thus increasing labour and product market tensions. Although unintended, this *ex post* pro-cyclical fiscal stance has been present throughout the last business cycle (Figure 2.1).

Figure 2.1. **The fiscal stance has been mainly pro-cyclical**

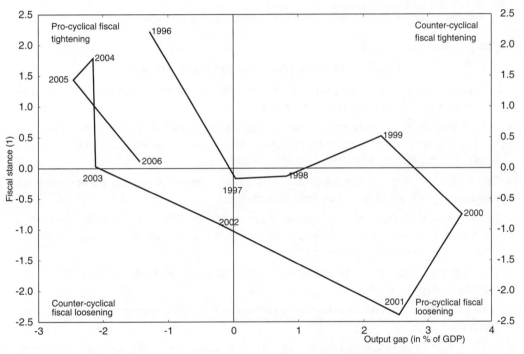

StatLink ᵐᵌᴸ *http://dx.doi.org/10.1787/186250176074*

1. Fiscal stance is measured by the change in the CAPB (cyclically adjusted primary balance) excluding natural gas revenues.

Source: OECD, Economic Outlook No. 82 Database.

In this light, resuming fiscal consolidation in 2008 appears particularly important. The budget for 2008, presented in September, implies an improvement of the structural balance, indicating a fiscal tightening. However, most of this is related to a return of natural gas revenues to a more normal pattern. The government balance will further benefit from higher revenues arising from economic development. Once the government balance is corrected for these influences, shown as the robust EMU balance, the improvement disappears (Table 2.2). The effects of revenue-raising measures are offset by new spending initiatives and increases in tax credits (see Box 2.1). For the 2009-11 period the fiscal stance is expected to be mildly restrictive.

Table 2.2. **The government balance and gross debt, 2006-2011**

In per cent of GDP

	2006	2007	2008	2009	2010	2011
EMU balance	0.6	−0.3	0.7	1.1	1.0	1.1
Central government	0.8	0.1	0.6	1.7	1.5	1.5
Local government	0,0	0.0	0.0	−0.1	−0.1	−0.2
Social security	−0.2	−0.4	0.1	−0.5	−0.4	−0.3
Structural EMU balance (CPB method)[1]	0.8	−0.7	0.0	0.4	0.5	0.9
Robust EMU balance[2]	−0.1	−1.0	−1.1	−0.7	−0.3	0.2
Gross government debt (EMU)	48.1	46.8	44.8	42.2	39.7	37.1

1. In most years the structural EMU-balance according to the EC-method is somewhat higher than the number shown here.
2. The robust EMU balance equals the structural EMU balance corrected for interest payments, interest and dividend receipts and gas revenues. The CPB estimates are used to secure consistency with the longer projections that are needed to assess the sustainability of public finances. It should be noted that the CPB method assumes a three quarters lag before the budget balance react to changes in economic activity.

Source: *Actualisatie Economische Verkenningen, 2008-2011*, CPB Document No. 151, September 2007.

Box 2.1. **Tax measures in the 2008 Budget**

In September 2007 the government presented the 2008 budget and the plans for the entire cabinet period. The main tax measures are:

● In 2008 and 2009, the government will increase environmental taxes by introducing a tax on air tickets and on packaging materials. Also taxes on leased cars and excise taxes on diesel, LPG, alcohol and tobacco will be raised.

● The social housing corporations will start paying corporate tax on all activities (as opposed to paying it only on commercial activities).

● In 2009, the VAT rate will be increased from 19% to 20%. The additional revenue generated by this measure will be partly used to lower the unemployment insurance premium for employees to zero in 2009.

● The working tax credit will be increased in 2008 and partly phased-out from 220% of the minimum wage onward.

● From 2009, the government will start to phase out the transferability of the general tax credit over 15 years.

● In 2008, resources will be earmarked to finance increases in the elderly and earned income tax credit and reductions in income taxation and the unemployment insurance premium.

● The tax credit for the working elderly will be raised both in 2008 and 2009.

● The general tax credit will be increased in 2008, but subsequently reduced in 2009 and 2010, until it returns to its 2007 value thereafter.

● Deductibility of pension premiums will be capped for incomes of € 185 000 and above.

● Imputed rent will be increased to 2.35% of house values, for properties worth more than € 1 million, and the earlier ceiling will be removed.

During the cabinet period, the ongoing programme of administrative simplification will be complemented by other efficiency-enhancing measures, such as the planned reduction in the number of civil servants (Box 2.2). Although the EMU balance is not expected to improve further from 2009, the underlying adjusted balance shows fiscal tightening taking place over the entire 2009-11 period. In 2009 the general VAT rate will be increased from 19% to 20%, which is partly offset by the reduction to zero of the premium employees pay for unemployment insurance (WW). The government expects that this shift of the tax burden from labour to consumption will increase labour participation and thus contribute to an improvement in the sustainability of public finances, although over the longer term this effect is likely to be relatively small as both higher income and indirect taxes have a similar impact on the overall tax wedge. Even though the recent turmoil on global financial markets and the likely slowdown of growth in the OECD area call for some caution, the adoption in 2008 of a fiscal stance that is neutral when corrected for the effects of increasing natural gas revenues does not seem to be well timed, as the output gap is likely to be positive.

Box 2.2. **Simplifying administrative rules and procedures**

Over the last four years, measures were taken to simplify administrative rules and procedures and further simplification is contemplated for the cabinet period (until 2011). The programme of the government to reduce regulatory costs is based on quantitative indicators (essentially calculating compliance time in terms of hours needed for various administrative tasks) with clear targets (linked to the budgetary cycle) and supported by a coordinating central unit in the Ministry of Finance and an external review body (OECD, 2007b). The programme is estimated to have already reduced the regulatory burden by 25% (some € 4 billion). For example, there has been a 42% reduction in the number of individual licenses achieved by greater use of ICT tools and scrapping obsolete or superfluous licenses. In parallel, there is an e-government programme that is also based on a similar framework with central coordination and local implementation combined with clear objectives (OECD, 2007c).

While Dutch economic growth could remain above trend, the uncertainty surrounding the short-term outlook has increased and the distribution of risks is now clearly skewed to the downside. If European growth weakens, the Dutch economy will be adversely affected. In case of a significant slowdown, the authorities will be walking a tightrope, having to avert the risk of pro-cyclical fiscal restraint on the one side and running the risk of excessive deficits on the other. Since fiscal policy is not a well-adapted tool to fine tune the business cycle, the authorities should allow the free play of automatic stabilisers, as laid down in the fiscal framework. This will imply that the short-term nominal target may no longer be within reach and the return to growing surpluses thereafter could be somewhat postponed.

More than in most other countries, the Netherlands is exposed to the risk of running pro-cyclical fiscal policies. The deviation of the actual budget deficit from its structural value is high in international perspective, which is caused in part by a higher variability of output (Figure 2.2). Another reason is that the sensitivity of the budget balance to changes in the output gap is high by international comparison (Girouard and André, 2005). In particular, there is a high elasticity of income tax receipts to household earnings, partly

Figure 2.2. **Difference between actual and structural budget balance and output variability**

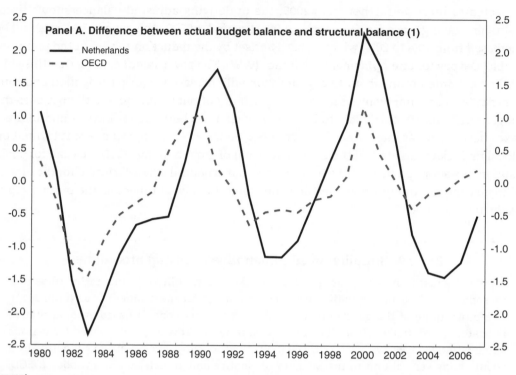

Panel A. Difference between actual budget balance and structural balance (1)

— Netherlands
- - - OECD

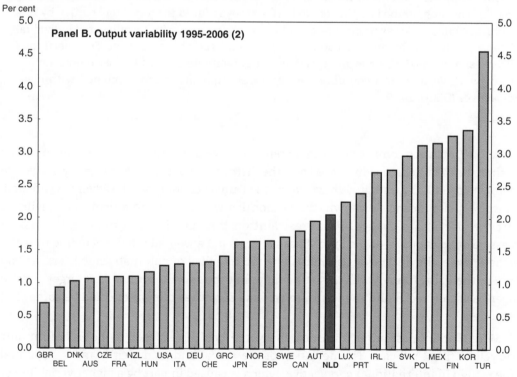

Per cent

Panel B. Output variability 1995-2006 (2)

StatLink http://dx.doi.org/10.1787/186256617220

1. Government net lending (% of GDP) minus cyclically adjusted government net lending (% of potential GDP).
2. Standard deviation of the output gap; 1995-2006, except for Czech Republic (1999-2006).

Source: OECD, Economic Outlook No. 82 Database.

OECD ECONOMIC SURVEYS: NETHERLANDS – ISBN 978-92-64-04076-2 – © OECD 2008

related to the extensive second pillar pension system. Pension contributions, which are tax deductible, have been negatively correlated to the output gap during the first half of the 2000s. The economic downturn and the parallel decline in asset prices put the solvency of pension funds at risk after the burst of the equity bubble; most pension funds had therefore no other choice than to sharply hike contributions (Box 2.3). The opposite effect took place during the boom years in the second half of the 1990s, when pension funds lowered contributions, resulting in lower tax exemptions and thereby boosting tax revenues. A post-crisis reform in pension fund supervisory rules, which reduced the share that pension funds are allowed to invest on equity markets and extended the period to assess solvency requirements, should help avoid a return of these pro-cyclical features, although this new approach is yet to be tested. An opposite effect on the budget has come from the tax deductibility on mortgage interest payments. During the economic upswing, increased housing demand pushed up house prices, leading to a rise in mortgage debt and interest payments and thus increasing associated tax expenditures from 1.7% to 2.3% of GDP over the past decade.

Box 2.3. **The second pillar pension system and the business cycle**

A main contributor to the decline in disposable income during the economic slowdown in the first half of the decade was the increase in pension fund contribution rates from an average of 7% in 2001 to 12.8% four years later. This was made necessary to restore pension funds' solvency, following the sharp stock market correction and the fall in interest rates. This led to a fall in the average funding ratio from 132% in 2000 to 101% in 2002 (Ponds and van Riel, 2007). Since then, two structural measures have been taken by many pension funds in the second pillar pension system to secure the long-term viability of the system and avoid future abrupt changes in the contribution rate. Firstly, indexation of pension rights (i.e. all liabilities) have been made solvency-contingent, implying that pension funds can erode the real value of pension payments if there is a mismatch between their assets and liabilities. This reduces the risk of under-funding (i.e. better control of solvency risks) and means pension funds can rely less on increasing premiums in order to restore solvency, which implies that negative effects on the business cycle should be smaller in the future. Secondly, most pension funds have moved from final-pay to average-wage schemes, where benefits are based on average wages over a number of years rather than being related to end-of-career pay.

As a consequence of these measures, the second pillar pension system has moved from being mostly a defined benefit system to becoming a hybrid system (Ponds and van Riel, 2007). It has also become less generous (Kakes, 2006). The changes have allowed the funding ratio to recover to 135% in 2006. Some authors have argued that this is still somewhat short of the necessary 140% to secure the real value of pensions (Ponds and van Riels, 2007). Moreover, few if any pension funds have formally moved away from the generous pension promises, which imply that members of a fund that abstain from indexation one year can expect that the fund will restore the real value of their pension payment at a later point in time. An additional issue is that older active members of a pension fund may have insufficient time to boost their alternative savings if the fund is unable to restore the real value of the pension. Thus, although substantial progress has been to secure the long-term stability of the pension system, additional adjustments may be required to secure all pension promises.

Given the sensitivity of the budget to the business cycle, there is a medium-term risk that the free play of automatic stabilisers might be impeded by the "signal value", which has been reduced from a deficit of 2½ per cent to 2% of GDP. The "signal value" implies that, when the deficit exceeds 2% of GDP, measures are to be taken so as to restrain expenditure below the ceilings previously agreed, and avoid breaching the Maastricht limit. A steady improvement of the structural budget balance is necessary, so as to provide enough room between the actual balance and the "signal value".

Fiscal policy framework

The recent consolidation of public finances was helped by the fiscal framework. The Dutch fiscal framework is rather unique by international standards because it has been consistently endorsed by successive governments. Perhaps this support results from a design that relies not only on strict rules, but also on national institutions that are able to adapt policies to changing circumstances (Bos, 2007).[3] The current approach, which was largely put in place by former Minister of Finance Zalm in 1994, is known under the name of "trend-based budgeting", because it seeks to keep public spending on a path of stable and controlled growth, and insulate the spending side of the budget from the influences of political changes, revenue windfall gains or attempts to fine tune the business cycle. The main policy tool used by the framework is the adoption of multi-annual ceilings for public expenditures, which are designed to break the link between annual changes in tax revenues and actual spending. At the start of any new coalition government, expenditure ceilings are established for the entire term of government (four years), based on expected revenues, and few changes to the ceilings are allowed subsequently. Thus, unexpected revenue windfall gains cannot be easily spent by the government; on the other hand, the government spending programme is generally protected in case of unexpected slowdown. Moreover, a requirement is in place that new tax measures must be off-set by compensating revenue measures to secure a neutral impact on the budget balance. Under this framework, automatic stabilisers are allowed to play freely on the revenue side. This appears to be a sound approach to finance functioning of public services, which are kept immune not only from short-term fiscal changes but also from evolving political preferences in the coalition government.

Recently, an official advisory group on budgetary principles brought together senior officials to work on ways to strengthen the framework and further reduce the pro-cyclicality of fiscal policy (Study Group on the Budget Margin, 2006). The group proposed: a) to remove interest payments from the expenditure ceilings; b) to break the link between the volatility in natural gas revenues and FES investments through a fixed funding level over the cabinet's term; c) to begin annual reporting on tax expenditures broadly defined (including the costs of tax deductions on mortgage interests and pension contributions); and d) to maintain the cautious economic growth assumptions for the medium-term framework. In addition, the group advised that part of the strategy to put public finances on a sustainable path should include structural measures to control ageing-related spending (such as health care and state pensions) and broaden the tax base. The government initially endorsed all of the proposals to strengthen the fiscal framework, except that it decided to use trend-based growth assumptions, rather than cautious economic growth assumptions, so as to reduce the bias towards windfall tax revenue gains and the derived political pressures on spending. When presenting the 2008 budget, however, the government failed to report on all tax expenditures. While the measures taken are improving the framework, further adjustments should be made.

The inclusion of unemployment insurance benefits under the spending ceiling brings an element of cyclicality, which requires offsetting changes to abide by the expenditure targets. For example, an economic downturn increases unemployment claims, thus requiring cutbacks in other items, perhaps at an inopportune time. The government should therefore consider excluding spending on unemployment insurance and other cyclically-sensitive expenditures from the expenditure ceilings. The issue was studied by the expert group, but it concluded that spending on unemployment insurance and government wages together exhibit no cyclical pattern. While this may be true in the medium term, due to the generally slow reaction of wages to economic developments the two variables do not fully cancel out in the shorter term, leading to additional spending pressure. Furthermore, including certain revenue items under the expenditure ceiling (such as dividends and central bank profit) should be reconsidered, as this allows greater spending in good times.

A significant part of government spending takes place in the form of tax expenditures. The fiscal framework includes a requirement that new tax measures are off-set by compensating revenue measures. Nonetheless, tax expenditures constitute a costly and growing form of government intervention. The tax expenditures listed in the budget amount to € 11 billion in 2008.[4] Although all tax expenditures are periodically reviewed by the relevant ministries, the system does not seem to be successful in bringing total tax expenditure down. A periodical review of all tax expenditures by an independent organisation, as done by the Congressional Budget Office (CBO) in the United States, could be a way to reduce tax expenditure and increase fiscal spending efficiency. Furthermore, as several large tax expenditures, such as the mortgage deductibility on owner-occupied housing and tax-exemption on pension contributions, are not listed in the 2008 budget, contrary to earlier recommendation by the OECD and the Study Group on the Budget Margin, this reporting should be implemented swiftly.[5] In addition to recording all tax expenditures and improving the review process, the government could consider making some of them subject to the expenditure ceilings when they are close substitutes to alternative government spending.

Long-term sustainability

In 2006 the effects of population ageing were estimated to increase public spending by about 7¼ percentage points to GDP by 2040, mostly as the result of higher pension and health care expenditures (Table 2.3). The ageing problem in the Netherlands peaks in 2040, when the old-age dependency ratio will have risen by about 20 percentage points to 43.4%, before falling back slightly. Despite the decline in the medium-term interest payments (related to the lower public debt to GDP ratio), the projections show that, in the absence of corrective measures, there will be a severe deterioration in general government balances and public debt levels in the longer term (van Ewijk *et al.* 2006). Lower interest rates and reduced wealth of pension funds have made the necessary correction larger than it was perceived to be in earlier calculations.[6] Requirements for securing long-term fiscal sustainability have increased further since 2006 as projections for life expectancy have been revised upward.

Table 2.3. **Public finances without budgetary measures in the baseline projection**

	2006	2011	2020	2040	2060	2100
	% of GDP					
Expenditure						
Social security	12.0	12.4	13.5	15.5	14.5	14.9
Public pensions	4.7	5.3	6.6	8.8	7.8	8.2
Disability benefits	2.0	2.1	1.9	1.6	1.6	1.6
Unemployment benefits	1.2	1.0	1.0	1.0	1.0	1.0
Other benefits	4.1	4.0	4.0	4.1	4.1	4.1
Health care	8.8	9.3	10.3	13.1	12.5	12.6
Education	5.4	5.5	5.4	5.8	5.7	5.8
Other expenditure, excluding interest payments	19.2	18.5	18.4	18.2	18.3	18.3
Primary expenditure	45.3	45.7	47.8	52.5	51.0	51.5
Interest payments	2.5	2.0	1.5	2.5	4.2	7.2
Total	47.8	47.7	49.3	55.0	55.2	58.7
Revenues						
Income tax and social security contributions	21.8	23.1	23.7	25.3	24.9	25.2
Of which on pension income	1.8	1.9	2.5	3.6	3.4	3.6
Indirect and other taxation	14.9	15.6	15.9	17.3	16.7	16.8
Of which on consumption by population aged 65 and older	1.9	2.2	2.9	4.2	3.6	3.7
Corporate income tax	2.6	2.6	2.5	2.4	2.3	2.3
Natural gas revenues	1.6	1.2	0.8	0.1	0.0	0.0
Other income	5.2	5.3	5.2	4.9	4.7	4.4
Total	46.1	47.9	48.1	50.0	48.6	48.8
EMU balance	−1.7	0.2	−1.1	−5.1	−6.6	−9.9
Primary EMU balance	0.7	2.2	0.4	−2.6	−2.4	−2.7
EMU debt	54.4	47.7	41.0	74.5	126.4	213.3
Government total wealth	60.3	64.2	61.0	17.6	−37.0	−125.0

Source: van Ewijk et al., 2006.

In January 2007, before the new coalition government took office, the sustainability gap (the difference between the projected government balance and the balance required to restore sustainability) was estimated to reach 2½ per cent of GDP in 2011. This was based on the assumption of unchanged policies. The government stated in its coalition agreement that it plans to close one third of this sustainability gap during its time in office, leaving the remainder to subsequent governments. A combination of structural measures decided in the coalition agreement, notably the increase in social security contributions for pensioners that retire early and the phasing-out of the transferability of the general tax credit (see below and Chapter 3) has reduced the sustainability gap by 0.7%. However, the "robust balance" (the structural balance corrected for natural gas revenues) that the government is expected to reach in 2011 is 0.6% lower than calculated in January, leaving the sustainability gap roughly where it was before the coalition took office. Thus, a sustainability gap of about 2¼ per cent of GDP will still have to be closed in 2011, so as to put the public finances on a sustainable path.

Policy options for restoring fiscal sustainability

Fiscal sustainability can be achieved through a pre-funding strategy, through implementing structural reforms to control the cost of ageing or through widening the funding base through higher labour market participation. The pre-funding strategy has the drawbacks that achieving large budget surpluses over a long period can be difficult in political economy terms; the risk that government surpluses would generate demands for short-sighted spending increases or tax cuts would be non-negligible (OECD, 2007a). A more robust sustainability strategy should rely more on structural measures to raise labour market participation and widen the tax base as well as measures to dampen the effects of ageing on public spending.

Expanding the labour supply through higher immigration has ambiguous effects. Although it could temporarily reduce the dependency ratio, in the long-run migrants will also claim pensions, making this policy option an unlikely long-term solution (OECD, 2007a). Alternatively, the tilting of the age structure could be achieved through higher fertility, but the factors behind fertility are poorly understood, making it difficult to design policy measures in this area to influence long-term fiscal outcomes.

A powerful measure would be to increase the effective retirement age, as this both expands the labour supply and reduces ageing-related costs (pension spending). This seems a logical option given that life expectancy at birth has increased by more than 6 years since 1957, the year when the current public pension was introduced. Van Ewijk *et al.* (2006) calculated that an increase in the official retirement age to 67 years in two steps in 2015 and 2025 would lower the sustainability gap by ½ per cent of GDP, assuming that the 65 and 66 year-olds have the same (low) labour market participation rate as today's 64 year-olds. However, as life expectancy is likely to increase further, a more structurally robust measure would be to increase the statuary retirement age in steps to 67 years and thereafter let it follow developments in life expectancy (Oliveira Martins *et al.*, 2005). To increase the beneficial impact of raising the retirement age, further enhancing participation incentives for older workers would be necessary. The abolition of tax incentives for early retirement has already induced a considerable increase in the participation rate of older workers (see Chapter 3). A further step in this direction is the government proposal of introducing full social contributions for pensioners unless they have continued to work until the official retirement age, providing strong incentives for higher participation until the retirement age without changing the tax incentives for those that choose to work until the statutory retirement age (see Chapter 3).[7]

In terms of controlling ageing-related costs, structural reforms have already been implemented to control health care costs, although health care expenditure is still rising rapidly (Box 2.4).[8] The other substantial ageing-related public spending category is state pensions, which was originally introduced to counter old-age poverty. Government spending on state pension is 4½ per cent of GDP per year and increasing rapidly. There are several ways to reduce the cost of state pensions, including the above-mentioned increase in the statutory retirement age.

Another effective way to reduce the ageing related cost and increase participation incentives would simply be to scale down the first pillar pension. The build-up of the extensive second pillar pension system has reduced the importance of the state pension pillar in countering age-related poverty. Calculations by the Secretariat using an overlapping generation model, as described in Chapter 3, show that lowering the replacement income provided by the first pillar pension from the current 31% to 25% of the average earnings would, in the longer term, increase average labour participation and improve government finances substantially (Table 2.4). A minimum replacement income of this level would still be generous in an international perspective. However, as rigorously scaling down the pensions would lead to a substantial reduction in incomes for vulnerable groups, it might be politically unattractive.

Box 2.4. **Early lessons from the health care reform**

A new *Healthcare Insurance Act* was introduced 1 January 2006, with the aim of guaranteeing that health care remains accessible, efficient, affordable, and of high quality (Ministry of Finance, 2006b). The reform introduces (a gradually phased-in) competition in the health care insurance sector, so as to curb the trend of rising health care costs, arising from the triple influence of higher incomes, new and costly technologies and ageing (Nederlandse Zorgautoriteit, 2006). The key characteristics of the reform are: health care insurance is mandatory; children do not have to pay a premium, low-income households are helped with an allowance (implying a fiscal cost of about € 4½ billion in 2006 and expected to rise to € 5½ billion in 2008); health insurance companies must accept all applicants; and health providers have a duty of care. More than 6 million households receive an income-dependent health care allowance to compensate for the higher nominal health insurance premiums and most households pay a maximum of 5% of their incomes on health (Ministry of Finance, 2005). Moreover, to prevent adverse-selection, a risk-equivalence fund is in place to compensate health insurance funds for their high risk patients (including about 30 major diseases). The reformed health care system is based on regulated market forces, where prices, volumes and quality are subject to substantial regulatory oversight. The system is supervised by a sector regulator (The Dutch Health care Authority).*

The first step of the reform was to allow competition between providers of health care insurance services. This induced an intense premium war for market shares, leading average insurance premiums to fall 7½ per cent below prior estimates (Teulings, 2006). Moreover, nearly one-fifth of all clients used their right to switch insurer once a year to change to a different health insurance company, almost four times more than expected. Most of the changes in consumer behaviour (fund switching and negotiation of lower premiums) have been achieved collectively through various organisations, such as membership of housing associations, unions, or through the workplace. Dutch insurance policies offer either free-choice policies (patients can freely choose their health care provider), or managed-care policies (companies enter into special deals with selected providers). Clients have mostly chosen free-choice policies, as price-differences between the policies were small and managed-care policies are considered as an inferior product because of the restricted choice, thus reducing the value of an important tool for insurance companies to negotiate lower health care prices.

In 2007, insurance premiums rose by some 8%, with another increase of 13% expected in 2008. Health insurance funds have implemented cost-saving measures, such as mergers, but over the longer term, the lower premiums can only be preserved if the health insurance funds are able to negotiate lower prices or better care with the health service providers. As part of the phasing-in of managed competition, the proportion of prices for health care services that are freely negotiated will double to about 20% of the more than 20 000 registered treatments by 2008. In addition, yardstick competition will be introduced in 2009 to increase the efficiency in hospitals. Looking forward, the main obstacles to a substantial lowering of health care costs are that individual consumers are not participating in seeking lower costs, that there is insufficient information about the quality of care and the limited number of freely negotiated prices. Dutch consumers probably have a higher awareness of the costs of their health care insurance than in many other OECD countries, but this is not matched by a similar awareness of the costs of health care provision (partly because of the patients' relatively infrequent use of care facilities). Independent evaluation institutions could be helpful in addressing such asymmetric information issues and the replacement of the current no-claim bonus (€ 255) by an annual own contribution of € 150 from 2008 could improve cost awareness. Still, a larger reliance on patients' co-payments would further enhance patients' incentives for purchasing low cost/high quality health care services. The limited share of freely negotiated prices needs to be extended substantially and should follow a fixed time table to allow forward planning by the involved parties.

---

* In addition, the sector is subject to a number of other supervisory bodies. The Health care Inspectorate (IGZ) monitors the quality of health care. The competition authority is responsible for competition policy issues (merger control, cartel activities, abuse of dominant position, etc). The central bank supervises the integrity and solvency of health insurance companies. The Netherlands Authority for Financial Markets has the task of the supervision of other financial market issues. The Data Protection Board ensures compliance with the Personal Data Protection Act. In general, managed competition requires complex and sophisticated organisations to mange medical practices and the administrative costs can be substantial (Hsiao, 2000).

Table 2.4. **Impact of pension reforms on labour supply and fiscal spending**

	Current pension system	Lower state pension to 25% of average earnings	Income-test state pension
Labour participation rate	75.2%	75.8%	75.3%
Average hours worked	32.2	32.1	32.4
Pensions (average replacement rate)	74.1%	61.5%	74.5%
Change in government balance	..	2.8%	3.6%

Note: The table compares the impact of various pension reforms on labour participation, average hours worked, the average replacement rate and the change in the fiscal burden with the current state pension system. The pension reforms considered are: i) a lowering of the state pension from the current 31% to 25% of the average income, which is still somewhat higher than the minimum income for people above 65 in Belgium, Germany or France; and ii) the introduction of an income-test for the state pension, at the full AOW-level with a 100% withdrawal rate with respect to other pension-income.
Source: Secretariat's calculations.

An alternative possibility could be to make the first pillar pension conditional on other income, in line with the social assistance scheme already in place. Such a measure would in effect provide a top-up for those with an income below the current level of the state pension. As currently poor and well-off people alike receive this old-age income support, such a reform would improve efficiency of public spending. If the mandatory social contribution to the public pension pillar is partly redirected towards the second pillar, the pension income of the average retiree would not change. However, it should be noted that means-testing of state pension in general creates important inactivity traps, requiring careful design and implementation. Simulations of such a scheme, based on individual income (due to modelling restrictions), are shown in the third column of Table 2.4. The simulation indicates that within this simple model public finances would improve substantially under this scenario. Moreover, if eligibility of the state pension would be made dependent on family income and on other income components similar to the scheme in place for social assistance, the simulation indicates an even stronger improvement in public finances. Although such simulations have a high level of uncertainty, the results suggest that reforming the state pension by merging it with the social assistance scheme could make a considerable contribution to securing the sustainability of public finances in the Netherlands.

Conclusion

The fiscal framework has been improved by removing some of its pro-cyclical elements, but more could be done to better allow the automatic stabilisers to play their stabilising role if necessary. That is particularly appropriate in the current uncertain conjectural situation. On the other hand, the lowering of the signal value to 2% may present a problem in case of a more prolonged downswing as the Dutch output variability is relatively high, implying a risk that pro-cyclical measures have to be implemented earlier than previously. Moreover, this risk has increased with the adoption of the CPB realistic, opposed to cautious, projections as this implies a higher possibility of lower-than-expected tax revenues. Hence, the Dutch government needs to continue improving the structural balance, thereby creating more room for the automatic stabilisers to work and improving the sustainability of public finances. At the same time, the government should also prevent pro-cyclical fiscal policy from exaggerating business cycle developments, which could either lead to overheating or the need for consolidation. Thus, the current strategy of achieving a 1% structural budget surplus over the medium-term looks appropriate, although further fiscal consolidations will have to take place after 2011. Additional measures to secure fiscal sustainability gap should be aimed at boosting participation or reducing ageing-related costs. With respect to the latter, reforming the first pillar pension, either by lowering the overall generosity or by further increasing the effective retirement age seem to provide promising directions for further reform. A more detailed set of recommendations is presented in Box 2.5.

Box 2.5. **Policy recommendations for securing sustainable public finances**

Fiscal consolidation should be implemented as planned without hampering the full function of the automatic stabilisers

The government plans to improve the structural balance by over 1 percentage point during the cabinet period. The full implementation of this programme is important as part of the strategy to achieve sustainable public finances. However, at the same time, the automatic stabilisers should be allowed to function fully in case of an economic downturn.

The fiscal framework could be further improved

To reduce the possible exacerbation of the economic cycle due to pro-cyclical fiscal policy, as seen during the last decade, the government should exclude items which behave pro-cyclically from the expenditure ceilings, notably spending on unemployment benefits. Moreover, including certain revenue items in the expenditure ceiling (such as dividends and central bank income) is questionable, as this allows greater spending in good times.

Tax expenditures constitute a costly and growing form of government intervention. Reporting on tax expenditure in the annual budget should be improved, notably on the income-tax allowance for mortgage interest payments and pension premiums, and a periodic review of these expenditures by an independent body should be considered, so as to improve fiscal spending efficiency. Furthermore, the government could consider including under the expenditure ceilings tax expenditures that are close substitutes to alternative government spending.

Measures to secure fiscal sustainability should include reforming the state pension

To improve sustainability of public finances the government should focus on enacting further reforms aimed at increasing labour participation (see following chapters) and reform age-related institutions. The government should raise the official retirement age in several steps to 67 years and thereafter link it to developments in life expectancy. To further reduce the cost of ageing, the government should evaluate various policy solutions aimed at reforming the public pension. Model simulations show that reducing the level of the first pillar pension would substantially raise labour participation and improve public finances.

Notes

1. The measures included tax cuts of € 2 billion and additional outlays of € ½ billion. The tax cuts consisted of an increase in the general tax credit, a reduction in employees' unemployment insurance contributions by more than ½ percentage point (a slightly larger cut for part-time workers), reductions in property taxes by abolishing the user element for people renting, and unchanged excise duties on petrol and other vehicle fuels rather than being raised in line with inflation. Likewise, the annual charge for domestic electricity users will be held at the 2005 level.

2. The tax measures included tax rate adjustments in the first two brackets of the income tax system, an increase in the general tax allowance, and a lowering of the corporation tax rate.

OECD ECONOMIC SURVEYS: NETHERLANDS – ISBN 978-92-64-04076-2 – © OECD 2008

3. However, the fiscal framework is not incorporated in a budget law as in some other countries, such as Sweden, where the legal basis in considered to increase long-term commitment (Heeringa and Lindh, 2001).

4. Some examples of major tax expenditures are the tax deductions for self-employed, reduced VAT-rates in the catering industry and public transport, and exemptions on certain rights on payments from capital insurance.

5. On similar arguments, other measures similar to tax expenditures, like the cost of exempting pension and housing wealth from the net wealth tax applicable to other private wealth could also be included.

6. The lower interest rate and fall in the wealth of pension funds imply lower future tax revenues. Moreover, the lower interest rate affects the applied discount rate, which in this context means more weight to the future cost of ageing. Another negative factor in the context is that, government debt is higher than projected in the 2000 study on fiscal sustainability. Moreover, the present study is less optimistic about future female participation. On the other hand, the disability reform has had larger-than-expected effects.

7. Abolishing the tax exemption from state pension contributions without the linkage to continued work would reduce the sustainability gap by about ¾ per cent of GDP (van Ewijk et al., 2006).

8. The reform was accompanied by other measures, such as greater use of cheaper generic drugs, inducing a 40% fall in their prices in 2005 (Ministry of Finance, 2006). Also the paring down of the insurance package of not strictly medical treatments had a favourable effect on health spending. Nevertheless, public health spending has increased due to higher demand for hospital services and the liberalisation of physiotherapy.

Bibliography

Bos, F. (2007), "The Dutch fiscal framework – History, current practice and the role of the CPB", *CPB Document, No.* 150, CPB, Den Haag.

Ewijk, C. van, N. Draper, H. Ter Rele and E. Westerhout (2006), "Ageing and the Sustainability of Dutch Public Finances", *Special Publication, No.* 61, CPB, Den Haag.

Girouard, N. and C. André (2005), "Measuring cyclically-adjusted budget balances for OECD countries", *OECD Economics Department Working Papers*, No. 434, OECD, Paris.

Heeringa, W. and Y. Lindh (2001), "Dutch Versus Swedish Budgetary Rules: A Comparison" in Banca d'Italia (eds.), *Fiscal Rules*, Banca d'Italia, Rome.

Hsiao, W. (2000), "What Should Macroeconomists Know About Health Care Policy? A Primer", *IMF Working Paper*, No. 136, IMF, Washington.

Kakes, J. (2006), "Financial behaviour of Dutch pension funds: a disaggregated approach", *DNB Working Paper*, No. 108, DNB, Amsterdam.

Ministry of Finance (2005), *Budget Memorandum 2006*, Den Haag, September 2005.

Ministry of Finance (2006a), *Budget Memorandum 2007*, Den Haag, September 2006.

Ministry of Finance (2006b), *Stability Programme of the Netherlands – November 2006 Update*.

Nederlandse Zorgautoriteit (2006), *Strategy of the Dutch Healthcare Authority – Creating and monitoring properly functioning healthcare markets*, NZA, Utrecht.

OECD (2007a), *Economic Outlook No. 81*, OECD, Paris.

OECD (2007b), *Cutting Red Tape – Administrative simplification in the Netherlands*, OECD, Paris.

OECD (2007c), *OECD e-Government Studies – Netherlands*, OECD, Paris.

Oliveira Martins, J., F. Gonand, P. Antolin, C. de la Maisonneuve and K-Y. Yoo (2005), "The Impact of Ageing on Demand, Factor Markets, and Growth", *OECD Economics Department Working Papers*, No. 420, OECD, Paris.

Ponds, E.H.M., B van Riel (2007), "The recent evolution of pension funds in the Netherlands: The trend to hybrid DB-DC plans and beyond", February 2007.

Study Group on the Budget Margin (2006), *Ageing and sustainability*, Den Haag.

Teulings, C. (2006), "Emergency: liberalise health-care prices to improve competition", *CPB Newsletter*, June 2006, CPB, Den Haag.

ISBN 978-92-64-04076-2
OECD Economic Surveys: Netherlands
© OECD 2008

Chapter 3

Coping with labour shortages: How to bring outsiders back to the labour market?

The Dutch labour market is functioning well, with employment and labour participation rates above OECD averages. Nevertheless, there are sizable pockets of under-activity, including social benefit recipients representing 17% of the working-age population, which could be mobilised in order to address short-run labour shortages and the long-run ageing-related reductions in the labour supply. Reintegrating these benefit recipients would also help to reduce spending on labour market programmes, which is among the highest in the OECD. Policies should continue to tackle the high inactivity of these groups. For people on social assistance and older workers, job search requirements should be strengthened and the authorities should continue making the tax-benefit system more work-friendly. For women with low-earning capacities, existing work disincentives should be eliminated. For (partially) disabled people, it is important to envisage labour market re-integration at an early stage. For the long-term unemployed, policies should be further strengthened by adjusting the unemployment benefit and the employment protection systems, as well as further improving current profiling and training measures.

Like other OECD countries, the Dutch economy has started to feel the effects of population ageing – older people are exiting the labour market in increasing numbers – weighing down on the growth of labour supply and weakening long-run growth prospects. If this trend persists, there is a risk that the potential supply of labour will stagnate, with detrimental effects on relative living standards. These prospects make it all the more important to mobilise existing pockets of under-activity, which are large by international standards, in particular among groups of social assistance recipients, low-skilled females, disabled people, older workers and the long-term unemployed (Figure 3.1). Income replacement schemes, targeted to people staying outside the labour market, were initially put in place as an attempt to address the adverse effects of large economic shocks and industrial restructuring, notably in the 1970s and 1980s. High replacement rates and corporatist administration of insurance systems led to a rapid increase in the number of beneficiaries. These schemes were subsequently reformed and inactivity fell rapidly over the 1990s, contributing to an expansion of labour supply. Nevertheless, around 1½ million recipients still access some form of replacement income due to their health characteristics (sick leave, disability benefits), labour market situation (unemployment benefits, social

Figure 3.1. **Incidence of inactivity remains large**[1]

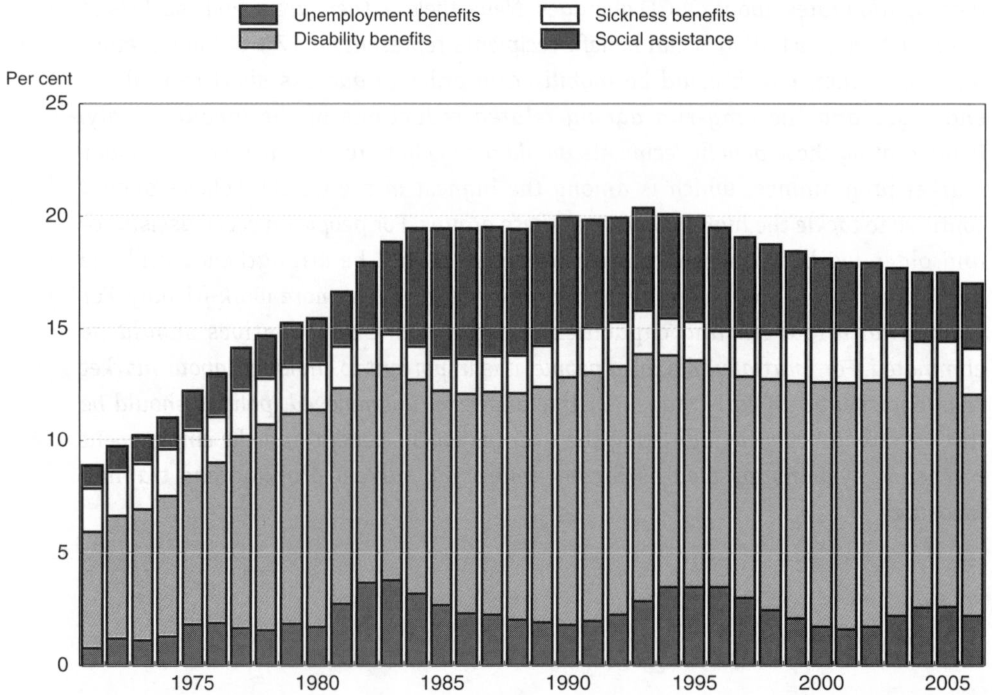

StatLink http://dx.doi.org/10.1787/186277830727

1. In per cent of working-age population.
Source: CPB.

assistance) or age (early retirement). Past efforts to activate these groups have been only partially successful notably because people have moved from one category of inactivity to another, including to long-term unemployment.

Bringing outsiders back to employment would go a long way towards addressing the challenges of population ageing. For instance, increasing older workers' participation to Swedish levels could raise the overall labour force participation rate by 4.3 percentage points. Similarly, raising prime-age female participation to the Danish level would lift the overall participation rate by 2.1 percentage points. Together, this would help to overcome the ageing-related reduction in the labour force over the medium-term and would stabilise labour supply in the long run, compared to current levels (Figure 3.2). Fully exploiting this potential would, however, require activating groups with weak labour market attachment. This is not an easy task, as resuming productive work requires appropriate economic incentives, as well as sometimes new investment in human capital and rebuilding professional skills. The authorities are aware of these challenges and have discussed policy measures at a recent "Participation Summit", which gathered the Dutch social partners and government representatives. In the light of these talks, the present chapter discusses measures to improve the work incentives faced by inactive people and to strengthen activation strategies. It reviews successively the situation of social assistance beneficiaries, low-skilled women, disabled persons, older workers and the long-term unemployed. Policy recommendations are summarised at the end of the chapter (Box 3.8).

Figure 3.2. **Labour force projections: current projections vs. projections with increased labour participation[1]**

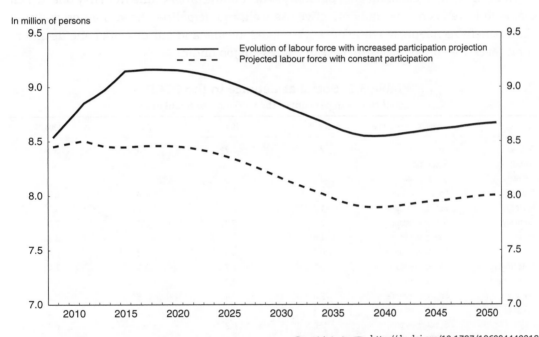

StatLink ⌦ http://dx.doi.org/10.1787/186284440318

1. The chart shows the evolution of the projected labour force both with current labour force participation projections and with increased labour force participation projections. The projected participation increase has been assumed to take place at an annual rate of 2% to reach a participation rate of 83% (similar to Sweden) in 2014.

Source: CPB, Secretariat's calculations.

Activating social assistance beneficiaries

Like most other countries, the Netherlands has a social assistance scheme providing support to people with insufficient financial resources to meet their essential living costs. The Work and Benefit Act (WWB) requires that people take on employment to support themselves, but provides a topping-up benefit to those who are unable to earn enough. The Act ensures that everyone receives at least the national assistance level, set at € 865.80 per month for a single person (€ 618.43 per month for those who share their rents) and € 1 236.86 per month for a couple as of 1 January 2004.[1] The budgetary and implementation responsibilities of the scheme were transferred to the municipalities in 2004 (apart from the establishment of benefit levels, which remain centralised). In addition, it was decided that the municipalities could use budget surpluses in this area for other purposes, thus enhancing the financial incentives for municipalities to monitor and activate benefit recipients.

There has been a decline in the number of persons receiving social assistance benefits since the 1990s, including during the most recent period, but the proportion of recipients in the labour force remains high by international standards (Table 3.1). Although the stronger economic situation has undoubtedly played an important role, it is widely acknowledged that the new incentive structure has stimulated municipalities to become more effective in screening new applicants and activating benefit recipients. Various tools have been used to enhance the incentives for job-search and help the labour market reintegration of recipients. The gate-keeper functions have been strengthened, so as to encourage applicants to accept temporary jobs or go back to schooling, rather than enrol under the scheme. A "work-first" strategy has been widely adopted by municipalities, whereby the benefit claimants are put in a job or training programme from day one, which seems to have been especially effective. As well, municipalities have the possibility to allow benefit recipients to combine work-related income and out-of-work benefits and to grant "back-to-work bonuses" in case of successful job finding.

Table 3.1. **Social assistance in the OECD**

Beneficiaries in per cent of the working-age population

	Type of programme	1990	1995	2000	2004
Australia	Lone parent	2.2	2.7	3.1	3.3
Canada	Social assistance	2.1	2.9	1.7	...
Denmark	Social assistance	3.3	2.9	2.5	...
Finland	Social assistance	0.4	0.3	0.4	0.3
France	Social assistance	1.7	2.9	3.2	3.4
Germany	Social assistance	2.1	2.2	2.2	2.5
Ireland	Lone parent	1.6	2.7	3.4	3.3
Japan	Social assistance	0.3	0.3	0.3	0.4
Netherlands	**Social assistance**	**5.1**	**4.7**	**3.2**	**3.1**
New Zealand	Lone parent	4.3	4.3	4.3	4.1
Norway	Social assistance	2.6	3.4	2.6	2.2
Portugal	Social assistance	...	...	7.3	...
Spain	Social assistance	0.0	0.2	0.3	0.3
Sweden	Social assistance	1.3	2.1	1.9	1.7
United Kingdom	Lone parent	2.2	2.9	2.4	2.0
United States	Lone parent	2.3	2.5	0.9	0.6

Note: Non-categorical social assistance is not available in all OECD countries and is often substituted for by income support for people with weak earnings capacity and children.
Source: Carcillo and Grubb, 2006.

While the success of the reform should encourage other OECD countries to implement similar measures, the incentives to return to work could be strengthened further, in particular to avoid a new stock of recipients from building up in an economic downturn. In this context, current plans to exempt lone parents with children under the age of 5 years from job-search requirements appear to go in the wrong direction.[2] Under these new plans, such persons would still be obliged to participate in training schemes to prepare for future labour market participation, but they would not be expected to work immediately. Such a measure is unlikely to have the intended effect and would be more costly than immediate participation on the labour market with support provided in the form of guaranteed child care.

Tax measures that discourage low-skilled women from working

Despite high female participation rates at the aggregate level, low-skilled women tend to remain at the margin of the labour market. This is particularly so for married low-skilled women, who are discouraged from participating by the tax system, despite the fact that they would like to work and that there is a strong demand for their labour, particularly in the service sector (Jaumotte, 2003). Policies have focussed in the past on removing impediments to full-time work such as raising the provision and subsidisation of childcare services but disincentives remain.

A tax measure particularly hampering female participation is the transferability of the general tax credit. Although the Dutch tax system has largely been individualised, the general tax credit of non-participating partners is transferable within couples, for taxpayers with low to moderate incomes. This increases the effective tax rate at the participation margin for the second earner, creating inactivity traps that cause women, especially low-skilled women, to stay at the fringe of the labour market. According to OECD estimates, reducing marginal effective tax rates of the low-wage second earner to the same level as for the first earner would increase the female participation rate by 2.4 percentage points (Burniaux, Duval and Jaumotte, 2004). In its coalition agreement, the Dutch government has recognised this transferability of the tax credit as a problem for female participation and decided to individualise it, thus making work pay more for low-skilled women. The phase-out of transferability will, however, take place over a period of 15 years, which seems unduly long. In addition, the phase-out will only apply to tax payers born after 1971 and mothers with children under the age of 6 years will be exempted, limiting the overall impact of this policy change. Given the important effect of a full phase-out, which is estimated to increase overall female labour participation by 6.6 percentage points (Table 3.2), the transferability should be eliminated more rapidly and without exemptions.

Unconditional child benefits and the income-tested child tax credit discourage participation, in particular of lower-income women (OECD, 2006a, p. 130). Currently, the unconditional child benefit per child is € 1087 *per annum*.[3] The income effect of granting unconditional child benefits provides incentives for low-income mothers to withdraw completely from the labour market. In addition, households are eligible to a child tax credit of up to € 939.[4] On the other hand, a small individual child credit (combination credit) of € 146 and an additional child credit for second earners, of € 700, are in place in order to stimulate women to combine work and child care activities. According to CPB calculations (Table 3.3) either a fully individualised targeted child tax credit for parents with a low income (column 3) or a child tax credit targeted specifically at the second earner (column 4) could increase female participation by 1.2%. As the latter measure is better targeted, the

Table 3.2. **Long-run impact of an individualisation of the tax credit on labour supply**

In per cent, unless otherwise indicated

Labour supply in total hours worked	1.0
Primary earners	0.1
Secondary earners	4.8
Single persons	0.4
Female participation rate (percentage points)	6.6
Employment	
Low skilled	0.7
High skilled	1.3
Unemployment (percentage points)	
Low skilled	0.1
High skilled	0.1

Source: De Mooij, 2006 and Secretariat's calculations.

distortions imposed on other groups as a result of the increased financing burden would be less severe. Following this analysis, the government has decided to make the additional tax credit for second earners income dependent (with no phase out) and to increase its maximum amount. In order to further stimulate female participation, the authorities should consider shifting more of the family-income based child tax credit to the individual or second earner children tax credit.

Table 3.3. **Long-run impact of reforms in child allowances on labour supply**

	General child allowance	Child credit for low incomes	Child credit for working couples
Labour supply in total hours worked	−0.4	−0.4	0.1
Primary earners	−0.3	−0.4	−0.1
Secondary earners	−0.6	0.0	1.0
Single persons	−0.4	−0.3	−0.1
Female participation rate (percentage points)	−0.5	1.2	1.2
Employment			
Low skilled	0.1	0.5	0.3
High skilled	−0.7	−0.9	0.1
Unemployment (percentage points)			
Low skilled	−0.1	0.0	−0.1
High skilled	0.0	0.0	0.0

1. Changes are measured in per cent if not otherwise indicated.
Source: De Mooij, 2006.

Reforms of disability benefits

Several reforms introduced since the 1990s have successfully reduced the inflow into the disability benefit (DB) scheme, notably the Gatekeeper Act in 2002, the application of tighter testing criteria in 2004, and the Labour Capacity Act in 2006. Entry into the disability benefit programme is now subject to more rigorous medical tests, and there is a required sickness absence period of two years paid by the employer. As a consequence, inflows into the DB scheme have decelerated substantially, while gross outflows continue at a much higher rate, leading to a net outflow of recipients from the system (Figure 3.3).[5] Nevertheless, the number of DB beneficiaries remains high in international comparison, mainly due to a high incidence of partial disability (Figure 3.4). Moreover, the decline of

Figure 3.3. **Net flows in and out of the disability benefit scheme, 1998-2006**

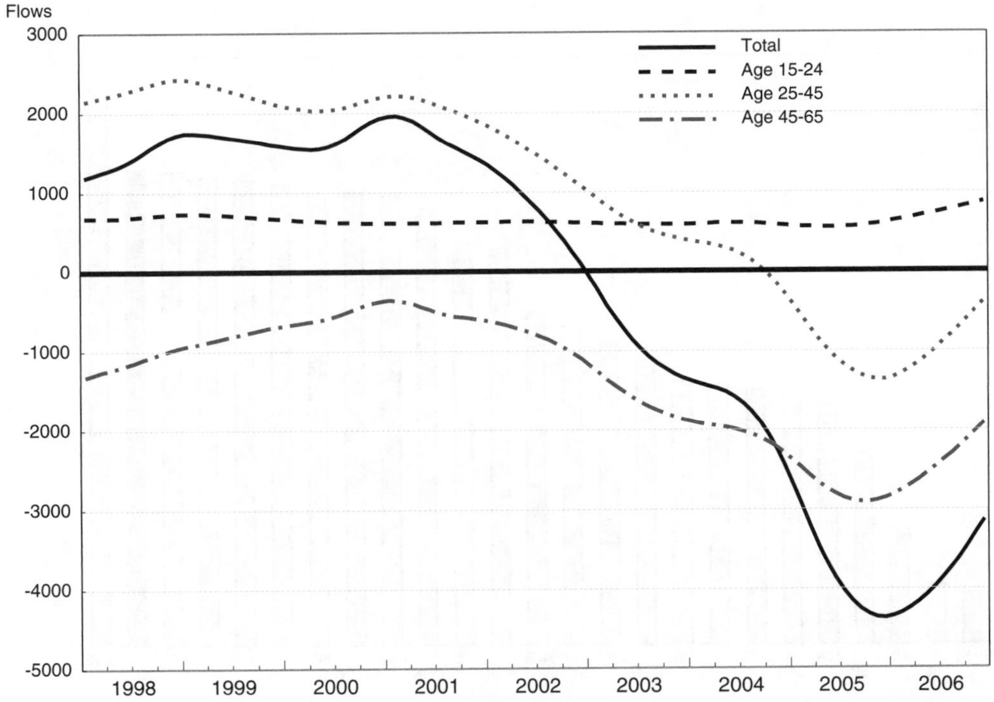

StatLink ⟪≣⟫ http://dx.doi.org/10.1787/186302187602

Source: Statistics Netherlands.

inflows into the DB scheme has been concentrated in the age group 25-45. For the disabled of both older and younger age groups, less progress has been achieved in activating and partially reintegrating the benefit recipients into the labour market. Finally, little is known about where those who have left the DB scheme have moved to; in particular, no structural assessment of labour market reintegration is available, making it difficult to evaluate the success of the DB reform for raising labour supply.

Medical reassessment and stricter access criteria of newly disabled workers have helped to bring down the aggregate rate of (partial) disability. However, most of those formerly classified as disabled have been out of the labour force for too long to be quickly returned to employment. It is, therefore, essential for this group to receive early activation and re-integration services. New entrants may even receive activation during their period of sickness leave if their current employer cannot offer suitable alternative occupations with the firm. In this regard, the government enacted several measures to strengthen work incentives and to facilitate reintegration of currently partially disabled people (Box 3.1), some of which having been further developed after the recent Participation Summit. Incentives to take up work after entering the partial DB scheme could be strengthened even further if the initial period during which benefits are based on previous earnings unrelated to the remaining partial work capacity, would be limited further, or phased-out altogether. Despite current difficulties in increasing participation of partially disabled workers more forcefully, regular assessments remain essential. In this respect, the recent decision to lower the maximum age at which beneficiaries under the old scheme are subject to the new, stricter medical testing criteria from 50 to 45, is unfortunate. This group

Figure 3.4. **Incidence of disability in the OECD**

Per cent of population aged 20-65 years, 2003-2004[1]

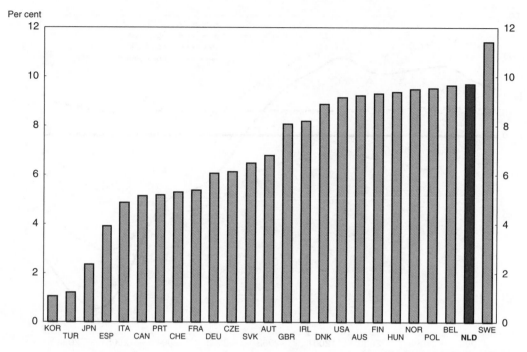

StatLink 🔢 http://dx.doi.org/10.1787/186313606001

1. 2003 for the Czech Republic, Finland, France, Germany and Italy.

Source: OECD, Going for growth, 2006.

Box 3.1. **Reforms to strengthen work incentives for partially-disabled people**

The government enacted a series of measures in order to ensure that the DB reform leads to an overall reduction in the stock of inactive people, and not only to a transfer from one benefit scheme to another. In particular, reintegration incentives have been strengthened through:

● an extension from one to two years of the initial sick leave period to be covered by the firm, which increased incentives for employers to find alternative job opportunities within the firm;

● the introduction of a "no-risk policy" whereby the UWV (uitvoeringsinstituut werknemersverzekeringen) covers sickness payments for employers who keep a (partially) disabled employee at work in case this person becomes sick again within five years;

● strengthening the incentives to take up work by introducing DB replacement rates that are dependent on the hypothetical earnings capacity of the benefit recipient. Upon entering the WGA scheme, those who have worked during 26 out of the last 36 weeks receive a replacement income (the loongerelateerde uitkering) that covers 70% of the difference between the current and the last wage (up to a ceiling). This benefit runs out after an age-dependent period of a maximum of 5 years, after which it is replaced by the loonaanvullingsuitkering, which is set as a function of the former wage and the hypothetical wage that the disabled person may still be able to achieve, if a person earns at least 50% of his hypothetical wage. Otherwise, the benefit is replaced by a vervolguitkering, which is based on the minimum wage.

remains, however, liable to periodic medical reassessment under the old criteria. Only new cases above 45 will be tested and reassessed under the new, stricter medical testing criteria. Medical and technological innovations may offer new opportunities to participate – at least partially – in the labour market and hence lower inactivity among DB recipients.

There has been a sharp increase in the number of younger people entering into disability under the *Wajong* scheme (mostly younger people with unspecified psychological disorders). The stock of recipients increased from 1.5% to 1.9% of the labour force during the last seven years. The *Wajong* scheme does not offer similar incentives (including reintegration services) as the DB system for prime-age workers so; recipients run the risk of permanently failing to integrate into the labour market. At the same time, weak activation and few medical reassessments of *Wajong* beneficiaries seem to have encouraged young people with lower educational backgrounds to apply for these benefits. The government should consider reacting quickly to signs of further inflows by adjusting its medical access criteria for certain types of disability. Moreover, incentives for the UWV to bring these people into employment (and off the benefits) are low as they usually lack labour market experience and may require the heavy use of reintegration services. In its current discussions on the reform of the *Wajong* scheme, the government should therefore include improving the incentives for school-to-work transition of younger people by requiring (except in cases where the impossibility of ever being able to work is obvious), that those who register under the *Wajong* scheme first apply for Social Assistance benefits and be available for activation measures and job market integration before they qualify for disability benefits.[6]

Continued work at older age

The participation of older workers in the labour market is still low in international comparison (Figure 3.5) though it has increased substantially in recent years, in particular among the age group 55- 59, reflecting the removal of tax incentives for early retirement (Table 3.4).[7] Adding to this effect is the complete elimination of pre-pension schemes, which increased the effective age of retirement. Moreover, as the removal of remaining tax incentives for early retirement schemes only applies to new retirees and a transition scheme has been put in place for those who turned 55 before 1 January 2005, a further increase of participation and employment rates for the elderly above 60 years can be expected. To further stimulate participation of the elderly the government plans to increase the work-related tax credit for workers that continue working after 62 and until retirement.

Still, continued work at an older age is discouraged by several factors. Although older unemployed people have been subject to job-search requirements since 2004, and the duration of employment benefits has been shortened, the maximum duration of unemployment benefits is still long and unemployment can be used as a transition to retirement. Severance payments can be high after long tenure (as a rule they are equivalent to 1 month of salary per year of service; until the age of 40. After that, each year accounts for 1½ months salary until the age of 50. Thereafter, each year worked accounts for 2 months of salary. These severance payments can be used to top-up unemployment benefits. Furthermore, workers are often not able to keep working after the age of 65. In most cases labour contracts legally end at 65 by collective agreement. Even for those not covered by collective agreements, the strict employment protection – and hence the obligation to pay high severance payments – stops at the 65th birthday.[8] In addition, the

Figure 3.5. **Old-age participation rates in the OECD**
1995 *vs.* 2005

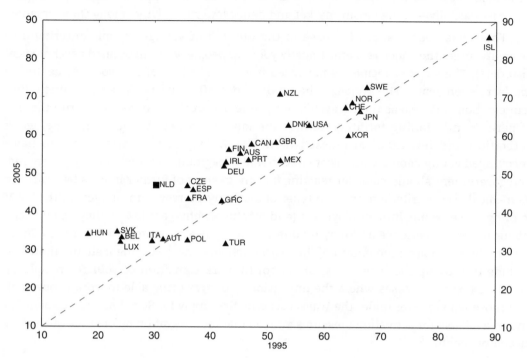

StatLink ᓫᔿᐧᑲ *http://dx.doi.org/10.1787/186333375046*

Source: OECD *Labour Force Statistics.*

Table 3.4. **Participation of older workers**
In % of the working-age population

	1995	2000	2005	2006
Men and women				
55-59	39.1	48.9	55.4	58.1
60-64	11.2	15.5	18.3	20.8
Total 55-64	25.8	33.6	39.7	41.7
Total 15-64	57.8	64.5	63.2	64.5
Men				
55-59	57.5	66.8	72.2	73.2
60-64	17.6	23.9	25.1	28.8
Total 55-64	38.8	47.4	52.3	53.8
Total 15-64	71.6	76.6	72.1	73.1
Women				
55-59	20.4	30.5	38.3	42.7
60-64	5.1	7.3	11.5	12.8
Total 55-64	13	18.8	26.9	29.5
Total 15-64	43.5	52	54.1	55.8

Source: Statistics Netherlands.

obligation to pay wages for the first two years of sickness also applies to employees above 65 years of age, which private insurers are hesitant to insure. Combined together these features provide strong incentive for employers to lay off their workers on this particular birthday. In order to strengthen labour demand for older workers after their

65th birthday, the government should consider abolishing the requirement to pay wages during long periods of sickness leave for workers above the age of 65. Finally, participation incentives for older workers could also be strengthened by indexing the official retirement age to life expectancy, thus further edging up the effective exit age from the labour market.

Existing tax-favoured savings schemes create an additional hurdle to old-age labour participation. Currently, employees have the choice between a general tax-favoured savings scheme (*spaarloonregeling*) and a competing life-course savings scheme (*levensloopregeling*) that is set up explicitly to finance a temporary withdrawal from the labour market (Box 3.2). The latter plan is particularly popular among older workers, but in principle both plans can be used to finance early-retirement before the age of 65.[9] In order to stimulate a further rise in the effective exit age from the labour market, the government should eliminate the possibility to use this tax exemption to finance early exits from the labour market. If the government considers that the current tax system unduly discourages the accumulation of savings with potentially useful externalities (such as to finance periods of retraining or pay for the education of children), it could consider raising the level above which financial assets are subject to the 1.2% wealth tax to, say, € 100 000, rather than grant tax exemptions targeted to specific schemes, such as life-course savings.[10] This would not only reduce possible distortions in the allocation of savings, but also reduce administrative complexity.

A Beveridge-style state pensions system (AOW) provides an old-age pension income to people who are aged 65 and over and have lived in the Netherlands for most of their lifetime,[11] irrespective of past contributions, similarly to the scheme in place in

---

Box 3.2. **The life-course savings scheme**

As part of the tripartite agreement to phase-out tax advantages favouring early retirement systems, it was agreed to introduce a life-course savings plan (*levensloopregeling*, LCS) to allow employees to save part of their income in a fund out of which, a period of up to 3 years of labour market withdrawal can be financed (early retirement, sabbaticals, paternity leave or other family obligations, training and educational leave). A maximum of 12% of the gross wage can be deducted annually from the taxable income so as to build savings, subject to a total accumulated saving ceiling of 210% of the gross wage. Taxation on such saving is deferred until the fund is drawn down. Due to the progressivity of the tax system, this can generate a substantial tax advantage, in particular in higher income brackets. A further tax incentive stems from the exemption of the life-course savings from the net wealth tax, which equals 1.2% and is applicable to most other financial assets. Moreover, for each year of participation in the scheme, the holder of the fund is entitled to a fixed tax credit. When the fund holder reaches the official retirement age at 65, the fund can be transferred (without the tax credit) to second pillar pensions, thereby increasing taxable income and raising the implicit tax on continued work.

Currently, with the system entering only its second year, the inflow into this new savings scheme has been limited as savers have to choose between the LCS and the older, tax-favoured savings scheme (*spaarloonregeling*), although the system is expected to continue maturing. However, the system experiences a relative success among older workers. Moreover, in contrast to the original intention to allow employees to adjust their labour supply to their personal circumstances at any point during their working life, a recent survey reveals that savers currently intend to use the plan to retire earlier.

New Zealand. Eligible single pensioners receive a first pillar monthly pension of € 956.18 and retired couples receive € 1609.91. This AOW pension constitutes a social safety net and represents 34% of pensioners' average earnings (OECD, 2006b). Such a system runs the risk of weakening labour participation incentives, in particular for low-income and second earners, as inactivity does not penalise access to the AOW pensions. The government should consider reforming the current state pension system in order to strengthen the participation incentives. The WWB Act already provides a social safety net ensuring a net minimum income to every resident, including pensioners. A separate social safety net therefore does not appear necessary. For people with life-time careers, the well-functioning second pillar pension funds provide adequate old-age retirement income. A reduction in the AOW pension is likely to increase participation through postponed (early) retirement, without aggravating poverty among pensioners (Bruinshoofd and Grob, 2006). More generally, a budget-neutral reduction of both the pension entitlement and income tax rates would substantially reduce the net present value of the tax burden over the working life, in particular for lower-income earners (Figure 3.6). For instance, a reduction in the replacement rate from 30% to 25% would help to increase labour participation, in particular of the 55-65 age group, by 3% and the average working time for this age group by almost 10% (Box 3.3). Any changes to the pensions system, however, should be introduced gradually in order to allow future recipients to make alternative savings.[12]

Incentives to postpone retirement are also affected by the fact that pensioners do not pay social security contributions for state pensions. This tax exemption allows a reduction in the tax rate of 17.9 percentage points for all income in the first two income tax brackets,

Figure 3.6. **Net present value of tax liabilities when lowering state pension**[1]
Actual tax-benefit system *vs.* pension reforms

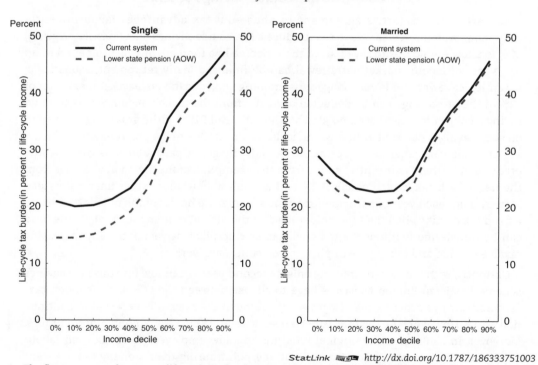

StatLink 🔗 http://dx.doi.org/10.1787/186333751003

1. The figures present the average life-cycle tax burden across income deciles in the current system, compared with the life-cycle tax burden after a reduction of the gross state pension of € 161 per month.

Source: Secretariat's calculations.

OECD ECONOMIC SURVEYS: NETHERLANDS – ISBN 978-92-64-04076-2 – © OECD 2008

Box 3.3. **Simulations of pension system reforms**

Reforms in the public and private pension systems involve changes in participation incentives over the life-cycle. In order to simulate such effects, an overlapping-generations model has been estimated and calibrated for 10-income deciles of the Dutch economy, similar to the approach used by Kotlikoff and Rapsojn (2006). On the basis of the current tax-benefit system, the model produces a labour force participation rate of 75.8% and a supply of working hours of around 32 hours a week, matching the observed values (see Annex 3.A1 for details on the model and its results).

The model considers the impact of three different types of taxes on incentives to participate and to expand working hours: taxes on consumption, on labour earnings and on capital income. In addition, the model introduces various social benefits and tax breaks available to households, including the general tax credit and tax exemptions for pensioners. The equilibrium distribution of the aggregate capital stock across different households then allows to calculate the net present value of tax liabilities (presented in the text) that a household in a certain income bracket faces.

When simulating the reforms to the pension system, a balanced-budget rule has been imposed: additional budgetary resources made available by lowering replacement rates or raising the marginal tax rates of pensioners are redistributed to households via lower consumption taxes. Alternatively, this higher primary surplus could have been given back to households in the form of lower marginal income tax rates, thereby possibly even increasing the beneficial effects presented above.

---

implying an increasing implicit tax on continued work before the age of 65. In addition, the exemption constitutes a substantial redistribution towards pensioners of about 0.5% of GDP (Stevens, 2005). As first pillar pensions are linked on a net basis to the social minimum income, a removal of this tax exemption would increase state pensions on a gross basis, yielding the same net disposable income as before. Consequently, the current tax break exclusively benefits pensioners who also have access to second pillar pensions (van Ewijk, 2004). Hence, removing the tax break would not lower net disposable income for pensioners who only receive the first pillar pension but would raise the tax burden for those who also have access to second pillar pensions. The government currently plans to strengthen participation incentives for older workers above a certain income level by introducing a new levy that reduces the value of the tax break for those who stopped working before the age of 65. While this measure is welcome, its contribution to long-term fiscal sustainability will be small (see preceding chapter) and the impact on labour participation limited as life-cycle tax liabilities do not substantially decline (they even increase for married earners, see Figure 3.7). The full impact of removing the tax break depends on how the additional tax revenues will be used to strengthen participation incentives for the working-age population.

Activating the unemployed

Despite favourable employment trends, long-term unemployment remains high in comparison to countries with a similarly low overall rate of unemployment. This may be related to the transfer of persons from the above-mentioned categories to the pool of the unemployed, following their activation, immediately or after a short period of work. Long spells of unemployment discourage job search efforts, and encourage the unemployed to

Figure 3.7. **Net present value of tax liabilities when removing pensioners'
tax exemptions**[1]

Actual tax-benefit system *vs.* pension reforms

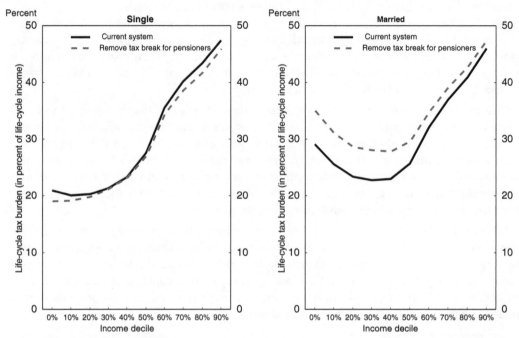

StatLink ⬛ http://dx.doi.org/10.1787/186358207352

1.   The figures present the average life-cycle tax burden across income deciles in the current system, compared with
     the life-cycle tax burden when removing the tax exemption for pensioners on the first and second income
     bracket.

Source: Secretariat's calculations.

eventually withdraw from the labour market altogether. The employability of workers
diminishes rapidly in the early months of unemployment (Lechner and Vazquez-Alvarez,
2006). Thus, activation and reintegration are essential at an early stage particularly to off-
set declining search activity.

The duration of unemployment benefits was reduced from 5 years to a maximum of
38 months at the end of 2006, in an attempt to increase job search incentives. Nevertheless,
benefit duration remains long in international comparison. Moreover, income replacement
rates do not decrease much with the length of the unemployment spell, even though they
are initially at similar levels as in other OECD countries. Declining replacement rates have
been shown to be an effective tool to strengthen job search incentives and to prevent
unemployment from becoming structural, in particular when benefit duration is long
(Bassanini and Duval, 2006). Hence, although unemployment benefits contribute to
improving the quality of job matches (OECD, 2007), the combination of long duration and
non-decreasing benefits is likely to dampen incentives for job search. The government
should therefore consider shortening the pay-out period of unemployment benefits
further, possibly to a period of 2 years, as in other countries. In addition, net replacement
rates should decline with the length of the unemployment spell. A consequence of phasing
down benefits could be that the initial replacement rate would be increased in order to
provide a sufficient margin for a steeper taper rate.

Reforming severance payments

Long-term unemployment is also likely to be raised by employment protection, which is strict in international comparison, thus reducing labour market turnover and prolonging unemployment spells for those at the margin of the labour market (Lalive *et al.* 2004). Under current procedures, firms face a dual dismissal system (Box 3.4). Smaller enterprises usually choose the administrative route, which avoids the payment of severance payments, but has the disadvantages of being lengthy and not always successful. Larger employers prefer the judicial route, which is generally quicker and less uncertain, but comes at an important financial cost in terms of severance payments. As a rule, these severance payments are based on the seniority of the employee (see above).

Box 3.4. **The dual system of the Dutch dismissal law**

Lay-offs can occur through two channels: 1) employers can address their request to the local public employment service (CWI) to obtain prior permission or 2) they can request a local court to dissolve the individual employment contract. In the first case, employers are faced with long notice periods (depending on the tenure of the employee) and a more bureaucratic and time-consuming dismissal procedure. The second route is faster, but also more expensive as firms are faced with much higher severance pay obligations, especially for long job tenures. Nevertheless, this route has increasingly been taken, in particular by large companies, as the costs for an individual layoff rapidly declines relative to the CWI-route when the salary of the person concerned increases, as it usually does with the size of the company (SER, 2005).

After a recent Participation Summit, the cabinet had put forward a proposal to review the current dismissal system and replace it with a more predictable scheme, which would regulate the level of severance payments. The new system would have specified severance payments in law and allow appeal of dismissals to local courts only as an *ex post* option, in case one of the parties is unfairly treated. This proposal would have made court decisions, and hence the level of severance payments, more predictable. The social partners failed to unanimously endorse this proposal, and the Cabinet finally decided not to pursue the reform of the dismissal law for now, but to establish a commission to advice on how to raise participation. However, the proposed reform would have been a welcome initiative to decrease the procedural inconveniences of the current system. The authorities should continue to assess the possibilities to reform the dismissal law. In a new proposal, the authorities should consider to limit the maximum amount of severance payments that seemed to be high in the earlier proposal, as it could have reached up to € 100 000 for older workers with long job tenure and even more for workers with annual incomes above this level,[13] which constitutes a serious financial risk, in particular for smaller companies.[14] Instead, the government should aim at legislating a minimum amount of severance payments – possibly dependent on the job tenure – that is well below proposed levels, leaving it up to social partners to negotiate any additional severance payments. This would help to reflect better sectoral and individual differences in the willingness of firms to grant severance payments to their employees. Moreover, the current proposal suggests letting rights to severance payments accumulate at a faster rate for workers above 50 years. This is likely to decrease employment chances for older workers and the government should aim at aligning severance payments rights between different categories of workers. The dismissal reform could also take example at the Austrian severance payment system, in particular as regards the objective to lower payments for dismissed workers with long seniority (see Box 3.5).

Box 3.5. **Reform of the system of severance payments in Austria**

The Austrian dismissal system used to share aspects found in the Dutch system, particularly the reliance on court decisions. The system was reformed in 2003 in order to address concerns about the lack of flexibility and for equity reasons (only of all employees benefited from severance payments). The reform aimed, in particular, at lowering firms' financial burden of dismissals and at limiting the additional costs resulting from an extension of the system to small- and medium-sized enterprises, which effectively had not been subject to the earlier severance payment scheme.

As a result, individual savings accounts have been opened for each new employment contract signed after January 2003, managed by one of nine privately run funds. Under the new system, employers are obliged to contribute 1.53% of gross monthly salary to these accounts. The rate was set such as to guarantee 12 months pay after 37.5 years of contributions, although there are signs that the rate is set too low. Contributions to the fund are tax free, but withdrawals are subject to a 6% flat rate. Dismissed employees can draw on their individual accounts, provided that they have been with their former employer for at least three years. Voluntary quits and dismissals after shorter tenures are not covered but the accumulated fund remains in the individual account, which can be taken over to the next employer. Any accumulated fund can be accessed at the legal retirement age or after five years of quitting the labour market (for instance, for child caring or expatriation).

The new system is claimed to have enhanced job mobility, lowered dismissal costs and reduced litigation over unfair dismissals. However, job mobility is mainly enhanced from the point of view of employees who no longer face loss of accumulated rights to severance payments when switching jobs. For employers, the new system mainly removes the liquidity risk of severance payment obligations during economically difficult times without reducing the overall financial burden of the system. Dismissal rates are unaffected, as the contribution rate is not linked to the number of lay-offs (such as with unemployment benefit experience rating in the US). What is more, the higher non-wage costs resulting from severance payments are likely to be internalised over time, except for employees at the minimum wage. The system resembles a savings device but with limited competition between the nine severance funds as the employers choose for the employees in which fund they accumulate the severance payment rights.

Enhancing activation schemes

Activation schemes have experienced some streamlining recently (see Box 3.6) but further improvements of activation schemes would help stimulating additional outflows from the unemployment pool and reduce the incentives of long-term unemployment (Boone and van Ours, 2004). Job search assistance is provided by the CWI (*Center for werk en inkomen*), which acts as a gatekeeper by placing the newly registered unemployed into different activation categories, depending on the perceived risk of long-term unemployment. The UWV, on the other hand, administers the earnings-related unemployment insurance benefits, activates long term unemployed and applies sanctions in case of insufficient job search efforts.

> ## Box 3.6. **Recent developments in activation policies**
>
> In order to place the newly unemployed into different activation programmes, the CWI used to establish a profile of the job seeker on the basis of a point system (called the "chance-meter") reflecting the job seeker's difficulties to reintegrate into employment. Each of the four profiles was characterised by a particular activation strategy and certain reintegration programmes to which the job seeker had access; however, once placed in a certain category, a job seeker only had access to programmes belonging to his or her particular profile, even if some other programmes may have been more appropriate. Similar profiling systems are in place in other OECD countries to avoid using expensive active labour market measures for the easy-to-place unemployed (Frölich *et al.*, 2003). However, there was and continues to be scope for improving the system as the predicted time of exit from unemployment was properly assessed in only 60% of all cases. The implication was that too many unemployed were left alone for too long without proper activation and that there was too much spending for those who turned out to find a new job more easily (Tergeist and Grubb, 2006). In addition, reflecting the lack of full integration of employment services provided by the CWI, the UWV and the municipalities, the latter two institutions carry out their own profiling of job seekers into target groups that are contracted out to private replacement providers, creating substantial administrative overlays. In order to reduce this administrative burden and in an attempt to improve the accuracy of the profiling, the government has consequently reduced the number of profiles from four to two.

The current profiling system employs only two profiles whereby everyone is deemed capable of seeking for a job (stream A) unless there is a situation where individual characteristics prevent immediate job seeking (stream B) which (temporarily) hinders job search activities. Job-seekers in stream B generally need special reintegration programmes that focus on removing obstacles and restoring their daily life. The need for profiling may be reduced when there are economic incentives for the unemployed to self-select into different activation groups. This could be achieved, for instance, by offering two different forms of unemployment benefits and assistance. An unemployed person could choose a combination of minimal monitoring of job search efforts and relatively high, but steeply declining unemployment benefits, or the person could choose a package with lower, but less rapidly declining unemployment benefits, combined with tight job search controls and stiff sanctions. This would allow the unemployed to reveal their own assessment of reintegration chances and support the CWI in properly targeting reintegration measures.

International evidence suggests that profiling may not be sufficient for activation measures to be successfully applied, and should be replaced by selecting activation programmes according to their success in bringing individual job seekers back into employment (Frölich *et al.*, 2003). This implies that, for each job seeker, all available programmes are initially considered and only those programmes are applied that promise to generate the highest individual chance of return to employment. An advantage of this approach is that it avoids excluding job seekers from certain programmes that belong to a different activation category, even though they may be more appropriate in the individual case. The current profiling system goes a long way in following this approach. Nevertheless, the government should consider abolishing profiling altogether and moving instead towards a full targeting system in order to reduce misclassification.

Most job placement and reintegration services are delivered by private providers as the result of the SUWI Act compelling the UWV to rely on outplacement.[15] The introduction of this quasi-market for reintegration services has helped to reduce the stock of unemployment and social assistance beneficiaries in a cost-efficient way. Nevertheless, further improvements of the quality of reintegration service are possible (Box 3.7). First, part of the tendering process is organised at the level of the 467 municipalities, and there are no clear performance ratings, contributing to a lack of transparency and the risk that some of these municipalities may get stuck with a "preferred" provider (Tergeist and Grubb, 2006). Moreover, in the absence of central standards, the transaction costs in terms of contract design, awarding provisions and monitoring are high. In addition, minimum requirements regarding placement success of private providers have been set very low, close to rates at which the benefit recipients flow out even without placement (Dykstra and de Koning, 2004). Overall, the current set-up has led to a very fragmented market with more than 1 800 providers for reintegration services of which 1 200 are self-employed. The tendering process and the incentives for the reintegration companies should therefore include not only the placement fee but also include a success criterion regarding the duration of the new job (Tergeist and Grubb, 2006) Moreover, constant evaluations of reintegration services are necessary to evaluate the effectiveness across providers with different case load characteristics. Preferably, these evaluations should take into account the past track record in terms of achieving placements, possibly using the Australian "star ratings" to provide a clear benchmark (Grubb, 2004). In addition, the UWV could follow up regularly on successfully placed job seekers to get feedback from the new employer regarding the relevance of the particular reintegration service in the hiring decision.

Box 3.7. **The market for reintegration services**

The selection of private providers has been a concern with the outplacement of reintegration services. In order to ensure the quality of these services, the SUWI Act stipulates that public institutions can only contract with service providers that operate according to certain basic quality standards.* In addition, the association of training providers (*Borea*) has developed a more elaborated quality certificate, which is granted to providers that meet 13 criteria and accept semi-annual audits and has been obtained by 72 providers (60% of the market volume). Reputation effects and the market selection mechanism are then supposed to guarantee that the most efficient providers will be selected by the UWV and the municipalities. This, however, does not seem to be the case: the market share of private providers did not evolve according to the placement success, even though some improvement in this respect seem to have been observed more recently (De Graaf-Zijl *et al.*, 2005; Groot *et al.*, 2006). What is more, even the *Borea*-certificate is no signal for performance as providers both with and without the certificate experienced similar reintegration success rates (De Graaf-Zijl and Groot, 2005). Moreover, while private providers seem to excel in rehabilitating groups with weak labour market attachments, they are less successful at contracting with employers and matching job seekers with unfilled vacancies. A first step to assess the contribution of different providers to reintegration success has been undertaken by the publication of purchaser satisfaction rates by the Council for Work and Income (RWI), albeit not yet on a regular basis.

* Service providers need to have a complaint procedure and a client privacy register.

Strengthening sanctions

A third policy tool for reducing the high incidence of long-term unemployment is to apply sanctions in case of insufficient job search and administrative infractions. By international comparison, Dutch public employment services (PES) have a long and precise list of sanctions at their disposal, which they use consistently and to a similar degree as PES in certain other countries, such as in Switzerland and the United States (Tergeist and Grubb, 2006; Gray, 2003). In 2007, a new system of measuring job search was introduced, based on individual targets that are periodically verified by the CWI case manager. The system allows the case manger to take the economic situation into account, weakening job search obligations considerably in less favourable times for up to 6 months, when the initial definition of a suitable job is widened. International evidence suggests, however, that sanctions should be applied earlier, ideally after 3 months, together with a gradual broadening of the definition of suitable jobs – as is currently planned – and the requirement that part-time workers accept a full-time job if no alternative exists (Graversen, Damgaard and Rosdahl, 2007). Moreover, maximum commuting requirements should be widened after longer unemployment spells, as the current 1.5 hour limit in each direction is relatively restrictive when taking into account the high incidence of commuting difficulties in the densely populated parts of the Netherlands. Some countries such as Norway or Sweden even require relocation, depending on the family situation of the job seeker. Finally, proper monitoring of job search efforts requires reliable information. In this respect, it seems that fixing quantitative goals (four applications in a four-week period) has led to job seekers sending out applications regardless of their potential to satisfy the qualifications specified in the vacancy note. Moreover, some unemployed have resorted to performing poorly on purpose during job interviews. Hence, the CWI needs to strengthen its assessment regarding the quality of job applications of the benefit recipient and should follow up on job interviews more intensively by contacting employers for feedback information.

Box 3.8. **Labour market participation: recommendations**

Continue activating social assistance beneficiaries

Job search requirements for current social assistance benefit recipients should be strictly enforced. The authorities should not introduce exemptions for lone parents as is currently planned.

Encourage participation of women with weak labour market attachment

The authorities should implement – as planned – the phase-out of the transferability of the tax credit for second earners. However, they should consider a more rapid phase-out rate than the currently announced 15 years.

Shift more of the family-income based child tax credit to the individual or second-earner children tax credit.

Consolidate the successful reforms of disability benefits

The authorities should closely monitor the outflow of former disability benefit recipients in order to assess the success of the disability benefit reform in reintegrating them into the labour market.

Box 3.8. **Labour market participation: recommendations** *(cont.)*

Medical criteria for the young disabled under the Wajong scheme should be tightened. Preferably, the young disabled should first receive social assistance and be granted Wajong only as a top-up after a waiting period.

The authorities should continue retesting the existing stock of disabled under the new, stricter medical testing criteria, disregarding the age of the benefit recipient. Moreover, in order to allow fully and permanently disabled people to benefit from new employment opportunities, permanent disability should be re-examined on a regular basis.

New entrants into the partial disability benefit scheme should be activated early, possibly already during their sickness period. In addition, the authorities should consider further strengthening work incentives for partially disabled by shortening the initial period of the first-stage replacement benefit (the *loongerelateerde uitkering*).

Further increase participation of older workers

The use of tax-favoured savings schemes such as the recently introduced life-course savings scheme should be monitored closely. The authorities should consider phasing-out the tax exemptions for these schemes entirely.

The job search requirements for older workers should be strengthened and aligned with those for other unemployed.

The effective exit age from the labour market needs to increase. This can be achieved by indexing the official retirement age to the increase in life expectancy. In order to allow older workers to be employed after the age of 65, permanent contracts should be made transformable into temporary ones more easily.

The obligation to pay full wages during long periods of sickness for + 65 years should be reconsidered.

In order to strengthen participation incentives for older workers, the state pension system (AOW) should be reformed and possibly merged with the current Social Assistance benefit scheme.

Further enhance activation of the long-term unemployed

Unemployment benefits should be made more activating by further reducing benefit duration and allowing for a gradual decrease of the replacement rates with the length of the unemployment spell. This could imply an initially higher replacement rate for short unemployment durations.

In order to improve labour market dynamics and to lower long-term unemployment, employment protection should be lowered. This could be achieved by making the current dual system of dismissal simpler and more predictable. In particular, the rules governing layoffs should be clearly specified in law with appeal to local courts only possible as an *ex post* option, in case one of the parties feel unfairly treated. Moreover, in order to safeguard labour market chances for workers after the age of 50, the accumulation of their severance payment rights should be aligned with that of other workers.

The unemployed should be profiled directly into different programmes instead of different activation categories. Moreover, the authorities should consider the introduction of economic incentives to allow benefit recipients to self select into different programmes.

Activation should start no later than three months after the unemployed entered the system. Moreover, the government should implement its plans to widen the definitions of suitable jobs more rapidly with the length of the unemployment spell. This should also include requirements to relocate after 1 year of unemployment, depending on family circumstances.

Notes

1. For people aged 21 to 65. There are different assistance levels for younger and older persons.

2. In practice, lone parents with children are often not subject to job search requirements, depending on the municipality that is granting social assistance. In principle, however, every benefit recipient is expected to be available for suitable work.

3. This applies to children between 12 and 18 years old. Lower rates apply for younger children.

4. The child tax credit declines at a rate of 5.75% for a household income between € 28 521 and € 44 524.

5. For instance, the number of men aged 50-55 dropped from 90 000 to 65 000 between 2000 and 2005.

6. To strengthen incentives for municipalities to activate also young disabled people, Wajong could be granted as a top-up to Social Assistance, depending on the degree of disability and after some waiting period.

7. More generally, low old-age participation rates can be accounted for, in part, by substantially higher wealth accumulated by Dutch households – mainly in form of pension and real estate assets – which tend to lower the average exit age from the labour market (Bloemen, 2006). On the other hand, there is an offsetting cohort effect with younger generations working longer over their life-cycle than older ones.

8. Both – employer and employee – may agree upon a new (temporary) contract, in which case the new tenure period for severance payments starts from scratch. In cases where work is continued without a renewed contract and dismissals are brought to court in a later stage, the court normally assumes that the contracts have been renewed at the age of 65.

9. It should be noted that people who intend to use the life-course savings scheme as a top-up to unemployment benefits and severance payments loose the tax advantage.

10. This would mean raising the tax-free threshold by € 80 000, which equals about 210% of the average wage thus creating a similar saving flexibility as under the life-course savings scheme.

11. A 2% reduction is made on the full pension for each year spent outside the Netherlands between the age of 15 and 65.

12. Alternatively, first pillar pensions could be linked to years of contributions, allowing pensioners with longer contribution histories to receive a higher pension, while still guaranteeing a minimum pension (probably at a lower level). Such a modified system would still contain a redistributive element, which could be controlled for by a cap on either pension contributions or pension replacement rates.

13. The amount of severance pay was set at one month for every year of service with a maximum of one year salary or Euro 75 000 (or Euro 100 000 for older workers) in case the annual salary was below this income limit.

14. The proposal did provide for the possibility to have the amount of severance pay lowered by court decision in case it would jeopardise the financial health of the company. Moreover, the CWI-route would still have been available for dismissals due to business and economic reasons. In that case, no severance pay would have been paid.

15. Only very few courses are available in-house, mainly on the level of municipalities, which stopped to be obliged to outsource these services since 2006.

Bibliography

Bassanini, A. and R. Duval (2006), "Employment patterns in OECD countries: Reassessing the role of policies and institutions", *OECD Economics Department Working Paper*, No. 486.

Bloemen, H. G. (2006), "The impact of wealth on job exit rates of elderly workers", *IZA Discussion Papers*, No. 2247.

Boone, J. and J.C. van Ours (2004), "Effective active labour market policies", *IZA Discussion Papers*, No. 1335.

Bruinshoofd, A. and S. Grob (2006), "Do changes in pension incentives affect retirement? A stated preferences approach to Dutch retirement consideration", *DNB Working Paper*, No. 115.

Burniaux, Jean-Marc, Romain Duval and Florence Jaumotte (2004), "Coping with Ageing: A Dynamic Approach to Quantify the Impact of Alternative Policy Options on Future Labour Supply in OECD Countries", OECD Economics Department Working Paper, No. 371.

Carcillo, S. and D. Grubb (2006), "From inactivity to work: the role of active labour market policies", OECD Social Employment and Migration Working Papers, No. 36, OECD.

De Mooij, R. (2006), "Reinventing the welfare state", CPB Special Publication, NB. 60.

Dykstra, M. and J. de Koning (2004), "Competitive procurement of reintegration services in the Netherlands", in: M. Janssen (ed.), Auctioning Public Assets. Analysis and Alternatives, Cambridge.

Frölich, M., M. Lechner and H. Steiger (2003), "Statically assisted programme selection – International experience and potential benefits for Switzerland", University of St. Gallen.

Graaf-Zijl,. M. de, I. Groot, A. Heyma, J. P. Hop and L. Janssens (2005), "Marktwerking in de reïntegratie", Amsterdam: SEO Economisch Onderzoek.

Graaf-Zijl, M. de and I. Groot (2005), "Transparantie op de reïntegratiemarkt. Werkt het Borea-keurmerk?", Maandblad reïntegratie, Vol. 5/10, pp. 23-25.

Graversen, B.K., B. Damgaard and A. Rosdahl (2007), "Hurtigt i gang – Evaluering af et forsøg med en tidlig og intensiv beskæftigelsesindsats for forsikrede ledige.", Socialforskningsinstituttet, Rapport 07:10, Copenhagen.

Gray, D. (2003), "National versus regional financing and management of unemployment and related benefits: The case of Canada", OECD Social, Employment and Migration Working Papers, No. 14.

Groot, I., D. Hollanders and J. Hop (2006), "Werkt de reintegratiemarkt?", Amsterdam: SEO Economisch Onderzoek.

Grubb, D. (2004), "Performance measurement and quasi-competitive mechanisms for the Public Employment Service", LSE Lunchtime seminar, London.

Jaumotte, Florence (2003), "Female Labour Force Participation: Past Trends and Main Determinants in OECD Countries", OECD Economics Department Working Paper, No. 376.

Koning, P. and D. van Vuuren (2006), "Disability Insurance and Unemployment Insurance As Substitute Pathways. An Empirical Analysis Based on Employer Data", CPB Discussion Paper, No. 70.

Kotlikoff, L. J. and D. Rapson (2006), "Does it pay, at the margin, to work and save? Measuing effective marginal taxes on American's labour supply and saving", NBER Working Paper Series, No. 1253.

Lalive, R., J. C. van Ours and J. Zweimueller (2004), "How changes in financial incentives affect the duration of unemployment", IZA Discussion Papers, No. 1363.

Lechner, M. and R. Vazquez-Alvarez, (2006), "Stochastic labour market shocks and active labour market policies: A theoretical and empirical analysis", paper presented at the IFAU/IZA Conference on Labour Market Policy Evaluation, Uppsala, Sweden.

OECD (2006a), OECD Employment Outlook, Paris.

OECD (2006b), Pensions at a Glance. Public policies across OECD countries, Paris.

OECD (2007), OECD Employment Outlook, Paris.

SER (2005), "Ontslagpraktijk en Werkloosheidswet", advies 06/2005.

Stevens, L.G.M. (2005), "Naar een bestendig fiscaal pensioenbeleid", Economisch Statisch Berichten, No. 4465.

Tergeist, P. and D. Grubb (2006), "Activation strategies and performance of employment services in Germany, the Netherlands and the United Kingdom", OECD Social, Employment and Immigration Working Paper, No. 42.

Van Ewijk, C. (2004), "Pension savings and government finance in the Netherlands", OECD Economic Studies, No. 39, pp. 173-192.

ANNEX 3.A1

The tax-benefit system and life-cycle employment[1, 2]

Households make their labour supply decisions on the basis of the net present value of their tax liabilities net of benefits. As a consequence, the optimal labour input by households in equilibrium will also depend on incentives to save and build up wealth over the life-time. Hence, capital and consumption taxes directly impact upon savings incentives and thus labour supply. Moreover, pension rights and the interaction between private and public pension assets will impact on incentives for participating, especially at older ages. In addition, exit routes provided by the benefit system – for instance through social assistance or unemployment benefits – may allow a temporary or permanent exit from the labour market, several years before the official retirement age. In this regard, the combination of large private wealth (in form of occupational pensions) and exit routes in the benefit system have been shown to explain low participation rates of older workers (Bloemen, 2006).

In order to analyse the impact of the Dutch tax-benefit system for life-cycle participation and working hours decisions, an intertemporal model has been calibrated, with households taking simultaneously decisions regarding their consumption, participation and hours worked. This annex presents the methodology underlying this model and the results that have been presented in this chapter and the next.

An overlapping-generations model

A life of a cohort

The analysis of life-cycle labour supply decisions has been based on an overlapping-generations model, similar to the one introduced by Auerbach and Kotlikoff (1987) and more recently applied by Kotlikoff and Rapson (2006). The model embodies 83 cohorts, each of which is characterised by its age at year t, its cohort size N(t) and – during working life – by its average productivity level y(t). The average individual's economic life starts at age 18 and ends with certain death at age 100. The life span is separated into working life (age 18-65) and retirement (age 65-100). For each generation, the cohort size shrinks over time as only s(t)% of each cohort survive during the year.

During working age, each cohort comprises three groups: inactives, unemployed and employed people. Inactives have access to social assistance, unemployed will receive earnings-related unemployment benefits, while employees receive a wage that depends on their individual productivity ef(i) and their average cohort productivity y(t). Once a cohort reaches retirement age, all individuals of the cohort will become inactive and receive their base pension. This assumption is in line with observed household behaviour whereby only very few individuals continue to participate after their 65th birthday.

Besides earnings-related income, retired individuals also receive income from accumulated wealth. Individuals are supposed to not leave any bequest at the time of their certain death. The accumulated wealth of those who have died earlier is supposed to be distributed across the cohort. The model does not make a distinction between different asset types (such as housing, financial and pension assets), which are all assumed to yield the same rate of return.[3] However, capital income taxes are levied only on part of the accumulated wealth, assuming that the relative share of different asset types does not change over the life-time.

The optimal work and leisure choice of a representative household

The household maximises its intertemporal utility by making an optimal arbitrage between work and leisure over its life cycle. The optimal labour supply comprises two elements: a decision to participate and the number of hours worked as participation is costly (to reflect opportunity costs arising from commuting time, for instance), measured by θ_P. The household's utility function is supposed to be time-separable with a constant relative-risk aversion (CRRA). With the daily working time normalised to one, the objective function over the lifetime of the average working individual of cohort i therefore writes as:

$$U^i\left(c_t^i, P_t^i, h_t^i\right) = E_{t_0}\left[\sum_{t=1}^{100-17} \beta^t \left(\prod_{j=1}^{t} s_j\right)\left(\left(\frac{c_t^i\left(1 - h_t^i\right)^\eta}{\gamma}\right)^\gamma - \theta_P P_t^i\right)\right]$$

where c_t^i: consumption of cohort i, P_t^i: its participation rate and h_t^i: its optimal working hours. The household's intertemporal time preference rate is measured by β, its relative risk aversion by γ and the labour supply elasticity by $\gamma\eta$.

The household maximises its utility against the following dynamic budget constraint:

$$a_{t+1}^i = \left(1 + r_t\right)a_t^i - \tau^W\left(a_t^i\right) - \left(1 + \tau^C\right)c_t^i + Yd\left(w_t, P_t^i, h_t^i, \tau^L\right) + tr_t^i$$

where r_t: the real rate of return on wealth, a_t^i: the total wealth of cohort i, $Yd\left(w_t, P_t^i, h_t^i, \tau^L\right)$: its disposable income depending on the ongoing wage w_t, its labour participation P_t^i and working hours h_t^i and the labour income taxes τ^L. Unemployed workers (for whom $P_t^i = 1$ but $h_t^i = 0$) will receive unemployment benefits, while non-participation individuals that have not yet reached retirement age will receive social assistance. Households have to pay wealth and consumption taxes, τ^W and τ^C respectively, and receive transfers (in form of a base pension from 65 years on).

The household's problem is solved in two steps. First, the household makes a decision whether or not to participate given the capital stock in its last year of life and on the basis of its disposable income resulting from its labour market status. In a second step, for participating workers the optimal labour input conditional on being employed is determined, yielding the following optimality condition for consumption and hours worked:

$$\frac{\eta \cdot c_t^i}{1 - h_t^i} = \frac{\partial Yd\left(w_t, 1, h_t^i, \tau^L\right)}{\partial h_t^i}$$

where due to the progressive nature of the tax-benefit system the term on the right-hand side usually does not have a closed form expression.

The macroeconomic assumptions

Wealth accumulated by the household sector is used by firms for productive investment. Moreover, firms will decide upon total hours worked by opening vacancies to fill available jobs, taking the decision on average hours as given. Jobs are filled through a search and matching process on the labour market, leaving some matches unrealised and thereby generating unemployment even in steady state. In order to maximise the net present value of their profits, firms select their flows of investment $\{i_t\}_{t=0}^{\infty}$ and vacancies $\{V_t\}_{t=0}^{\infty}$. The optimal program for firms therefore writes as:

$$\pi_t = \sum_{t=1}^{\infty} \left(\frac{1}{1+r_t}\right)^t \left(Y(A_t,k_t,n_t,h_t) - w_t h_t n_t - i_t - \zeta w_t V_t\right)$$

subject to

$$k_{t+1} = (1-\delta)k_t + i_t$$
$$n_{t+1} = m(U_t,V_t) + (1-\sigma)n_t$$

with π_t: net present value of a firm's profits, k_t: the firm's capital stock, n_t: its employment level, h_t: average working hours, i_t: the firm's investment, w_t: the hourly wage rate, V_t: the firms open vacancies. The production function is supposed to be Cobb-Douglas: $Y(A_t,k_t,n_t,h_t) = k_t^{\alpha}(A_t h_t n_t)^{1-\alpha}$. Moreover, the matching process follows a standard constant-returns-to-scale matching function depending on the vacancy ratio $\theta = \frac{V}{U}$ (see Pissarides, 2000):

$$m(U_t,V_t) = q_0 U_t^{q_1} V_t^{1-q_1} \Leftrightarrow \frac{m(U_t,V_t)}{U_t} = \theta \cdot q(\theta),\ q(\theta) = q_0 \theta^{1-q_1}$$

Wages are negotiated at the firm level. As a first approximation to a Nash-bargaining distribution of profits, wages are determined as a weighted average between the marginal contribution of an additional worker to the firms' profits and the worker's fall-back option, i.e. social assistance. The bargaining power, ρ, is set to 0.48, in line with the average wage share in the Dutch economy. Moreover, the negotiated wages depend on the state of the labour market, measured by the vacancy ratio θ.

$$w_t h_t = \rho(Y_{n,t} + \zeta w_t h_t) + (1-\rho)SA \Leftrightarrow w_t h_t = \frac{\rho}{1 - \zeta\theta_t\rho - (1-\rho)R} Y_{n,t}$$

where R measures the replacement ratio of social assistance benefits[4] and $Y_{n,t}$ the marginal labour productivity.

In equilibrium, all firms behave symmetrically, hence the first-order conditions allow to determine the steady state as follows:

$$\bar{r} + \delta = \alpha \bar{k}^{\alpha} \left(\bar{A} \cdot \bar{h} \cdot \bar{n} \cdot LFPR \cdot POPT\right)$$
$$\frac{\bar{r} + \sigma}{q(\theta)} = \frac{1 - \zeta\rho\bar{\theta} - (1-\rho)R}{\rho} - \bar{h}$$
$$\bar{n} = \frac{\bar{\theta}q(\bar{\theta})}{\bar{\theta}q(\bar{\theta}) + \sigma} \cdot LFPR \cdot POPT$$
$$\bar{i} = \delta\bar{k}$$

where $\bar{r}$: equilibrium real interest rate, $\bar{n}$: equilibrium employment rate, LFPR: labour force participation rate (determined by households), POPT: working age population (exogenously given), $\bar{k}$: the economy's equilibrium capital stock, $\bar{i}$: equilibrium investment and $\bar{\theta}$: steady state vacancy ratio.

The tax-benefit system

Taxes

The schedule for marginal effective tax rates on labour income is taken from OECD (2006). This includes not only the statutory tax rates for different income brackets but also various social benefits, such as housing and child benefits. In addition, different tax credits – such as the general tax credit and the work-related tax credit – are also included. Given that some of these tax credits and benefits depend on the household situation, the tax burden has been assessed separately for an economy only consisting of single earners and one only consisting of married persons with two children. While this is clearly an abstraction, it allows to better identify how the burden of different tax-benefit reforms will affect different groups depending on their family situation.

In addition, households face a consumption tax in form of a VAT of 19% and a capital income tax ("Box 3 income") that is levied as a wealth tax at a rate of 1.2%. Given that the model does not differentiate between housing, pension and other wealth, the wealth tax is only applied on 1/3 of total wealth accumulated by the household, which corresponds to the current distribution of wealth between different asset types. Finally, the calculation of the wealth tax takes a 22.5% tax credit into account.

Benefits

In the Beveridge-type social security system of the Netherlands, benefits are exclusively financed out of tax revenues. Given that only one household type is considered, the selection of the benefits in the model is limited to the three major ones: unemployment insurance, social assistance and first-pillar pensions.

Social assistance

Social assistance is available for non-participating households subject to a capital income test (all capital income above 15% of the average wage is deducted from social assistance). In principle, households on social assistance face strict reintegration requirements and cannot simply withdraw from the labour market while receiving replacement income. These reintegration requirements, however, decrease with the age of the person. In order to integrate the idea that younger people face a higher risk of inactivity without any replacement income, we use the relative wage profile to adjust the replacement income accordingly.

Unemployment insurance

Unemployment insurance is granted for periods during which the individual is participating but without a job. The replacement income covers 70% of the last salary but limited to 130% of the average salary.

First pillar pensions.

First-pillar pensions are available as of the age of 65 years and amount to 30% of the average wage. In principle, the full amount goes only to people having lived a full 45 years in the Netherlands, which is assumed to be the case for all generations in our sample.

Calibration of the model

In order to obtain reliable estimates of the life-cycle tax burden and household's labour supply decisions, the model has been calibrated using the DNB Household Survey. In particular, in order to properly reflect distributional consequences of different tax-benefit systems, a Markov transition matrix between 10 different income deciles and in and out of unemployment has been estimated from the DNB Survey. This transition matrix indicates the probabilities with which individuals in different income strata persist at their current (relative) income level or move up or down one level during one year. As the transition probability changes over time, the matrix has been estimated in 5-years intervals over the entire working life span. Moreover, age-productivity profiles have been estimated (see Figure 3.A1.1 below) for an average worker and have been used to modulate the wage over each cohort's working age. Finally, the survival probabilities for each age group have been taken directly from Statistics Netherlands; for the last year (at age 100 years) it has been set to zero.

Figure 3.A1.1. **Productivity over the working life**

Productivity at age 20=100

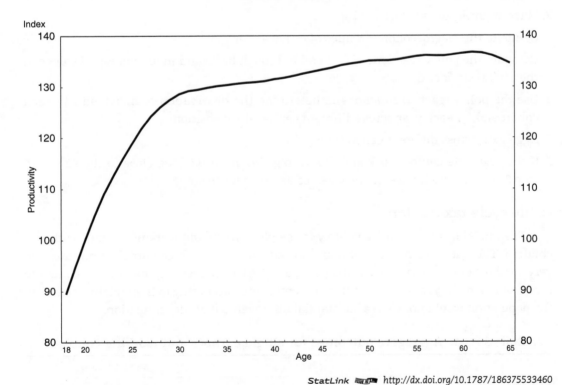

StatLink ⟨⟩ http://dx.doi.org/10.1787/186375533460

Source: Secretariat's calculations.

The parameters of the utility function, comprising the time preference rate β, the constant relative risk aversion, γ, and the labour supply elasticity, η, have been selected in such a way as to obtain in equilibrium a real interest rate of around 4%, a labour force participation of 75.8% and an average working time per week of 32 hours, which corresponds to the outcome of the current tax-benefit system.

Regarding the calibration of the macroeconomy, the parameters for the labour market matching function have been set using standard values found in the literature (see Pissarides and Petrongolo, 2001 for a survey), leading to an unemployment rate of 4%. The parameters on the capital-labour elasticity, α, and the capital depreciation rate, δ, have been taken from Ernst et al. (2006), while the parameters on vacancy costs, ζ, and employment destruction, σ, are taken from Merz (1995).

Determining the equilibrium distribution of work and leisure

Given that no cohort has individuals that live beyond the age of 100, a method called "finite value approach" has been chosen to calculate the equilibrium distribution of consumption and working hours. This algorithm calculates the optimal path of consumption and hours worked for each value out of a large, but finite number of average capital stocks. The equilibrium value is then determined by selecting the path with the highest net present value of the individual's utility. Concretely, the following steps have been carried:

1. Set up a grid of possible terminate capital stocks around the expected steady state average capital stock;

2. Make an initial guess of k_0 and h_0;

3. Compute the macroeconomic values of w, r, θ and n;

4. Compute the policy reactions of c, h, and P through backward induction for all values in the capital stock grid;

5. Use the policy reaction functions to determine the distribution of individuals in each cohort and for each year across different capital stock positions;

6. Aggregate across different generations;

7. If the aggregate capital stock and the average hours worked are close to the values in step 2 stop, otherwise use the new values and go back to step 3.

Average life cycle tax burden

The model has been run separately for single earners and working couples with two children. The outcome in terms of hours worked and labour force participation rates are very similar between the two set-ups (see Table 3.A1.1), suggesting that a more complete model where both types of households are represented according to their relative shares in the population would not yield a substantial improvement of the simulations.

Table 3.A1.1. **Aggregate outcomes for single earners and working couples**

	Single Earners	Married first earner
Participation rate	75.2%	75.2%
Hours worked	32.2 h	31.9 h
Pensions (average replacement rate)	74.1%	73.8%
Income inequality (Gini coefficient)	48.8	47.6

Source: Secretariat's calculation.

Reforms of the tax benefit system

Two different tax-benefit reforms are considered in this survey. The first reform scenario analyses the impact of different pension reforms on participation and hours worked. The second one discusses the effects of a reduced marginal tax burden on working hours, for instance, by introducing a flat tax system.

Pension reforms

Four pension reforms are considered. The first one corresponds to the actual government programme and consists of removing the tax break for pensioners that currently lowers the statutory tax rates for the first two income brackets. The second reform consists of a reduction in the replacement rate of the base pension by 17%. Currently, the base pension is calculated as to represent 30% of the average wage. In the reform proposal in the chapter, the replacement rate is reduced to 25%. A third reform proposal discussed in the survey consists of introducing income tests for the state pension. Finally, a convergence of the state pension and social assistance system is analysed whereby the state pension is replaced by the (means-tested) social assistance benefit system and the available resources being used to lift occupational (second pillar) pensions. The following table replicates the aggregate labour supply effects of these reforms as well as consequences for pension replacement rates and income inequality.

Table 3.A1.2. **Aggregate outcomes for single earners and working couples**

	Remove tax exemption	Lower state pension	State pensions with income test	Converge state pensions and WWB
Participation rate	75.1%	75.8%	75.3%	76.4%
Hours worked	32.2 h	32.1 h	32.4 h	33.0 h
Pensions (average replacement rate)	74.2%	61.5%	74.5%	58.1%
Income inequality (Gini coefficient)	49.7	48.6	49.6	51.3

Source: Secretariat's calculations.

Introducing a flat tax

In order to bring down the high marginal tax burden, the introduction of a flat tax system is suggested in Chapter 4. In order to simulate the effect of such a flat tax for labour supply over the life-cycle, two different tax rates have been simulated (at 34% and at 37%), keeping the current general tax credit at 15%. Moreover, it has been assumed that these new rates correspond to the new marginal *effective* tax rates; hence all benefits are subsumed under the new system. The VAT rate is assumed to adjust in order to balance the government's budget. Table 3.A1.3 summarises the labour supply effects as well as consequences for income of pensioners and income inequality.

Table 3.A1.3. **Aggregate outcomes for single earners and working couples**

	34% Flat	37% Flat
Participation rate	75.5%	75.3%
Hours worked	34.7 h	34.3 h
Pensions (average replacement rate)	73.6%	73.3%
Income inequality (Gini coefficient)	52.2	52.0
Increase in VAT rate	3.7pp	1.2pp

Source: Secretariat's calculations.

Notes

1. The annex and the simulations therein have been prepared in collaboration with T. Teuber (University of Bielefeld).

2. The authors would like to thank the Dutch Delegation to the OECD and Centre at the University of Tilburg to have generously granted access to the Dutch Household Panel in preparing the calibration of the model.

3. The model does not include aggregate uncertainty. Hence, households will invest in different assets so as to equalise the after-tax rate of return.

4. The Work and Benefits Act (WWB) defines social assistance by means of an absolute level. In reality, however, this level is set such as to guarantee at least 50% of the minimum wage, which has been used as a reference for calibrating the model.

Bibliography

Auerbach, A. and L. Kotlikoff (1987), Dynamic Fiscal Policy, MIT Press.

Bloemen, H.G. (2006), "The impact of wealth on job exit rates of elderly workers", *IZA discussion paper*, No. 2247.

Ernst, E., G. Gong and W. Semmler (2006), "Quantifying the impact of structural reforms", *ECB Working Paper*, No. 666.

Kotlikoff, L. and D. Rapson (2006), "Does it pay, at the margin, to work and save? Measuring effective marginal taxes on American's labor supply and saving", *NBER Working Paper*, No. 12533.

Merz, M. (1995), "Search in the labor market and the real business cycle", Journal of Monetary Economics, 36, pp. 269-300.

OECD (2006), *Taxing Wages*, Paris.

Pissarides, C. (2000), Equilibrium Unemployment Theory, Cambridge University Press.

Pissarides, C. and B. Petrongolo (2001), "Looking into the Black Box: A Survey of the Matching Function", Journal of Economic Literature, Vol. 39/1, pp. 390-431.

ISBN 978-92-64-04076-2
OECD Economic Surveys: Netherlands
© OECD 2008

Chapter 4

Increasing working hours:
Helping reconcile work and family

About two-thirds of Dutch female workers opt for part-time jobs, bringing down the country's average working time to one of the lowest levels in the OECD. It is often said that the preference of Dutch women for part-time work reflects a social norm strongly favouring family values. This chapter shows that the Dutch-specific prevalence of part-time work also reflects the influence of public policies, notably regarding the provision of childcare and the taxation of second earners. Recent government decisions have started to make it easier for people to work longer hours and take care of children at the same time. Facilities to help parents balance their work and care responsibilities have been expanded, such as with more abundant and cheaper childcare services, but not all obstacles have been removed. Moreover, the marginal effective tax burden on second earners remains high as social benefits are conditioned on family income, which creates incentives to work part time. Thus, more emphasis is needed in further reducing the marginal effective tax rate. This could include both measures to expand existing work-related tax credits as well as reconsidering the withdrawal of benefits when the income of second earners rises as they work longer hours.

A high proportion of Dutch women participate in the labour market, more than in most other OECD countries. This is particularly so for younger generations, which have higher participation rates than older ones (Figure 4.1). As this trend is likely to continue for some time in the future, female participation will help to mitigate the effects of population ageing.

Figure 4.1. **Female participation rates by cohorts**

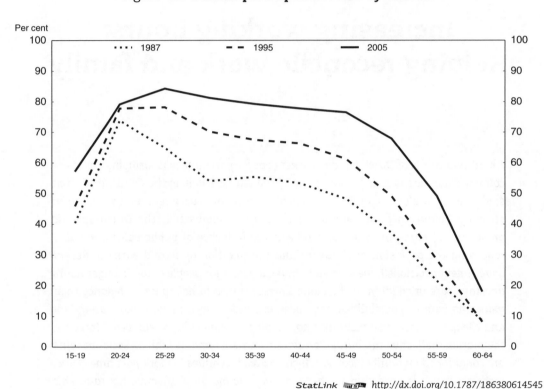

StatLink http://dx.doi.org/10.1787/186380614545

Source: OECD Labour Force Survey.

However, most working women opt for part-time jobs after the birth of children (Euwals *et al.*, 2006), pulling down average working time to one of the lowest levels in the OECD and reducing overall labour utilisation. The widespread incidence of part-time work has various downside effects both for the employees and the overall economy: it results in lower rates of return of investment to education, which appears to be damaging for female life-cycle career prospects and life-time earnings and may also have contributed to lower (trend) productivity growth.

The prevalence of part-time jobs in the Netherlands seems to reflect social preferences for non-market work activities, such as family care, although by international comparison, these preferences are not particularly strong and concern especially families with children (Albrecht *et al.* 2000). The present chapter suggests, moreover, that this collective choice has been influenced by government policies that have aimed at encouraging people to opt for part-time jobs. The provision of childcare services was restrained until recently and the tax system has discouraged women from increasing their individual working hours. The government has started to change the course of these policies and has attempted to make it easier for parents to reconcile family care and work responsibilities, for instance, by stimulating the provision of childcare services and revisiting some key aspects of the tax system. As this chapter argues, these policy steps go in a direction that should foster the greater utilisation of labour resources; a number of additional policy changes are suggested to go further in the direction of allowing a large number of women to opt for full-time jobs. Policy recommendations are summarised at the end of the chapter (Box 4.3).

A high incidence of part-time employment among female workers

The current average working time of 1362 hours annually per employee is the second lowest in the OECD, after Norway. The short duration of working time reflects first and foremost the widespread use of part-time employment. Nearly two-thirds of female workers opt for a part-time job, the highest preponderance among OECD countries (Figure 4.2). The prevalence of part-time employment has a depressing effect on the utilisation of the potential labour supply. Indeed, the labour supply would increase by nearly 30% if all part-time workers began to work full-time (Ministry of Social Affairs, 2007), which is nearly twice as much as if all the unemployed and inactive people were no longer

Figure 4.2. **Incidence of female part-time employment**[1]

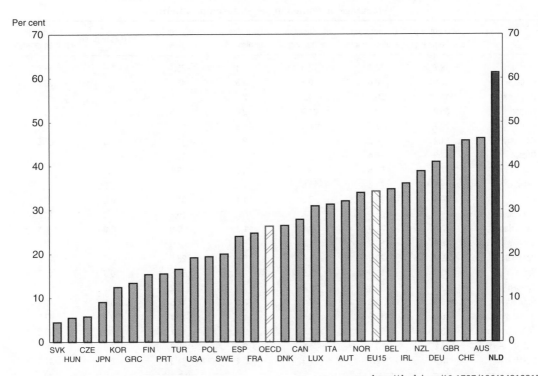

StatLink http://dx.doi.org/10.1787/186404812815

1. Share of female unemployment working part-time.

Source: OECD, *Average hours worked* 2006.

out of work (as discussed in the previous chapter). As the participation of female and older workers is set to increase in the coming years, the positive effect on labour supply of encouraging full-time employment is all the more important for the mobilisation of potential labour resources.

Encouraging part-time work seem to have been a long-standing feature of Dutch labour market policy. For instance, past governments promoted part-time employment mainly by providing subsidies to firms that would split full-time jobs into two or more part-time jobs (Visser *et al.* 2004). Policy measures have also sought to allow workers to freely adjust their working hours. In 2000, the Working Hours (Adjustment) Act introduced the right for every employee to opt for working part time without requiring the employer's approval; this was subject to certain conditions, which subsequently turned out not be very restrictive.[1, 2] In the view of policy makers, part-time employment brought several types of benefits: *a*) part-time employment was meant to help families better balance work and child care activities; *b*) part-time employment was considered useful to encourage certain categories of employees to participate; *c*) part-time employment was meant to support economic flexibility, especially in the service sector where employers can use part-time jobs to cope with peak loads; and *d*) part-time was seen as a way to share existing jobs across a larger labour force.[3]

The legislation of part-time employment may correspond to a strong social preference. Indeed, there is some indication that most women feel comfortable in part-time employment, and more so than in other countries (Table 4.1). Assessing the importance of social preferences is, however, difficult as only revealed preferences can be

Table 4.1. **Part-time employment by reasons, 2001**

Percentage of women in part-time employment

	Could not find a full-time job	Did not want a full-time job	In education or training	Own illness or disability	Other reason given	No reason given	Look after children or adult
Austria	9.7	16.5	3.8	1.1	25.1	..	43.8
Belgium	18.2	8.6	0.8	1.8	43.8	..	26.8
Denmark	14.8	59.0	23.5	2.3	..	..	..
Finland	35.9	22.5	24.9	2.4	4.3	..	9.6
France	22.7	67.0	5.8	4.5	..	..	..
Germany	11.2	16.2	4.6	2.0	..	3.5	62.5
Greece	43.9	36.4	..	..	13.3	..	..
Iceland	7.7	52.5	22.7	4.5	9.8	..	..
Ireland	9.9	73.6	13.0	..	..	2.6	..
Italy	30.4	28.1	2.8	1.1	31.6	6.0	..
Luxembourg	..	55.5	..	..	15.3	..	12.2
Netherlands	**2.0**	**72.9**	**9.5**	**1.1**	**0.9**	**6.0**	**7.5**
Norway	8.9	62.9	17.2	3.0	..	7.9	..
Portugal	19.7	20.0	4.1	16.5	26.5	..	13.2
Spain	21.2	10.5	4.9	..	50.5	0.9	11.7
Sweden[1]	23.5	52.3	10.4	7.0	6.2	..	..
Switzerland	3.1	19.8	7.1	3.0	14.5	0.5	52.1
United Kingdom	6.8	15.6	10.8	1.7	19.1	0.3	45.7
EEA	13.4	32.7	7.5	2.4	11.1	2.2	30.8
EUR-12	15.2	36.1	5.6	2.4	9.2	2.9	28.7
EU-15	13.4	32.1	7.3	2.4	11.3	2.1	31.4

1. 2000 data for Sweden.

Non-responses to the variable "Full-time/Part-time" distinction not considered.

Source: European Labour Force Survey 2001.

observed that typically include the reaction to the whole array of tax and benefit arrangements, social policies, labour market regulations and childcare provisions. In this regard, available evidence indicates that these play indeed an important role in explaining the high incidence of part-time work in the Netherlands (Jaumotte, 2003).

The perceived beneficial effect of part-time work has to be weighed against the likely costs for the workers and the overall economy. These include: *a)* increased fixed costs for employers of handling a larger pool of part-time workers (such as fixed office and human resource management costs); *b)* lower return from investment in human capital formation, as experience and learning-by-doing often require that employees are available for a certain number of hours on the job; and *c)* reduced labour utilisation as lower average hours worked have in general, not contributed to increases in employment rates (Hunt, 1998; Kapetyn *et al.*, 2000).

Moreover, working part-time appears to have detrimental effects on the professional prospects of workers, notably on female careers and wage progression over their life cycle (Figure 4.3). Women are more often found in lower-paying jobs than men. In addition, women only occupy a small share of executive management positions (Zandvliet, 2002; Rasmussen, Lind and Visser, 2004). Glass ceilings – preventing qualified and motivated women from reaching levels of responsibilities similar to their male colleagues – seem to lower their career prospects more than they do in other European countries (Arulampalam, Booth and Bryan, 2005). Partly this may be related to discriminatory practices. On the other hand, flexible part-time legislation allows women to withdraw at least partially from the

Figure 4.3. **Wage progression (males *vs.* females)**
Wages at age 18 = 100

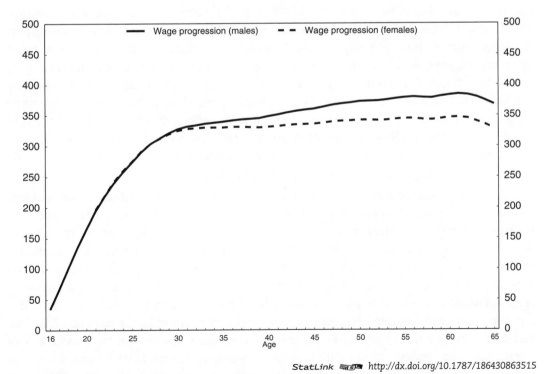

StatLink ᴍᴍᴍ *http://dx.doi.org/10.1787/186430863515*

Source: DNB Household Panel, Secretariat's calculations.

labour market, which constitutes a major obstacle for them to improve their life-time career prospects. Part-time employment is highly persistent – as indicated by internationally low transition probabilities from part- to full-time employment – which means that women do not use part-time work as a stepping-stone to a full-time job after a period of (partial) labour market withdrawal (Buddelmeyer *et al.* 2005). This contrasts with the experiences in Australia and New Zealand where women do not work part-time on a long-term basis (OECD, 2002 and 2004) and suggests that the substantially lower life-time career prospects after a (temporary) period of part-time work creates incentives for women to permanently lower their hours worked (Román, 2006).

Increasing the supply of childcare services to facilitate full-time work

One explanation of the incidence of part-time work could be the insufficient provision of childcare services. In past decades, childcare was supported by municipalities, through the granting of subsidies to local facilities. However, these facilities only covered about 10% of eligible children. In response, a reform of the childcare subsidy system was enacted in 2005 by the central government to allow a more flexible supply of childcare services. Instead of subsidising providers of childcare services, the new system offers (income-dependent) childcare benefits to households who purchase these services, irrespective of the type of provider (*e.g.* day care centre, nurses, etc.). The amount of childcare benefit is based on the consumption of childcare services and depends on the household work income, with a maximum reimbursable amount per hour of care. Since January 2007, employers are obliged to share at least one third of the overall financial burden for childcare through higher contributions to unemployment insurance, further reducing costs for both households and public finances. In addition, the government subsidy for childcare was increased. Consequently, households' own childcare costs represent 17.5% of the average earning (down from 29% in 2001), slightly above the international average (OECD, 2007). However, the share of childcare costs paid by parents rises rapidly as household income increases (Figure 4.4). This raises the marginal effective tax rate faced by second earners, who have to shoulder a large share of childcare costs if they intend to work longer hours. For instance, Figure 4.5 shows that the share of childcare costs paid by the household increases if the second earner works more than 14 hours per week, on the basis of a minimum wage remuneration. To remove this effect, the childcare benefit should not depend on the family's income. Alternatively, the government could consider linking the amount of childcare benefits to the number of hours worked, so as to more effectively target the fiscal support on full-time working families.

Concerns about the quality and the flexibility of centre-based childcare public services have restricted demand for such services. The subsidised local day-care facilities have been regarded as failing to offer quality services and lacking responsiveness to parents' demands. In response, the new Childcare Act puts emphasis on the respect of minimum requirements regarding the number of children per caretaker, the size of the group and the educational background of the staff members.[4] Nevertheless, availability and flexibility remain unresolved issues, as potential providers find it difficult to acquire new facilities and most childcare centres continue to have standard opening hours between 7.30 a.m. and 6 p.m., despite moves towards further extending hours in some centres; about 25% of the providers has opening hours until 6.30 p.m. Given frequent road traffic congestion, this lack in flexibility and availability of childcare centres (in particular in the evening) reduces parents' ability to work full time. The problem should become less severe over time, as new

Figure 4.4. **Childcare costs and income after the 2006 reform**

In per cent of childcare benefits

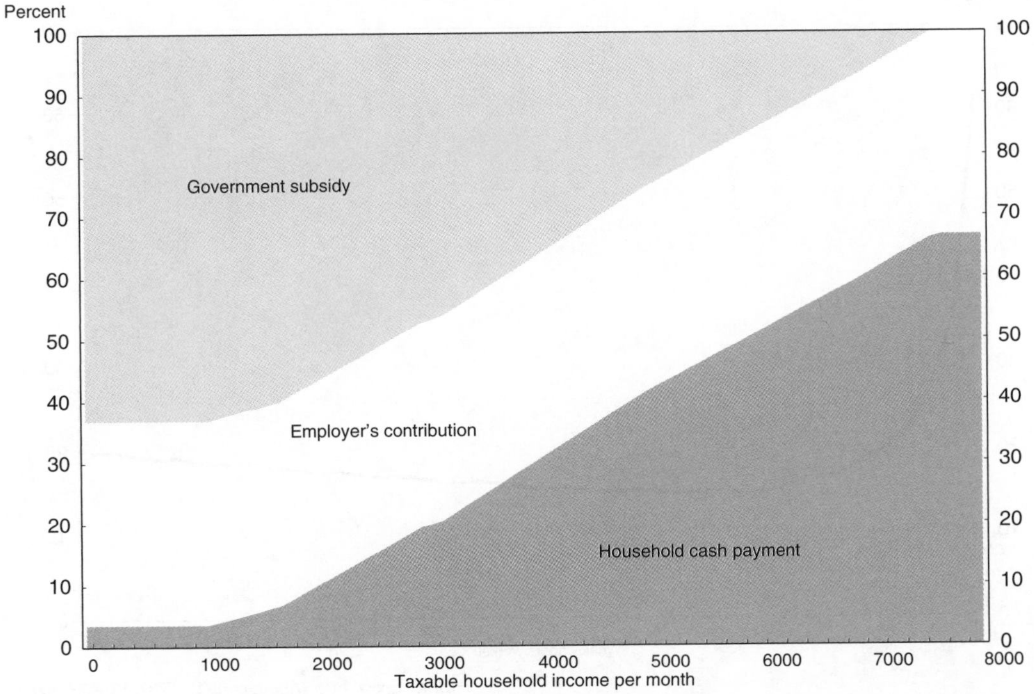
Percent
100
90
80
70
60
50
40
30
20
10
0
Government subsidy
Employer's contribution
Household cash payment
0
1000
2000
3000
4000
5000
6000
7000
8000
Taxable household income per month

StatLink http://dx.doi.org/10.1787/186446505055

Source: CPB, 2006.

private providers enter the market. Nevertheless, the government could help the market develop more rapidly by, for example, regulating a minimum number of opening hours. Alternatively, the government could offer a higher tax credit for the demand for childcare services outside normal working hours. Moreover, certain aspects of the current regulation are likely to impede a well-functioning market of childcare services. For instance, zoning regulations make it difficult for private childcare providers to find suitable premises at a convenient distance to either the workplace or the homes of their potential clients. To make supply of appropriate institutions more flexible, the government should therefore consider designating childcare as essential facilities in the zoning law as with other educational facilities.

Out-of-school hours care

As of the age of 4, children can be enrolled in primary education, and around 98% of all children of this age group are registered in school.[5] In principle, this should allow women to increase their hours worked. However, short school-opening hours, free afternoons on Wednesdays and Fridays, lunch at home (involving 1 to 2 hours breaks) and (for older children) cancellation of school hours at short notice make it difficult for women to engage in full-time participation.[6] A new law requires schools to facilitate the provision of care before and after school hours, starting with the year 2007-2008. Schools are obliged to organise care according to the parent's wishes. In every case, a proper solution has to be chosen. Care is organised by the school or by a child care provider. Parents receive a childcare benefit that covers all costs. In addition, the establishment of schools with

Figure 4.5. **Childcare costs in relation to second-earner income**[1]

Increase in the marginal effective tax rate for second earners

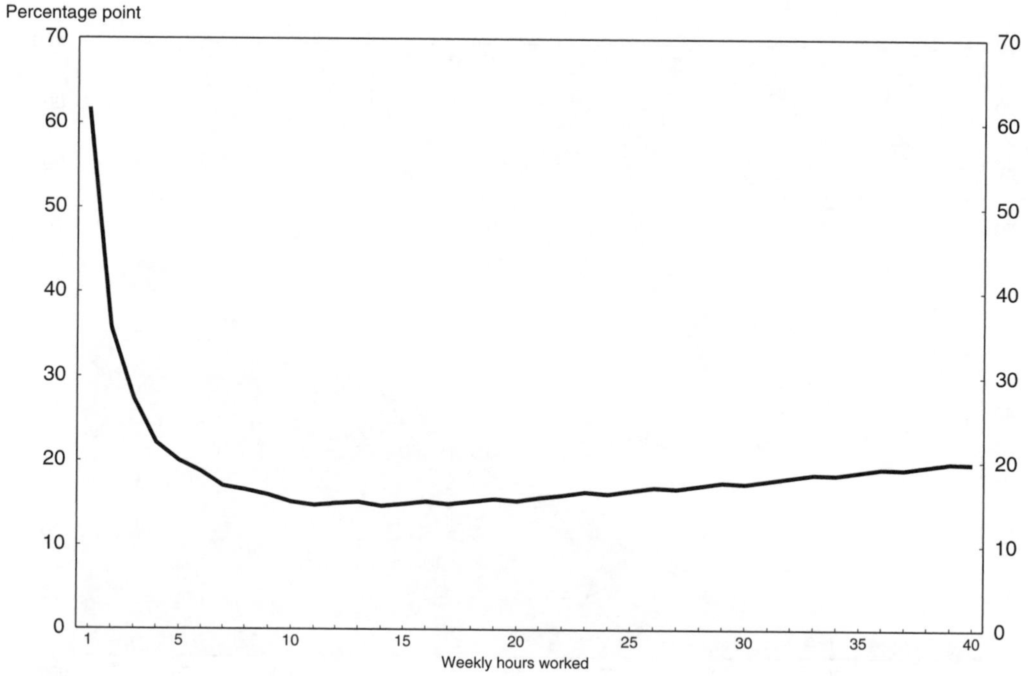

StatLink ⟪ms⟫ http://dx.doi.org/10.1787/186453087816

1. The childcare costs are assessed on the basis of a second earner at the minimum wage.

Source: CPB, Secretariat's calculations.

extended services (the so-called "brede school") will strengthen the cooperation between local care providers and schools and to this end, the government started to provide additional financial support, which will be phased in gradually until 2011, so as to cover around 1 200 schools (out of around 7 000).[7] The initiative could be strengthened further by securing faster implementation. More importantly, working parents need to be sure that childcare services are provided throughout the day. However, the new law does not cover exceptional circumstances such as teacher absences at short notice. The government should make it mandatory that schools are responsible for childcare services during the agreed opening hours, at least as a provider of last resort. In order to provide minimum services during the transition period after the introduction of the new law last August, the government should also extend these mandatory services to before- and after-school hours and to lunch breaks, with schools being free to outsource these care services to private providers. In a related vein, the government should undertake efforts to convince school boards to make school premises available for out-of school hours care services, which would allow such services to be offered at a relatively low price.

The marginal tax burden weighs on incentives to work longer hours

The incentive to work longer hours is weakened by relatively high marginal effective tax rates, with large effects on workers with relatively high labour supply elasticity, such as second earners (Table 4.2). The impact is even greater when long-run effects are taken into account: households are likely to base their labour supply decision on the expected net tax burden over the life-time, including during retirement (Blundell and Macurdy, 1999).

Table 4.2. **Marginal effective tax rates for different income groups and family types**

In per cent

	2005	2006
2 adults, 1 income, with child(ren)		
Minimum plus	69.5	60.8
Modal income	70.0	71.0
Twice modal income	59.3	52.8
2 adults, 2 incomes, with child(ren), income of lowest earner rises		
Minimum plus + half minimum plus	35.3	35.8
Modal income + half modal income	38.0	39.8
Twice modal income + modal income	50.0	48.0

Note: The table indicates the evolution of marginal effective tax rates between 2005 and 2006 at various income levels and for two different family types. The "minimum plus" income level corresponds to 60% of the modal income (€ 24 956). The modal income level corresponds to the most frequent income across the income distribution. The figures do not include childcare benefits.
Source: Ministry of Social Affairs and Social Security.

Indeed, a static view of the tax burden indicates that only 4% of the working age population is subject to the highest statutory marginal tax rate; but when evaluated in net present value terms, a substantially larger group is subject to high marginal tax burdens, due to the evolution of income over the lifetime (Figure 4.6). Past governments have adjusted tax credits and income-dependent benefits so as to mitigate these negative effects (Box 4.1).

Figure 4.6. **Life-cycle marginal tax burden**[1]

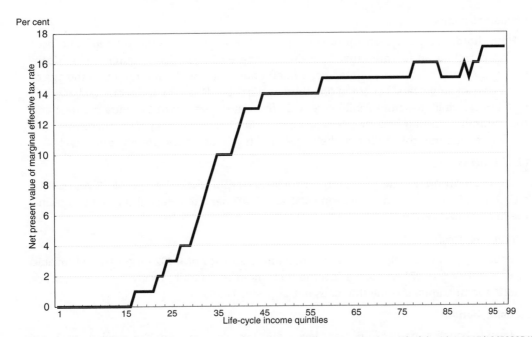

StatLink ⛓ *http://dx.doi.org/10.1787/186528354558*

1. The life-cycle marginal tax burden is calculated as the net present value of statutory marginal tax liabilities over the life-cycle (age 16-91) as a percentage of the net present value of income at a certain quintile. This assumes that an individual does not change the income quintile over the life cycle and that tax liabilities remain at their 2005 level. The net present value assumes a real interest rate of 3% *per annum*.
Source: DNB Household Survey, Secretariat's calculations.

Box 4.1. **An overview of family-related tax credits and benefits**

Several tax credits and allowances are granted to Dutch households in order to provide income support and to lower the tax burden. Some of them are income-dependent, thereby raising the marginal effective tax rate. When they are, they usually depend on the household income and not on the individual income.

Tax credits

The general tax credit

The (non-refundable) general tax credit of up to € 2043 reduces the tax burden to zero for the first € 6 070 annual income. The tax credit of a non-participating partner is transferable if income is below € 6 070.

Work-related tax credit

The work-related tax credit (*arbeidskorting*) can be deducted from tax liabilities. It reaches a maximum of € 1 392 when annual income reaches € 18 382.

Combination tax credit + Additional combination tax credit

Employees with children below 12 years receive an additional tax credit of € 149. An additional tax credit of € 700 is available for the second earner with the lowest income in families with children below 12 years.

Children tax credit

For families with children below 18 years, a child tax credit is available up to a maximum of € 939 that tapers off above an annual family income of € 28 978.

Benefits

Childcare benefits

Households with children up to the age of 12 receive an income related benefit of € 2 712 per child up to an annual household income of € 130 000 to purchase childcare services. Above this income related benefit, all households with children up to the age of 12 receive an employers' benefit of one third of the costs. The maximum annual benefit is € 16 173 per child (assuming child care of 52 five-days weeks with 11 hours per day) and the minimum annual benefit is € 5 581 per child (5 days a week). The maximum and minimum amounts correspond to the lowest and highest income groups, respectively.

Child benefits

An unconditional benefit is granted for every child until the age of 18 years. The quarterly child benefit varies between € 285 and € 405 per child, depending on the age and the number of children.

Health care benefits

A single-person household receives a maximum subsidy of € 432 for an annual taxable income below € 26 071. A double-income household or a family receives a maximum of € 1 223 for an annual income that does not exceed € 41 880.

Housing benefits

Housing benefits are based on rent levels and taxable income of the previous year. An income-dependent standard rent is defined that sets the minimum amount of rent a household has to pay. The maximum eligible rent for housing benefits is € 621. Households are eligible for housing benefits if their income is lower than € 20 300 for a single earner, or € 27 575 for a household. Slightly lower thresholds apply for retirees. Finally, the amount of the subsidy depends on the number of persons living in the household and the household income.

However, the provision of generous social benefits (to address equity concerns) and their rapid tapering-off (to address budgetary concerns) keep the marginal effective tax rates at a high level, thus weakening work incentives.

The benefit system raises incentives to work part-time

Even taking into account recent reforms to curb the marginal tax burden, second earners in families with children continue to face marginal effective tax rates that are high by OECD standards (Table 4.3). This is mainly related to steep taper rates at which benefits such as housing and childcare are phased-out. The phase-out rate of childcare benefits has already been lowered, but the withdrawal rate for housing benefits continues to be high.

Table 4.3. **Marginal effective tax rates for part-time employees**

2005, different working-hours transitions, in per cent[1]

Change in working hours	Part-time (50%) to full-time						Part-time (33%) to part-time (66%)						Part-time (66%) to full-time					
	No children			2 children			No children			2 children			No children			2 children		
	Single person	1 earner married couple	2 earners married couple	Lone parent	1 earner married couple	2 earners married couple	Single person	1 earner married couple	2 earners married couple	Lone parent	1 earner married couple	2 earners married couple	Single person	1 earner married couple	2 earners married couple	Lone parent	1 earner married couple	2 earners married couple
Australia	32	33	32	62	57	41	45	40	30	72	76	53	31	31	31	54	52	35
Austria	45	45	45	45	45	45	36	47	36	41	62	36	45	45	45	45	45	45
Belgium	56	51	55	56	51	55	57	47	58	57	45	58	56	51	55	56	51	55
Canada	34	36	31	60	60	39	32	39	29	44	52	39	34	36	31	64	64	41
Czech Republic	28	36	28	58	43	34	34	52	26	43	59	42	29	33	29	62	55	36
Denmark	48	49	43	60	71	49	82	74	49	75	93	60	50	46	43	61	59	43
Finland	42	58	42	61	76	42	64	93	34	63	100	34	44	44	44	57	64	44
France	39	29	35	34	33	32	34	35	36	55	55	31	35	29	32	24	23	31
Germany	54	45	53	60	58	53	51	58	50	81	78	51	55	50	54	54	52	54
Greece	31	31	31	25	25	26	17	17	17	16	16	17	38	38	38	30	30	30
Hungary	49	49	49	47	84	49	31	36	31	41	75	31	57	57	57	57	57	57
Iceland	41	40	41	47	45	48	42	72	41	47	72	48	41	41	41	47	47	48
Ireland	30	44	30	80	56	30	49	91	25	53	74	25	30	24	30	71	52	30
Italy	37	40	37	34	31	43	35	25	34	3	–7	49	37	42	37	49	53	39
Japan	21	20	21	40	45	24	19	52	19	86	94	26	21	20	21	20	20	20
Korea	12	12	13	12	30	11	9	20	9	48	69	9	14	13	14	11	11	12
Luxembourg	37	44	33	23	50	33	51	96	28	60	110	21	41	25	35	27	19	35
Netherlands	**39**	**46**	**39**	**50**	**51**	**40**	**69**	**81**	**43**	**54**	**76**	**43**	**34**	**31**	**34**	**37**	**36**	**35**
New Zealand	36	63	24	79	78	26	63	80	22	87	89	40	30	54	25	70	67	25
Norway	36	36	36	36	51	36	38	70	31	65	90	31	36	36	36	36	36	36
Poland	35	53	35	89	60	37	65	63	35	94	81	45	35	35	35	57	58	35
Portugal	29	22	28	28	37	29	20	33	23	33	75	24	32	22	30	32	21	30
Slovak Republic	30	15	30	29	15	30	23	23	33	22	27	33	30	16	30	29	16	30
Spain	30	26	30	26	24	28	25	14	25	19	16	20	30	28	29	26	24	29
Sweden	35	45	35	51	54	35	57	82	35	52	92	35	35	35	35	49	39	35
Switzerland	26	47	26	38	56	25	64	91	24	75	97	37	25	29	27	31	37	25
United Kingdom	35	43	33	69	72	33	58	69	33	84	84	33	33	33	33	59	63	33
United States	29	23	29	46	47	30	32	37	29	41	44	38	29	24	29	46	48	29

1. Hourly earnings correspond to the AOW level throughout so that a half-time employee would have earnings equal to 50% of AW. Social assistance and any other means-tested benefits are assumed to be available subject to the relevant income conditions. Children are aged 4 and 6 and neither childcare benefits nor childcare costs are considered. In-work benefits that depend on a transition from unemployment into work are not available since the person changing working-hours is already in employment prior to the change. For married couples the percentage of AW relates to one spouse only; the second spouse is assumed to be "inactive" with no earnings in one-earner couples and to have full-time earnings equal to 67% of AW in two-earner couples. Figures for Ireland and Korea are based on the APW (Average Production Worker wages).

Source: OECD (2007), *Benefits and Wages*.

Phasing the housing benefits out more gradually is expensive and the incentive effect of a lower taper rate has to be matched against a higher tax burden through alternative forms of taxation. Given that the elasticity for women is typically much higher than for men (Evers, De Mooij and Van Vuuren, 2005) even small differences in marginal tax rates for second earners are likely to have substantial effects on female labour supply incentives. In this regard, current calculations suggest that a more gradual phase-out of benefits could be revenue-neutral through strong effects on raising labour supply (De Mooij, 2006).

Other elements in the benefit system are also reducing incentives for full-time participation. Marginal effective tax rates for part-time working second earners are increased by the fact that some social benefits – such as childcare, housing and health care allowance – are not granted on an individual basis but with respect to household income. Hence, in order to strengthen work incentives, social benefits should be granted on an individual income basis, which would help to lower marginal effective tax rates for second earners. Particularly, the tapering off rate for housing and child benefits should be reduced further. Moreover, certain work-related entitlements and tax credits could be conditioned on the number of hours worked as done in some other OECD countries.

The government is considering extending the work-related tax credit (*arbeidskorting*) in order to further reduce marginal effective tax rates. The measure will be targeted to workers with low-to-moderate incomes, so as to stimulate their labour participation. However, the fiscal cost of this measure equals a 1 percentage point increase in the overall marginal tax rate. The positive labour supply effect resulting from increasing the tax credit for low-income workers has to be set against the adverse effects related to the phase-out of the credit for workers with moderate incomes and possible adverse effects on participation resulting from measures the government needs to take to finance this extension of the tax credit. The net effect of these measures will depend on the labour supplys elasticity of the different groups concerned by the measure. In this regard, it appears that a small increase of the tax credit that applies across-the-board may have more favourable long-term effects on second earners and female participation than a large, targeted increase, as the phase-out would occur at an income range with particularly high labour supply elasticity (Table 4.4). Moreover, if these measures were to be financed by an increase in income taxes, the overall effect on total hours worked is expected to be

Table 4.4. **Long-term effects of extending the work-related tax credit**

In per cent, unless otherwise indicated

	Targeted tax credit	Across-the-board
Labour supply in total hours worked	−0.4	−0.3
Primary earners	−0.5	−0.2
Secondary earners	0.1	0.5
Single persons	−0.4	−0.5
Female participation rate (in per cent)	1.0	1.6
Employment	0.0	0.1
Low skilled	3.2	1.0
High skilled	−1.2	−0.3
Unemployment rate (in percentage points)	−0.4	−0.6
Low skilled	−0.7	−0.2
High skilled	−0.3	0.0

Note: Both the increase in the targeted tax credit and in the across-the-board tax credit are assumed to bear the same fiscal costs.
Source: De Mooij, 2006.

negative, in both cases, as the positive labour supply effect at lower earnings is not sufficient to compensate the adverse effect of the general increase in marginal tax rates. The government should therefore seek alternative ways to reduce the marginal tax burden. Instead of extending the work-related tax credit, it could; for instance, lower statutory tax rates (see the discussion below). Alternatively, the government could finance such a measure by phasing-out some of the existing tax expenditure instead of raising general income taxation.

Statutory marginal taxes also reduce work incentives

The present government has stated in its Coalition Agreement that there is a need to continue lowering the high marginal tax burden. However, a main concern with respect to lowering taxes is whether such measures will be self-financing through an increase in labour supply. If not, strengthening labour supply incentives through changes in the tax code may require off-setting measures to ensure a revenue-neutral package. In order to address these issues, the Council of Economic Advisors (2005) recommended the introduction of a flat tax system, combined with a phasing-out of certain tax expenditures in order to finance the reduction of the marginal statutory tax rate across the board (Box 4.2).[8] Such a general overhaul of the tax system would help to restore labour supply incentives for women who currently face the highest marginal tax rates, but would also lower the marginal tax burden, even for lower income people. Over the life-cycle, the introduction of a flat tax would help to decrease the tax burden

---

Box 4.2. Proposal for a flat tax

As a stand-alone measure, a revenue-neutral flat tax runs the risk of increasing the marginal tax rate for certain groups with relatively high wage elasticity in their labour supply, such as women and older workers (Keen, Kim and Varsano, 2006).[1] Without off-setting measures, such a flat tax rate needs to be 37.7% (Table 4.5, column 1). This is 3 percentage points higher than the lowest tax bracket; hence reducing low-wage earners' incentives to supply labour (De Mooij, 2006). Many offsetting measures could be implemented. In the following, the case of a 1 percentage point higher VAT rate and phasing out the transferability of the general tax credit is considered. This would allow a flat tax rate of 36%, slightly higher than the currently lowest rate in the tax code; such a rate would imply lower marginal tax rates for all employees earning more than € 17 046, i.e. a bit more than half of all tax payers, but should help raising hours worked by around 4% (i.e. 1.8 h/week). More importantly, these measures are likely to increase the labour supply, particularly of females, who currently face steep marginal effective tax rates.[2] At the same time, the reduced marginal tax burden allows for lower labour costs, which should further expand labour utilisation through lower structural unemployment (Table 4.5, column 2). Using only one of the suggested compensatory measures would allow a smaller decrease in the marginal tax burden (Table 4.5, column 3 and 4) but would still lead to an increase in labour supply for all or most groups. A more radical approach would be to abolish most tax expenditures (including a reform of taxation of housing wealth and tax exemptions for pensioners), which could create budgetary scope to further reduce the flat rate to 28% (Council of Economic Advisors, 2005). Such a measure would also address some of the income distribution concerns as mortgage deductibility is mostly enjoyed by relative well-off households. Nevertheless, the reduction in marginal tax rates has to be set against an increase in after-tax income inequality.

Box 4.2. **Proposal for a flat tax** (cont.)

Table 4.5. **Labour supply and employment effects of alternative tax reforms**

	1	2	3	4	5	6
Female participation rate	0.12	7.07	−1.77	5.42	−1.66	5.30
Labour supply in hours	0.08	0.73	1.08	1.89	1.16	1.81
Primary earners	0.03	0.07	1.32	1.42	1.35	1.38
Secondary earners	0.12	3.43	0.03	3.58	0.15	3.46
Singles	0.07	0.25	1.05	1.37	1.12	1.30
Share of high-skilled labour supply[1]	0.01	0.01	0.85	0.88	0.87	0.86
Producer wage	−0.30	−1.10	−2.04	−3.44	−2.34	−3.14
Low skilled	−0.28	−0.97	0.10	−1.15	−0.18	−0.87
High skilled	−0.32	−0.15	−3.06	−4.54	−3.38	−4.21
Employment in enterprises	0.08	0.86	1.48	2.42	1.56	2.34
Low skilled	−0.01	0.68	−1.80	−1.13	−1.81	−1.12
High skilled	0.11	0.93	2.69	3.73	2.80	3.62
Unemployment rate[1]	0.01	0.02	−0.13	−0.10	−0.12	−0.11
Low skilled	0.03	0.03	−0.43	−0.37	−0.40	−0.39
High skilled	0.01	0.01	0.07	0.09	0.08	0.08
Share of long-term unemployment[1]	0.06	0.06	−1.03	−0.91	−0.97	−0.97

1. Percentage points.
Note: The following tax reforms are considered:
1) Higher VAT rate by 1 percentage point and lower income tax by 0.7 percentage points across the board.
2) Remove transferable credit for non-participating partners and lower income tax by 1 percentage point.
3) Flat tax of 37.7% to replace current progressive income tax structure.
4) Sum of the three columns (= flat tax rate of 36%).
5) Flat tax rate of 37% financed by an increase of the VAT rate by 1 percentage point.
6) Flat tax of 36.7% financed by a phase out of the transferability of the general tax credit.
Source: CPB calculations.

1. Besides lowering the marginal tax burden, a flat rate system has often been advocated on the basis of its administrative simplicity (Hall and Rabushka, 2007), thereby lowering the overall burden of the tax system.
2. The high marginal effective tax rates for women are mainly the result of high phase-out rates of income dependent benefits. Nevertheless, a lower statutory marginal tax rate would also help lowering the effective marginal rates for women.

substantially both for low and for high income groups, while it would increase it only moderately for medium-income households (Figure 4.7). Such a shift in the life-cycle tax burden would raise total hours worked by 6-8% (depending on the rate of the flat tax, see Annex 3.A1), which is more than suggested by a static analysis of changes in marginal income taxes alone. The flat tax proposal would have an even stronger impact if combined with measures to remove or phase-out certain tax expenditures, such as the mortgage interest rate deductibility or reduced tax rates for pensioners, as this would allow introducing a flat tax at a lower rate.

Other factors contributing to short working hours

In addition to the preponderance of part-time female participation, there are other factors contributing to short working time in the Netherlands. The average work week for full-time (prime-age) employees is short by international standards and its length has declined by around 4 hours since the mid-1980s for both men and women (Table 4.6). At unchanged employment rates, a return to the length of the standard full-time working

Figure 4.7. **Life cycle burden: actual system *vs.* flat tax**[1]

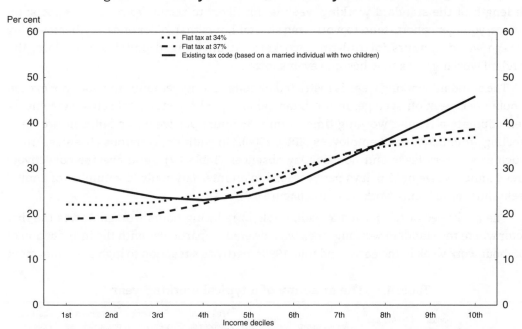

StatLink ᵐˢᵖ *http://dx.doi.org/10.1787/186530023345*

1. See Annex 3.A1 in the previous chapter for details on the calculation of life-cycle tax burden. The flat tax proposal is financed by an increase of consumption taxes, compared with the actual situation. A flat rate of 34% requires an increase of the consumption tax by 3 percentage points, a flat rate of 37% would require an increase by 1 percentage point.

Source: DNB Household Survey, Secretariat's calculations.

Table 4.6. **Average weekly hours for full-time employees at different ages**

	Total			Younger workers			Older workers		
	1985	1995	2005	1985	1995	2005	1985	1995	2005
Australia	n.a.	45.0	44.3	n.a.	41.5	41.2	n.a.	46.8	45.3
Austria	n.a.	41.4	43.4	n.a.	39.7	40.6	n.a.	44.2	45.2
Belgium	42.4	41.0	40.9	40.2	39.3	38.5	45.4	43.6	43.4
Czech Republic	n.a.	n.a.	42.7	n.a.	n.a.	41.1	n.a.	n.a.	42.5
Denmark	41.8	39.9	40.0	40.4	38.2	39.1	43.0	40.8	40.0
Germany	42.6	40.9	41.2	40.6	39.1	39.4	44.3	42.3	42.4
Finland	n.a.	40.2	40.4	n.a.	39.2	38.7	n.a.	41.6	41.3
France	42.2	41.5	40.8	40.2	40.0	37.7	46.0	43.3	43.1
Greece	45.8	45.5	44.7	44.8	44.8	44.4	47.8	47.3	45.7
Hungary	n.a.	42.2	41.0	n.a.	41.7	40.8	n.a.	41.8	40.9
Iceland	n.a.	47.9	n.a.	n.a.	48.3	n.a.	n.a.	45.2	n.a.
Ireland	45.0	44.6	41.2	41.7	41.4	39.5	49.8	48.8	42.5
Italy	41.5	41.8	42.0	41.0	41.6	41.3	42.3	42.8	42.9
Korea	n.a.	54.4	51.8	n.a.	52.3	50.0	n.a.	53.1	52.9
Luxembourg	42.0	42.1	40.5	40.6	40.7	39.6	44.7	44.1	41.3
Mexico	n.a.	49.2	n.a.	n.a.	48.4	n.a.	n.a.	50.2	n.a.
Netherlands	**43.0**	**40.5**	**39.3**	**40.2**	**38.6**	**37.6**	**45.0**	**43.1**	**39.9**
New Zealand	n.a.	45.2	44.3	n.a.	43.3	42.4	n.a.	45.4	44.8
Norway	n.a.	39.0	38.8	n.a.	38.0	38.0	n.a.	39.3	39.2
Poland	n.a.	n.a.	43.9	n.a.	n.a.	42.6	n.a.	n.a.	44.2
Portugal	n.a.	44.6	41.5	n.a.	43.8	41.1	n.a.	46.2	42.8
Slovakia	n.a.	43.2	41.8	n.a.	42.6	41.5	n.a.	42.8	41.8
Spain	n.a.	42.2	42.2	n.a.	41.7	41.6	n.a.	43.5	42.8
Sweden	n.a.	40.2	39.9	n.a.	39.3	38.2	n.a.	39.9	40.4
Switzerland	n.a.	n.a.	42.2	n.a.	n.a.	39.6	n.a.	n.a.	43.1
United Kingdom	44.1	44.7	43.0	41.8	42.1	40.6	43.7	44.5	43.1
United States[1]	41.1	41.9	41.6	40.2	40.1	39.7	40.9	41.7	41.7

n.a.: not available.

1. For the USA, hours worked are only available for dependent employees, not for self-employed.

Source: OECD, *Labour Force Survey*, 2006.

week prevailing in 1985 would increase average hours worked by 6.5%. Such an increase in the length of the standard working week is not likely to result from cohort effects: on average, younger cohorts tend to work even shorter hours than older ones, further lowering average working hours for full-time workers. At unchanged policies, therefore, the standard working week may become even shorter.

The standard working week is restricted by collective agreements and does not exceed 37 hours per week on average. In the financial and public sectors, collective agreements even stipulate a regular working time of only 36 hours per week for full-time workers, affecting around 37% of all employees (EIRO, 2006).[9] In addition, generous absentees' rules – such as sickness leave and non-holiday absences (Table 4.7) – and average collectively agreed annual leave of 25.6 days per year lead to an internationally low number of annual weeks, further reducing working hours (Figure 4.8).

The public sector has played a leading role in reducing hours worked. It was the first sector where the standard working week was lowered, in particular with the introduction of a 36-hour work week in the early- and mid-1990s, partly as a reaction to high unemployment

Table 4.7. **The anatomy of a typical working year**

	Annual working hours	Average weekly hours on all jobs	Annual weeks worked	Holidays and vacation weeks	Full week absences due to non-holiday reasons	Part-week absences due to non-holiday reasons	Absences due to sickness and maternity leave	Absences due to non-holiday reasons
	(a) = (b)*(f)	(b)	(f) = 52 − [(g) + (h) + (i) + (j)]	(g)	(h)	(i)	(j)	(h) + (i) + (j)
Austria	1 497	38.4	39	7.2	2.9	0.4	2.6	5.9
Belgium	1 451	36.3	40	7.1	2.4	0.5	2.1	5
Czech Republic	1 692	41.3	41	6.2	2.3	0.3	2.2	4.8
Denmark	1 410	36.3	38.9	7.4	2.8	1.1	1.8	5.7
Finland	1 491	38.8	38.5	7	2.8	1.6	2.1	6.5
France	1 467	36.2	40.5	7	2.2	0.5	1.9	4.6
Germany	1 480	36.5	40.6	7.8	1.9	0.3	1.4	3.6
Greece	1 816	40.7	44.6	6.7	0.2	0.2	0.2	0.6
Hungary	1 798	40.9	43.9	6.3	0.9	0.1	0.8	1.8
Iceland	1 714	43.2	39.6	6.1	2.8	1.6	1.9	6.3
Ireland	1 585	36.3	43.7	5.7	1.4	0.2	1	2.6
Italy	1 533	37.4	41	7.9	1.8	0.3	1	3.1
Luxembourg	1 582	37.9	41.7	7.5	1.4	0.2	1.2	2.8
Netherlands	**1 223**	**31.8**	**38.4**	**7.5**	**2.9**	**1**	**2.2**	**6.1**
Norway	1 339	37.3	36	6.5	4.8	1.1	3.6	9.5
Poland	1 817	41.8	43.4	6.2	1.2	0.3	0.9	2.4
Portugal	1 688	40.4	41.8	7.3	1.5	0.2	1.2	2.9
Slovak Republic	1 761	41.8	42.2	6.9	1.4	0.1	1.4	2.9
Spain	1 639	38.8	42.2	7	1.3	0.4	1.2	2.9
Sweden	1 349	38.1	35.4	6.8	4.2	1.8	3.8	9.8
Switzerland	1 586	37.5	42.3	6	1.7	0.9	1.1	3.7
United Kingdom	1 546	38.2	40.5	6.5	1.8	1.6	1.6	5
Total average	1 566.5	38.5	40.7	6.8	2.1	0.7	1.7	4.5
EU15 average	1 517.1	37.5	40.5	7.1	2.1	0.7	1.7	4.5

1. Annual leave entitlements and the number of public holidays are taken from the EIRO (2002), "Working Time Developments, 2002", *www.eiro.eurofound.ie/2003/03/update/tn0303103u.html*. In addition, hours not worked due to sickness and maternity leave, the second most important reason for absences, are corrected to account for an estimated 50% under-reporting in labour force Surveys compared to absences reported in health surveys and social security registers.

Source: OECD *Employment Outlook, 2004.*

Figure 4.8. **Average collectively agreed annual paid leave (2005)**

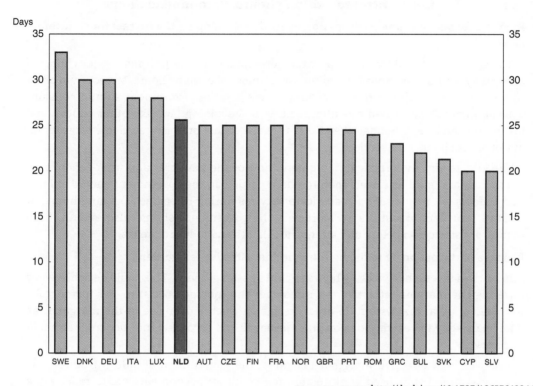

StatLink ⟨⟩ http://dx.doi.org/10.1787/186576423441

Source: European Industrial Relations Observatory, 2006.

rates at that time. An increasing share of public employees will be retiring soon, however, which could lead to the government being faced with increasing difficulties in hiring a sufficient number of employees in an already tight labour market (Ekamper, 2006; Høj and Toly, 2005). One way the government could ease the transition period is by introducing – at least for new hires – a longer standard working week, and phasing out the 4-days work week. Such a measure would also have a strong signalling effect for other sectoral agreements.

Despite short working hours, employers only make a limited use of overtime. In international comparison, the use of overtime is around 26 hours per worker per year, well below the more than 90 hours for the average European employee (EIRO, 2003). Partly, this can be related to overtime regulation that continues to be strict in international comparison despite some simplifications that have been introduced recently. The strictness concerns in particular the short time span over which deviations from regular working hours are permitted. Total working time cannot exceed 48 hours per week over a 16 weeks period, and 60 hours during one week, whereas in countries with a more flexible regulation, an annual ceiling of the maximum working hours is defined. Moreover, a substantial overtime pay premium is commonly agreed upon in collective negotiations, even though no universal national standard exists (McCann, 2005). In addition, some collective agreements require that the work council gives prior approval to overtime, making the process overly bureaucratic and inadequate to abrupt changes in demand. To stimulate more flexible working hours, the government should introduce a system with annual ceilings for overtime, as practised in France and Germany. In addition, the social partners should ensure a flexible approval process, which only in exceptional circumstances should involve others than those directly concerned.

Box 4.3. **Increase working hours: Recommendations**

Facilitate female full-time participation by further developing the market for childcare services

The government could help support the development of the new market for childcare services by setting provisions for a minimum number of opening hours. Moreover, in order to make supply of childcare services more flexible, the government should consider designating childcare as an essential facility in the zoning law, like other educational institutions and should undertake efforts to make school premises available for external out-of-school hours care services.

The effects and the practical implementation of the new pre- and after-school care requirements should be closely monitored. In particular, the government should enforce that schools are responsible for childcare services during the agreed opening hours, at least as providers of last resort. Moreover, the government should also extend these mandatory services to before and after-school hours and to lunch breaks.

Increase participation by reducing the marginal effective tax burden

Incentives to lengthen working hours should be strengthened. This could be achieved by lowering the marginal effective tax rates over the income spectrum, for instance by introducing a flat tax system. In order to finance such a decrease in the marginal tax burden, existing tax exemptions on state pensions and second-earner tax credits should be removed.

To lower high effective marginal tax rates, the government should introduce – as planned – an individualised work-related tax credit for second earners, to replace the current general tax credit. Moreover, the tapering off rate for housing and child benefits should be reduced further and certain work-related entitlements and tax credits could be conditioned on the number of hours worked as done in some other OECD countries.

To avoid the increase in marginal effective tax rates due to the recent childcare benefit reform, the government should consider introducing flat childcare benefits, irrespective of the family income. Alternatively, the government could consider conditioning the reimbursement rate for childcare services on the number of hours worked.

The marginal effective tax rate could also be lowered by reducing the rate at which certain benefits phase out, such as the housing or the children benefit. Alternatively, the authorities could consider broadening the existing work-related tax credit.

Strengthen incentives to negotiate a longer work week

In order to address pending problems in the public sector to find qualified employees in sufficient numbers, the authorities should consider negotiating longer standard working weeks for public sector employees, at least for new hires. This could also help the public sector to play a role model for other sectors.

Increasing the flexibility of working hours would also help expanding the average working week. This could be achieved by easing rules on overtime work further. In particular, the authorities should consider defining the maximum hours worked over a longer horizon (preferably over a year).

Notes

1. Policy makers in other European countries have followed the Dutch example, and favouring part-time employment is now part of the Lisbon agenda and the Broad Economic Policy Guidelines published by the European Commission to assess national reform strategies in EU member countries.

2. The law applies only to firms with more than 10 employees. Employers can refuse to convert an existing full-time into a part-time job if there is no staff available to cover the hours concerned or if this would lead to serious financial or organisational problems. In practice, this does not seems to be a strong restriction as in only few cases the original reduction in working hours has been denied (*Wet aanpassing arbeidsduur, Jurisprudentieonderzoek*, 2003). The influence of this law on the degree of part-time work is, however, ambiguous as the number of working hour reductions has not substantially increased (OSA Working Paper 2004-23). To some extent, the law may have confirmed an already existing practice.

3. See "promoting part-time work", Ministry of Social Affairs and Employment (*www.internationalezaken.SZW.nl*).

4. Compliance with these requirements will be monitored by local governments.

5. School is mandatory from age 5 on.

6. Teacher absences at short notice due to sickness or extra holidays that can be taken on short notice (the *ADV dagen*) occasionally force schools to send children back home unexpectedly. In principle, schools are obliged to find alternatives for such cases, but in practice they rely on the fact that most second earners work part-time.

7. Part of this program has been implemented under the initiative "*operatie Jong*", *http://www.operatie-jong.nl/*.

8. The proposed flat tax would include a tax credit to keep the progressivity of the tax system, at least as regards the average tax burden.

9. Reducing the length of the standard work week has become an objective for collective agreements with the onset of high unemployment during the 1970s and 1980s in an attempt to create jobs through work share agreements.

Bibliograhy

Albrecht, J.W., P.-A. Edin and S.B. Vroman (2000), "A cross country comparison of attitudes towards mothers working and their actual labour market experience", Labour, Vol. 14/4, pp. 591-608.

Arulampalam, W., A.L. Booth and M.L. Bryan (2005), "Is there a glass ceiling over Europe? Exploring the gender pay gap across the wages distribution", *ISER Working Paper*, No. 2005-25.

Blundel, R. and T. Macurdy (1999), "Labor supply: A review of alternative approaches", in: O. Ashenfelter and D. Card, Handbook of Labor Economics, Vol. 3, pp. 1559-1695.

Buddelmeyer, H., G. Mourre and M. Ward-Warmedinger (2005), "Part-time work in EU countries. Labour market mobility, entry and exit", *ECB Working Paper*, No. 460.

Council of Economic Advisors (2005), "De noodzaak van grondslagverbreding in het Nederlandse belastingstelsel", Tweede Kamer der Staten-Generaal, The Hague.

De Mooij, R. (2006), "Reinventing the welfare state", *CPB Special Publication*, No. 60.

EIRO (2003), "Overtime in Europe", available at: *http://www.eurofound.europa.eu/eiro/2003/02/study/tn0302101s.html*;

EIRO (2006), "Working time developments – 2005", available at: *http://www.eurofound.europa.eu/eiro/2006/08/update/tn0608101u.html*.

Ekamper, P. (2006), "Ageing of the labor market in the Netherlands: An overview", In T.S. Rocco and J.G.L. Thijssen (eds.). Older workers, new directions; employment and development in an ageing labor market. Miami: Center for Labor Research and Studies, Florida International University, pp. 41-54.

Evers, M., R. De Mooij and D. Van Vuuren (2005), "What explains the variation in estimates of labour supply elasticities?", *CPB Discussion Paper* No. 51.

Hall, R. and A. Rabushka (2007), "The Flat Tax", Hoover Institute.

Høj, J. and S. Toly (2005), "The labour market impact of rapid ageing of government employees: Some illustrative scenarios", *OECD Economics Department Working Paper*, No. 441.

Hunt, J. (1998), "Hours Reductions as Work-Sharing", Brookings Papers on Economic Activity, Vol. 1998/1, pp. 339-381.

Kapetyn, A., A. Kalwij and A. Zaidi (2000), "The Myth of Worksharing", IZA discussion paper, No. 18.

Keen, M., Y. Kim and R. Varsano (2006), "The 'Flat Tax(es)': Principles and Evidence", *IMF Working Paper*, No. 218.

McCann, D. (2005), "Working time laws: A global perspective", International Labour Organisation, Geneva.

Ministry of Social Affairs (2007), "Onbenut arbeidspotentieel", internal note.

OECD (2002), *Babies and Bosses*, Vol. 1.

OECD (2004), *Babies and Bosses*, Vol. 3.

OECD (2007), *Benefits and Wages*, forthcoming.

Rasmussen, E., J. Lind and J. Visser (2004), "Divergence in part-time work in New Zealand, the Netherlands and Denmark", British Journal of Industrial Relations, No. 42/4, pp. 637-658.

Román, A. (2006), Deviating from the standard: effects on labor continuity and career patterns, Dutch University Press, Amsterdam.

Visser, J. T. Wilthagen, Ronald Beltzer and E. Koot-van der Putte (2004), The Netherlands: from atypicality to typicality, in: S. Sciarra, P. Davies and M. Freedland (Eds.), Employment policy and the regulation of part-time work in the European Union: A comparative analysis, Cambridge University Press, pp. 190-223.

Zandvliet, K. (2002), "Vrouwen in hogere functies. Ontwikkeling benchmark", Report for the Ministry of Social Affairs.

ISBN 978-92-64-04076-2
OECD Economic Surveys: Netherlands
© OECD 2008

Chapter 5

Reaping the economic benefits
of immigration

The Netherlands has been an immigration country since the 1960s. In the past decade, poor economic integration and weak labour market performance of immigrants have induced policy changes aimed at making immigration policy more selective. More restrictive measures for family-related migration were introduced that led to a reduced inflow of immigrants from non-Western countries which, in combination with higher emigration of natives, resulted in net migration outflows in recent years. A new entry scheme was enacted to facilitate entry of high-skilled workers, but at this time it is difficult to ascertain whether this has led to an increase in the inflow of such workers. Rising labour market demand for low-skilled labour has mostly been filled by workers from the new EU member states, which seems to have had limited impact on labour market changes of native workers. This chapter examines how immigration policy could be further improved to meet the needs of the labour market and how the economic integration of immigrants could be enhanced.

This chapter deals with migration and integration in the Netherlands. First, a brief overview of migration in the Netherlands is given as well as an assessment of immigrants' labour market performance and economic impact. Next, recent changes in immigration policy are discussed. The chapter then deals with policies that affect the labour market integration of first and second-generation immigrants in the Netherlands. A set of policy recommendations concludes the chapter (Box 5.8).

Migration trends

Even though migration has contributed substantially to the labour supply, the share of foreign-born persons relative to the total population is not much different from that of neighbouring countries and much smaller than in Luxembourg and Switzerland and traditional settlement countries like Australia and Canada (Figure 5.1). Of the foreign-born persons, about two-thirds come from non-Western[1] countries, with the largest groups being of Turkish, Surinamese and Moroccan origins. Second-generation immigrants constitute some 10% of the Dutch population; those of German and Indonesian descents form the largest groups (Figure 5.2).

Figure 5.1. **Share of foreign-born in the labour force in selected OECD countries, 2005**

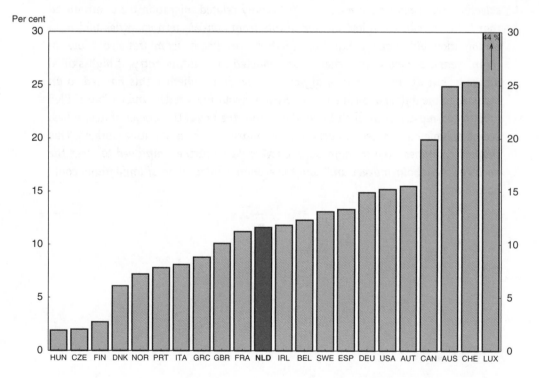

StatLink ⌨ http://dx.doi.org/10.1787/186601275652

Source: OECD Immigration Outlook, 2007.

Figure 5.2. **The population of first and second-generation immigrants in the Netherlands, 2006**

As percentage of the total

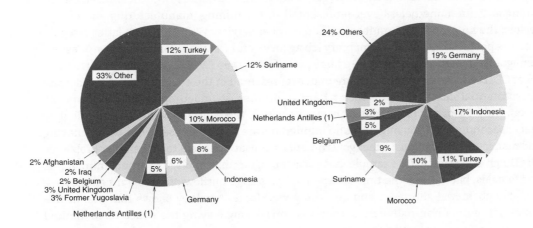

StatLink 🔚 http://dx.doi.org/10.1787/186603552247

1. Including Aruba.

Source: Statistics Netherlands and Secretariat's calculations.

Dutch immigration history after the Second World War has been heavily influenced by immigrants from former colonies and immigration through labour recruitment programmes. In the period 1945-65, 300 000 people moved from Indonesia to the Netherlands. At the same time, many Dutch nationals left the Netherlands, mainly for Australia and Canada, attracted by good economic prospects and stimulated by the government. It was only in the 1960s that the Netherlands turned from being an emigration to an immigration country, when foreign workers were recruited from the Mediterranean countries, initially mainly from Spain and Italy, later followed by workers from Turkey and Morocco, to alleviate labour market shortages in the booming Dutch economy. Return migration among Spaniards and Italians was significant, reflecting the economic development in their country of origin. On the other hand, return rates among Turks and Moroccans were far lower. Instead they preferred family reunification, leading to the immigration of spouses and children from these countries. It was only during the 1970s that the Dutch government started to discourage further immigration. Even though in the early 1980s many immigrant workers became unemployed due to industrial restructuring, immigration continued, largely based on family formation (marriage migration). Immigration from the Western colonies surged around 1975 when Surinam became independent and the Surinamese were given five years to choose between the Dutch and Surinamese nationality. Since the 1980s, immigrants that entered on humanitarian grounds have contributed significantly to the migrant population in the Netherlands. These immigrants came from many different countries; initially large groups came from Pakistan, Ghana and Sri Lanka, followed by refugees from Afghanistan, Iran, Iraq and the former Soviet Union and Yugoslavia. Most of these groups still have a substantial impact on the immigrant composition in the Netherlands.[2] Box 5.1 discusses where immigrants found employment.

Box 5.1. **Where are immigrants working?**

Although immigrants initially filled vacancies in sectors with shortages, such as manufacturing in the 1960s or horticulture in more recent years, the employment distribution of the foreign-born converges towards that of natives over time. Foreign-born immigrants are nonetheless over-represented in the mining, manufacturing and energy sectors, the hotel and restaurant sector and in other services (Table 5.1). The latter category includes people working for a temporary job agency or for cleaning companies; non-Western immigrants in particular constitute a large part of this group (WODC, 2007). Contrary to most other OECD countries, immigrants are under-represented in the construction sector despite the substantial shortages in this sector. Immigrants are also under-represented in the public sector. Only 3% of top management positions within the central government are filled by first or second-generation migrants and immigrants are under-represented in policy-making and management positions. Other government organisations seem to face similar problems. The Dutch police force, for example, has special programmes in place to attract immigrants and females, but at the same time is experiencing a large outflow of immigrant employees, despite substantial shortages and an ageing workforce. A survey shows that one in five policemen with a non-native background is considering leaving the police force; limited career opportunities seem to be a major cause.

Table 5.1. **Employment of foreign-born by sector**

2003-2004 average, percentage of total foreign-born employment

	Agriculture and fishing	Mining, manufacturing and energy	Construction	Wholesale and retail trade	Hotels and restaurants	Education	Health and other community services	Households	Administration and ETO	Other services
Austria	1.2	22.3	*8.8*	*14.4*	*12.0*	4.2	*8.8*	(0.4)	2.9	25.0
Belgium	1.2	17.3	6.9	13.6	*7.4*	6.2	*10.7*	0.6	9.1	*27.1*
Canada	1.2	*19.8*	6.0	14.1	*7.8*	5.5	9.6	...	3.6	*32.5*
Czech Republic	3.7	29.9	8.8	*18.2*	*4.6*	5.1	6.1	...	4.5	*18.9*
Finland	...	20.1	5.1	*14.5*	8.9	6.8	*13.6*	...	...	26.9
France	1.9	14.6	*10.3*	11.9	*5.9*	6.0	9.7	*5.8*	6.8	*27.2*
Germany	1.3	*32.0*	*6.4*	12.9	7.6	3.9	*10.1*	0.7	3.3	21.9
Greece	6.1	*16.3*	27.3	11.4	*9.2*	2.7	2.4	*13.4*	1.4	9.7
Ireland	2.2	16.6	8.4	11.5	13.2	6.4	*12.5*	...	2.9	*25.4*
Japan[1]	0.5	*58.7*	1.8	13.1	[1]	...	...	...	...	*25.9*
Luxembourg	1.0	*10.5*	16.0	*12.2*	*6.0*	1.9	6.3	4.2	12.2	*29.8*
Netherlands	**1.5**	***20.4***	**4.5**	**15.0**	***8.2***	**5.4**	**12.2**	...	**4.6**	***28.2***
Norway	...	13.7	4.5	12.6	8.6	8.0	20.7	...	3.7	27.0
Spain	*6.0*	13.6	16.3	12.2	*12.0*	3.6	*3.7*	12.2	2.0	18.5
Sweden	0.6	17.2	2.7	12.1	*6.6*	10.8	18.6	...	3.9	27.5
Switzerland	1.1	19.7	*8.4*	*15.2*	7.3	6.1	*13.4*	1.3	3.4	24.1
United Kingdom	0.4	11.8	4.3	13.6	*9.0*	8.4	*14.5*	*1.0*	5.2	*31.9*
United States	*2.5*	*14.3*	9.6	13.0	11.9	16.4	...	...	2.5	*26.6*

Note: The number in italics indicates the sectors where foreign-born are over-represented (*i.e.* the share of foreign-born employment in the sector is larger than the share of foreign-born employment in total employment). The sign ... indicates that the estimate is not reliable enough for publication.

1. Data refers to June 2002. The "Hotels and restaurants" sector is included in the "Wholesale and retail trade" sector.

Source: OECD *Employment Outlook*, 2007.

Recent developments

In 2003, net migration flows turned negative in the Netherlands for the first time since the 1960s, driven by a simultaneous decrease in immigration and increase in emigration (Figure 5.3). The economic downturn starting in 2001 was relatively strong and employment opportunities deteriorated quickly.[3] At the same time, social and political attitudes towards migration changed rapidly, causing migration policy to become stricter in the area of asylum migration and family related migration, in practice mostly affecting immigration from non-Western countries. Consequently, both the number of non-Western immigrants went down and the number of emigrants leaving the Netherlands went up. The largest share of non-Western immigrants leaving were Antilleans, whose Dutch nationality allows them to re-enter, and Somalis, who moved to other countries, mainly the United Kingdom. In addition, the number of Dutch-born emigrants went up strongly, probably reflecting the more adverse economic development relative to other countries. On balance, 50 000 more people born in the Netherlands left than returned in 2006, up from just over 10 000 in 1999.[4] More recently, the number of workers from the new EU member states filling low-skilled positions increased rapidly, reflecting on rising labour demand and the loosening of restrictions for labour mobility from these countries (see section on migration policy); these developments have taken place despite the high unemployment rates of immigrants already living in the Netherlands. In 2007, the government decided to regularise approximately 30 000 illegal immigrants who entered under the pre-2001 asylum policy, but had not left the country.

Impact and performance of migrants

Immigrants have added considerably to the productive capacity of the Dutch economy. In 2006, nearly 19% of the workers in the Netherlands were either first or second-generation immigrants. While the economy-wide benefits of this labour supply inflow are large, the gains for the native population are much smaller; most gains accrue to immigrants themselves in the form of labour income. Despite popular belief, there seems to be few signs of immigrants having a negative effect on the natives' labour market performance. Empirical studies suggest that effects on wages and (un)employment are generally negligible (Box 5.2).

As immigrants may differ from natives in their labour market behaviour, their presence potentially "greases the wheels" of the labour market. Through their high responsiveness to economic opportunities offered by different geographical areas, they can contribute to the overall efficiency of the labour market, resulting in a lower structural unemployment rate (Borjas, 2001). However, given the rigidity of the Dutch housing market (addressed in the last part of this chapter), these gains might not (fully) materialise. Immigrants can also improve the functioning of the labour market through their lower reservation wages, which may help accommodate labour force shortages in specific sectors (see, for example, the economic surveys of the Czech Republic, Greece or Spain). However, strict sectoral wage agreements and minimum wage requirements are likely to dampen these beneficial effects in the Netherlands.

Can migration help alleviate the burden of an ageing population? Increased immigration might lead to an increased number of relatively young workers and, in the near term, such immigrants could contribute positively to public finances by lowering dependency rates. Indeed, projections by Statistics Netherlands show that without immigrants, the dependency ratio in the Netherlands would reach 27% in 2050 instead

Figure 5.3. **Immigration, emigration and the impact on population growth**

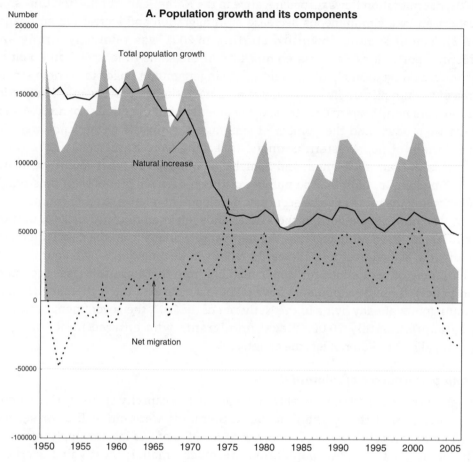

A. Population growth and its components

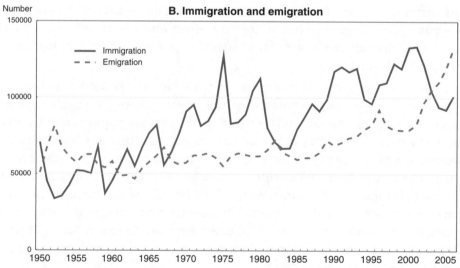

B. Immigration and emigration

StatLink ᴍ⩗ʟ http://dx.doi.org/10.1787/186605774054

Note: Immigration relates to all individuals arriving in the Netherlands whose arrival result in entries in a municipal population register (criteria is an expected residency of at least four out of the forthcoming six months). Emigration relates to all individuals departing from the Netherlands whose departure result in removal from those registers (criteria is an expected period abroad of at least eight out of the following twelve months). From 1977 the figures for emigration and net migration include administrative corrections. The components of total population growth may not always add up because of additional corrections not related to birth, death, immigration, emigration or administrative corrections.
Source: Statistics Netherlands.

OECD ECONOMIC SURVEYS: NETHERLANDS – ISBN 978-92-64-04076-2 – © OECD 2008

Box 5.2. **Economic impact of migration**

Immigration increases the labour force of an economy, thereby raising potential production. The distributional effects of immigration, however, are more complex. Theoretical models suggest that immigration creates only a small welfare gain for natives as the gains mainly accrue to the migrants in the form of wage income. Assuming that the capital stock is fixed, migration will put downward pressure on real wages of native employees. This, however, is more than offset by gains made by the owners of the capital stock. Together, this results in a small net total surplus (see *e.g.* Borjas, 1995). Empirical estimations for the Netherlands of a model which distinguishes between high and low-skilled workers are shown in Table 5.2. A 5% increase in the labour force increases production by around € 10 billion. However, the migration surplus that accrues to natives is much smaller, between € 0.3-0.5 billion. This model estimation, however, does not take into account possible complementary effects between foreign and local workers. When immigrants are complementary to natives or when economies of scale are present or dynamic efficiency increases, for example through innovation, the surplus created by immigrants can be far larger.

Table 5.2. **Simulation of economic effects caused by an inflow of workers in the Netherlands**

Redistribution effects of immigration assuming a fixed capital stock, in billions of euros[1,2]

	Only low-skilled immigrants	Immigrants' skills equal to residents	Only high-skilled immigrants
Change in total earnings of capital owners[3]	9.8	13.6	14.7
Change in total earnings of high-skilled residents	−3.3	−9.9	−12.6
Change in total earnings of low-skilled residents	−6.0	−3.4	−1.7
Change in total GDP	8.6	11.9	12.9
Immigration surplus[3]	0.4	0.3	0.5

1. It is assumed immigrants increase the labour force by 5%.
2. The GDP of the year 2000 is used (€ 402.6 billion).
3. Residents are assumed to own the entire stock of capital.
Source: CPB (2003), "Immigration and the Dutch Economy".

Another way immigrants might affect labour market changes of natives is through employment effects. Notably when wage flexibility is low, a labour supply shock can potentially lead to lower employment opportunities. However, a recent analysis of existing studies on the impact of immigration on employment shows a significant, but very small effect of immigration on employment of natives, which reinforces the broad consensus among economists that the impact of migration is rather benign (Longhi *et al.* 2006). The impact of immigration on employment is, however, bigger in the EU than in the US and greater for women than for men. This might be explained by the lower wage flexibility in the EU. Jean and Jimenez (2007) conclude that immigrants have no long-run impact on the unemployment rates of natives, but anti-competitive product market regulations and stringent employment protection magnify the persistence of an initial impact. No specific studies are available for the Netherlands on this subject.

Box 5.2. **Economic impact of migration** (cont.)

Besides employment effects, immigration can have an impact on wages. Longhi et al. (2005) shows that the impact of migration on wages is negative, but small. An empirical analysis for the Netherlands by Hartog and Zorlu (2005) concludes that immigrants in the Netherlands have a small negative effect on wages of low-skilled natives, while exhibiting a positive effect on wages of high-skilled natives (Table 5.3). These results seem to suggest that immigrants in the Netherlands are somewhat complementary to high-skilled natives, which also appears to hold in several other countries.

Table 5.3. **Effect of immigrants on wages of natives at different skill levels**

Elasticity of wage to the share of immigrants

	Low-skilled	Medium-skilled	High-skilled
Netherlands	**−0.036**	**0.031**	**0.058**
Norway, 1996	0.025	0.020	−0.013
Norway, 1989	0.070	0.092	−0.088
United Kingdom	−0.005	−0.014	0.018

Source: Hartog and Zorlu (2005).

of the current projection of 24%. However, durably tilting the population structure towards younger ages would require immigration levels that are unprecedented in most countries (OECD, 2007a). Moreover, in the longer term immigrants will also grow older and qualify for pension, health and long-term care spending. The fiscal contributions of immigrants are thus best looked at in net lifetime terms. For the Netherlands, the net lifetime fiscal contribution of an immigrant entering is estimated to be negative (CPB, 2003). This result largely depends on the labour market characteristics of the immigrants; an immigrant entering the Netherlands with the average labour market characteristics of a non-Western immigrant currently in the Netherlands would negatively contribute to public finances irrespective of the age of entry. On the other hand, a high-performing immigrant would contribute positively when entering between age 5 and 50. The negative lifetime fiscal contributions of large groups of immigrants are also found in similar calculations done for Denmark and Sweden, but contrast with results from Canada and Australia and the new immigration countries, Spain and Italy.[5] One reason behind the negative fiscal contribution of immigrants in the former countries seems to be the larger extent of fiscal redistribution, notably the lower tax contribution of low-income earners. As well, the weak tax contribution of immigrants reflects the poor labour market performance of immigrants relative to natives in these countries.

Indeed, labour market participation of immigrants is weak in the Netherlands. The average participation rate of the foreign-born is low on an international perspective, especially relative to that of native workers (Figure 5.4). The participation gap (between migrant and native workers) can almost entirely be explained by the low participation of non-Western immigrants; for this group, the gap is over 20 percentage points. In the traditional immigration groups, the participation rates of Turkish and Moroccan women are the lowest, with less than 30% of Moroccan women participating in the labour market for more than 12 hours a week. On the other hand, women from Surinam

Figure 5.4. **Participation rates of immigrants and natives in OECD countries, 2003**

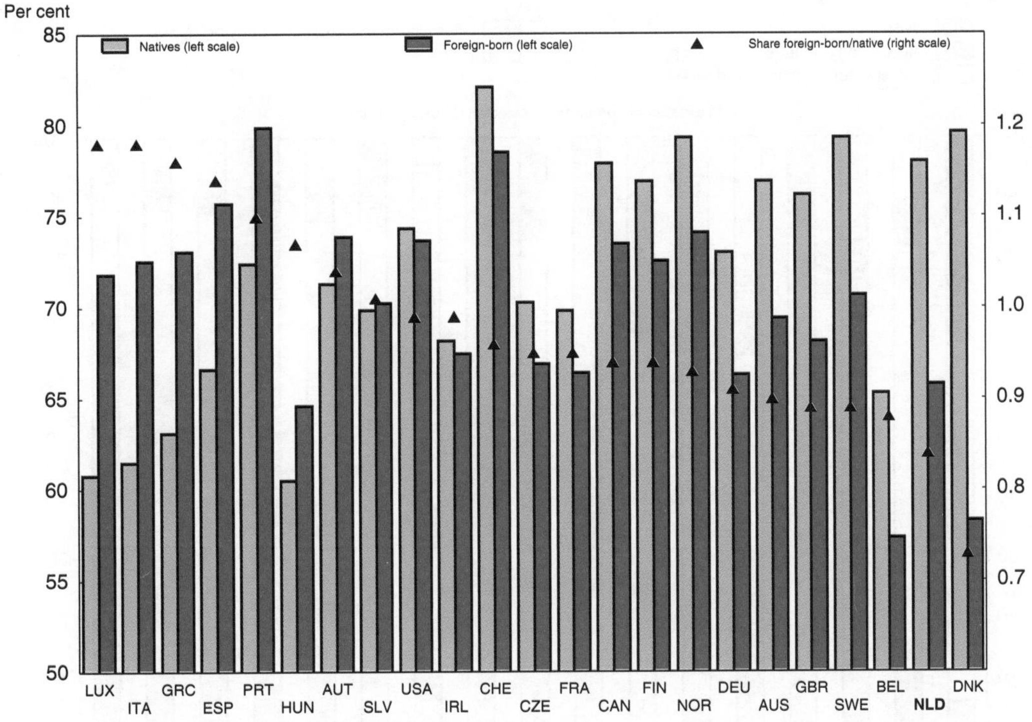

StatLink ⌷⌷⌷ http://dx.doi.org/10.1787/186614854551

Source: OECD, *International Migration Outlook*, 2006, Secretariat's calculations.

and the Antilles have higher participation rates than native women. Besides participating less on the labour market, immigrants are also more likely to be unemployed. Although the absolute unemployment rate of immigrants in the Netherlands does not stand out on an international perspective, the share of immigrants in unemployment relative to their share in the labour force was 2.3 times higher than that of natives in 2003-04, the highest rate among all OECD countries. Also, benefit dependency is significantly higher among immigrants, especially among those with a non-Western background. Where 15% of the native Dutch population receives some sort of social benefits (disability, unemployment or social assistance benefits), this number is twice as high for the Turkish and Moroccan population. Especially the share of persons relying on social assistance benefits is high for all groups of non-Western immigrants (Snel *et al.*, 2007).

An important factor influencing labour market performance is the nature of immigration. Countries attracting migrants with family-related, rather than work-related motives tend to show less favourable results (OECD, 2007b). The share of work-related immigrants in the Netherlands is not high by international standards and has increased only marginally over the last decade. The share of immigrants coming in for family formation or reunification is rather constant over the last decade, while the share of immigrants entering for asylum purposes has decreased sharply (Figure 5.5).[6]

Figure 5.5. **Immigration by category of entry**

Percentage of total inflows, 2004

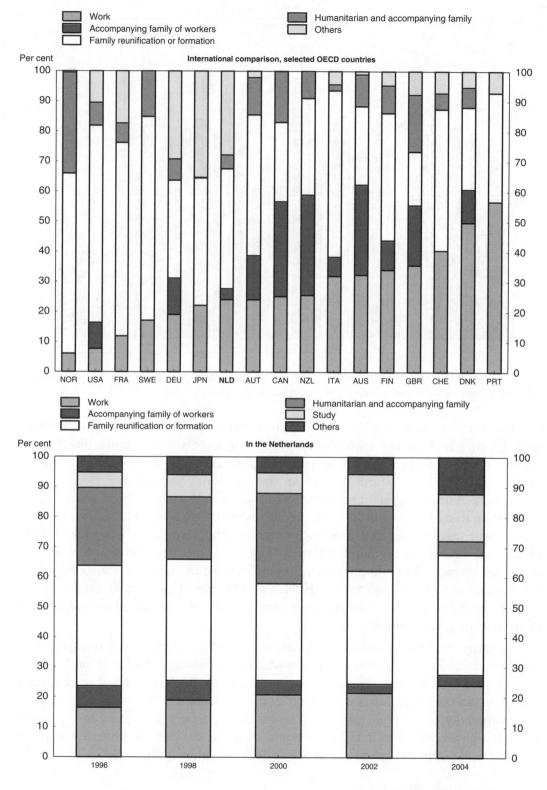

StatLink ᔕ http://dx.doi.org/10.1787/186648051588

Source: OECD, International Migration Outlook, 2006, Statistics Netherlands, Secretariat's calculations.

Migration policy

An important tool to influence the number and composition of migrants is migration policy. Since 2000, migration policy in the Netherlands has seen marked changes. On the one hand, immigration policy has become stricter; on the other hand, policy has become more selective towards (skilled) migrant workers (Table 5.4 shows major policy changes).

Table 5.4. **Overview of changes in Dutch immigration policy**

1995	Foreign Nationals Employment Act introduced
1998	Introduction of Civic Integration Programmes. *Immigrants coming to the Netherlands are obliged to follow a one-year language and integration course.*
2001	Introduction of the New Aliens Law 2000. *Asylum procedures are shortened and possibilities for appeal are curtailed.*
2003	Act on Dutch Citizenship introduced (RWN). *Mandatory language and culture test introduced for naturalisation.*
2004	Income and age requirements for family formation become stricter. *The minimum age is raised from 18 to 21 years for both parties and the income requirement is raised to 120% of the minimum wage.*
2004	Scheme for knowledge workers introduced. *Work permit requirement abolished for employees with an income above € 45 000 (€ 33 600 for workers younger than 30 years).*
2006	Law "Inburgering buitenland" introduced. *Passing a civic integration exam (culture and language test) is required before a visa (MVV) for the purpose of family formation can be obtained.*
2006	Policy view "to a modern migration policy" published. *Government presents plan to streamline and improve existing immigration policy.*
2007	Government decides on regularisation of (former) asylum seekers. *A regularisation programme is enacted for (former) asylum seekers that filed their asylum requests before 2001.*
2007	Restrictions lifted for workers from the new EU member states. *The work-permit requirement for workers from the ten EU member states that entered the EU in 2004 is abolished, but it remains in place for workers from states that entered the EU in 2007 (Romania and Bulgaria).*
2007	Social Economic Council presents advice on labour migration policy.

Due to rising concerns about economic and social integration, especially of non-Western immigrants, the government introduced several policies in recent years to stem the inflow of immigrants. The New Aliens Law 2000, enacted in 2001, shortened asylum procedures and limited the possibility for appeal, leading to more applications being rejected and a reduction of the inflow of asylum seekers. In 2004, the age requirement for immigrants who want to enter for family formation was raised from 18 to 21 years, while the income requirement was raised from 100% to 120% of the minimum wage. In 2006, a language and culture test was introduced that has to be taken in the country of origin before a visa for family formation can be obtained. These policies contributed to a halving of immigration from non-Western countries since 2001, while during the same period immigration from Western countries did not decline.

Concerning labour migration, policy has become more selective. The current system for labour migration in the Netherlands is demand-driven, similar to its European neighbours. Since the introduction of the Foreign Nationals Employment Act in 1995, migrant workers from outside the EEA are only admitted after a strict labour market test to verify that there is no job-seeker available within the Netherlands or the EEA to fill the job. In 2004, policy was introduced to facilitate the entry of knowledge workers. In 2006, restrictions on access for workers from the new EU member states were loosened and completely abolished in 2007 as a response to increasing labour market demand, as discussed in more detail below. When the new government reached its coalition agreement in February 2007, it decided to naturalise those persons who entered the Netherlands under the pre-2001 asylum policies and were still residing in the Netherlands in 2006. Further changes to immigration policy are being prepared as stated in the government's policy memorandum "Towards a modern immigration policy" (Ministry of Justice, 2006). Immigrants' contributions to society are a basic principle for the further modernisation of migration policy. The government aims to overhaul the large number of existing entry procedures and create a new entry system based on five "residence tiers".[7] In early 2007, the Social Economic Council (SER), an advisory body of social partners and independent experts, sent its advice on migration policy to the government stating the necessity to make policy for labour migrants more welcoming, especially for highly-skilled workers. The council proposes the introduction of a points system for highly-skilled migrants without an employment contract (SER, 2007).

Policies to attract high-skilled workers from outside the EU

In 2004, a scheme to attract highly-skilled workers was introduced following the advice of the Innovation Platform, established by the government to design policies aimed at stimulating innovation in the Dutch economy. Under this scheme, workers earning more than € 45 000 are exempt from the work permit requirement that is in place for workers from outside the EEA. A lower income requirement exists for employees under the age of 30; PhD students, post-doctorate researchers and professors under 30 face no income requirements. In addition, migrants under this scheme are granted a residence permit for 5 years (unless their contract has a shorter length) and there are no residence or work permit requirements for accompanying family members. Though the income criterion does not guarantee that migrants are actually working in knowledge-intensive sectors, a first evaluation shows that a large majority are.[8] In 2006, nearly 4 000 entry visas were granted to knowledge workers, making up for almost 10% of all entry visas distributed to immigrants from outside the EEA. Although the scheme is increasingly used it is hard to determine the net impact of the scheme, i.e. whether the scheme is successful in attracting additional skilled migrants, as not sufficient data is available to separate out the effects of other factors, such as the business cycle. Nonetheless, the new system does seem to be effective in reducing bureaucracy. To further increase the supply of highly-skilled workers, the government recently reduced restrictions on the labour market access of international students who graduate from Dutch universities (Box 5.3).

Additional measures aimed at attracting skilled workers are welcome as the average educational attainment of first and second-generation immigrants in the country is rather low (Table 5.5). Countries like the United Kingdom or Ireland have been more successful in attracting highly-skilled migrants, perhaps partly due to the more attractive tax rates in these countries,[9] although tax incentives for skilled workers are in place in the Netherlands. These tax breaks could, however, be made more transparent and targeted (Box 5.4). International comparison shows that migration policy can play an important role in determining the skill mix of immigrants. Traditional settlement countries other than the United States are examples in this respect. According to a 2001 census, 38% and 43% of the immigrants in Canada and Australia held a tertiary degree (OECD, 2007b). Contrary to schemes in these countries, the Dutch knowledge workers scheme is demand-driven in nature. Introducing a supply-led immigration scheme for workers without a job contract, as advised by the Social Economic Council, has several advantages. It would increase the direct availability of high-skilled workers for employers, as skilled workers without a labour contract can enter the country. Furthermore, it would increase the migrant worker's

Box 5.3. **Entry of foreign students**

International students graduating from Dutch universities are a readily available source of highly-skilled workers. These students are by definition highly skilled and already have experience with Dutch culture and language. The number of international students in the Netherlands is below the OECD average (Figure 5.6), but rising rapidly. Of the 10 800 study permits issued between January 2005 and August 2006 to students from outside the EEA, 23% were for Chinese nationals. Until recently, students from outside the EEA had to find a job within 3 months of graduation, which was rather strict given that the majority of native students do not find a job within this period. Following the advice of the Advisory Committee on Alien Affairs (ACVZ) and the Social Economic Council the search period has recently been extended to one year and income requirement for these groups under the knowledge worker scheme was lowered to € 25 000.

Figure 5.6. **International students as a percentage of all tertiary enrolment**
2002-04

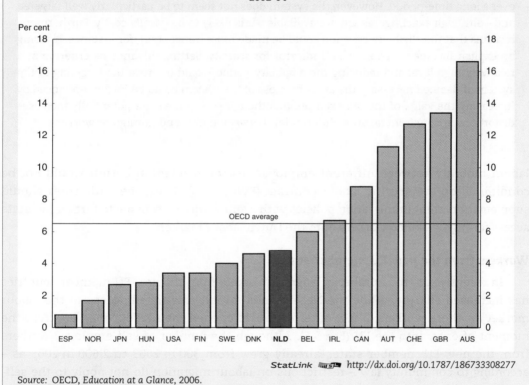

StatLink ᘈᗩᔿ *http://dx.doi.org/10.1787/186733308277*

Source: OECD, Education at a Glance, 2006.

Table 5.5. **Educational level of natives and immigrants (first and second generation) aged 15-64, 2005**

	Primary education (%)	Lower secondary education (%)	Higher secondary education (%)	Tertiary education (%)	Higher tertiary education (%)
Natives	8.0	24.9	41.0	17.1	8.9
Western immigrants	7.0	18.4	44.3	14.1	16.3
Non-Western immigrants	21.4	24.3	40.0	6.7	7.6

Source: Statistics Netherlands and Secretariat's calculations.

> **Box 5.4. Tax measures to attract highly-skilled workers**
>
> Tax incentives are in place to attract highly-skilled foreign nationals to the Netherlands. The so-called "30% rule" enables employers to pay foreign employees working in the Netherlands a tax-free allowance of up to 30% of regularly received employment income and a tax-free reimbursement of school fees for children attending international schools for up to 10 years. To qualify for the tax-free allowance the foreign employee needs to bring skills that are scarce on the Dutch labour market; the criterion is based on educational attainment, relevant work experience and the wage level. Although no explicit wage criterion is defined, private tax consultants suggest an annual salary of € 45 000 generally provides adequate proof to qualify for the latter condition. This scheme is similar to the scheme in Sweden that was introduced in 2001, where 25% of income is exempt from taxation. On the other hand, tax incentives for high-skilled foreign workers in Denmark are larger, but of a shorter duration. Here, foreign researchers or employees earning more than DKK 60 100 (around € 8 000) per month can profit from a flat tax rate of 25% for a maximum period of 36 months. The Dutch system seems attractive, as the tax-exemption is fairly large and can be received over a long time-period. However, the system does not seem to be particularly well targeted and – although exact figures are not available – it is likely to be fiscally costly. Furthermore, it seems that the eligibility criterion could be made more transparent, for instance, by using an explicit income criterion as an indicator for scarcity. Setting this income criterion at a relatively high level and reducing the eligibility period would improve the targeting of the system. If deemed necessary the attractiveness of the system could be further enhanced by increasing the value of the tax exemption, although such a measure potentially increases distortions arising from taxation differentials between native and immigrant workers.

labour mobility between different employers as the residential permit would not be conditional on the specific labour contract (PWC, 2006). Thus, the authorities should supplement current immigration policies with a supply-driven scheme to further facilitate access for highly-skilled workers onto the Dutch labour market.

Workers from the new EU member states

In recent years, the number of migrant workers from the new EU member countries has increased sharply. While the Netherlands initially restricted access to the labour market for these workers, a few other countries opened their labour markets from the moment of entry into the EU (Box 5.5). Although the number of self-employed workers from the new EU member states already grew from 300 in 2003 to 2 600 in 2005 as – according to community law – restrictions on labour migration do not apply to the self-employed, restrictions for employees were only eased in 2006. This was introduced in response to increased hiring problems faced by employers. These workers mainly took up low-skilled positions in sectors like horticulture, industry and international transport. In early 2007, the labour market test was dropped in 40 sectors, comprising about 70% of the Dutch labour market. As a consequence, the number of work permits granted for this group rose rapidly, reaching nearly 24 000 in the first quarter of 2007. First indications for the Netherlands show that the impact of these immigrants on the wages and employment of natives is minimal and the impact on production and public finances is positive. Furthermore, employers have reported their satisfaction about the loosening of the search requirements as it enables them to attract the necessary workers for vacancies for which they have difficulty finding Dutch workers.

Box 5.5. **Experience with workers from the new EU member states in the United Kingdom**

When the 10 new countries entered the EU in 2004, only three of the old EU members (Ireland, Sweden and the United Kingdom) fully opened their labour markets to these workers (Table 5.6). While in Sweden the number of workers from the new EU member states has remained extremely small, the United Kingdom and Ireland attracted many more. The inflow to the United Kingdom amounted to approximately 500 000 (1.3% of the UK working-age population) between May 2004 and late 2006. In addition, the booming Irish economy attracted many new immigrants from these countries; their share reached 2.8% of the working-age population in the second quarter of 2006. First evaluations show that the experiences in the United Kingdom are predominantly positive. The economy has benefited from the pool of new workers which contributed to prolonging their economic upturn, while there is no evidence that these immigrants have led to a rise in unemployment claims. Moreover, the inflow of workers is likely to have reduced the natural rate of unemployment in the UK over the past few years, either by filling skill gaps or by tempering wage demands of other workers. Given that these immigrants contribute more to supply than demand, at least in the short run, they are thought to have had a dampening effect on inflation (Blanchflower, 2007). A model simulation of the inflow of workers into the UK economy (Iakova, 2007) shows both total and per capita output and consumption increases in the medium-term, as immigrants become more productive over time and investment growth accelerates. Because the average age of the immigrants is relatively low, the fiscal expenditure to GDP falls and the dependency ratio declines.

Table 5.6. **Restrictions on workers from new member states**

	Entry of EU8 workers		Entry of workers from Bulgaria and Romania[5]
	May 2004 to April 2006	May 2006 to April 2009	2007-08
Austria	Restricted	Restricted	Restricted
Belgium	Restricted	Restricted	Restricted
Denmark	Restricted	Restricted	Restricted
Finland	Restricted	Open	Open
France	Restricted	Restricted[1]	Restricted[1]
Germany	Restricted	Restricted	Restricted
Greece	Restricted	Open	Restricted
Ireland	Open	Open	Restricted
Italy	Restricted	Open[2]	Restricted[3]
Luxembourg	Restricted	Restricted	Restricted
Netherlands	**Restricted**	**Open[4]**	**Restricted**
Portugal	Restricted	Open	Restricted
Spain	Restricted	Open	Restricted
Sweden	Open	Open	Open
United Kingdom	Open	Open	Restricted

1. Except for health care, transport, construction, hotels and catering.
2. Since July 2006.
3. Procedures for obtaining work permits are simplified in certain sectors.
4. Since May 2007. Between May 2006 and March 2007, the Dutch labour market was open to EU-8 workers in a large number of sectors.
5. Bulgarian and Romanian workers also face restrictions in Hungary and Malta.

Source: EU survey, European Commission and www.euractiv.com.

Reflecting continued tightening of the labour market, the work permit requirement for workers from the new EU member states (except Bulgaria and Romania) was completely abolished in May 2007, in effect granting these workers full access to all sectors of the Dutch economy. Although there is substantial uncertainty concerning the remaining pool of workers from these countries, anecdotal evidence suggests that it is becoming harder to find suitable workers. An illustrative example is the Dutch trucking sector; while concerns about crowding out of natives were high during previous years, the sector is currently facing substantial shortages. Should labour market shortages persist, the government could consider abolishing the work permit requirement for workers from Romania and Bulgaria in sectors that are facing shortages (such as transportation and horticulture), as was done in previous transition arrangements.

Temporary work permits and the labour market test

Persons from outside the EU who do not qualify for the knowledge workers scheme need a work permit. Since 2003, the number of permits has declined for this group, especially relative to the rising number of workers coming in from the new EU member states (Table 5.7). In about half of the applications a work permit is only issued after a labour market test has been passed proving that no job seeker is available within the EU. Generally, the employer has to post the vacancy at the Centre for Work and Income (CWI) and its European counterpart for five weeks and actively search during this period; thereafter, the CWI has five weeks to process the request.

Table 5.7. **Number of working permits (WP) issued as a share of working age population**

	WP total (%)	WP new EU (%)	WP non-EU + Bulgaria and Romania (%)
2001	0.30	0.07	0.23
2002	0.34	0.11	0.24
2003	0.38	0.13	0.25
2004	0.44	0.25	0.19
2005	0.46	0.29	0.17
2006	0.75	0.59	0.16
2007[1]	1.09	0.96	0.13

1. Annualised data based on Q1.
Source: Centre for Work and Income Netherlands and secretariat's calculations.

The bureaucratic way in which the labour market test attempts to shelter native workers from competition and the inability of the system to respond to unexpected peak demands makes the whole process time-consuming and costly. In addition, the large increase in the number of workers who entered once the labour market test was abolished in certain sectors for residents of new EU member states shows a high revealed demand for low-skilled workers in the Dutch economy. The government should therefore consider shortening the procedures, for example by abolishing the search requirement for the employer, and automatically granting a work permit if the employment agency does not find an appropriate candidate within several weeks of the request being posted at the CWI.

To meet demand for seasonal workers or to fill temporary shortages, temporary work permits can be a useful instrument. In its recent policy report on the future of immigration policy the government proposes introducing permits for temporary workers issued for a year with no right to family reunion or to draw social benefits; these may only be renewed from the country of origin (Ministry of Justice, 2006). If the migrants' return can be assured, for example by creating an opt-in' arrangement, where social security and pension premiums are paid out once the worker has returned to the country of origin, the fiscal risks of such an arrangement would be low and the work permit requirements could be loosened. However, imposing a strict maximum of one year might make the scheme too rigid to be attractive for employers.

Labour market integration

The contribution of immigrants to the economy depends to a large extent on their performance on the labour market, which is generally poor in the Netherlands; participation rates are low and unemployment rates high and volatile. As in other countries, the government has put increased emphasis on integrating newly arrived immigrants into society through language and culture courses.

In recent years the responsibility for integration has been increasingly put on immigrants themselves. It will be the immigrants' own responsibility to find, register and pay for integration courses and, eventually, pass a mandatory language and culture test. The new government that took office in 2007 stressed the importance and necessity of mandatory integration of new and old immigrants. Moreover, it has transferred integration policy to the Ministry of Housing and Spatial Planning, reflecting a stronger focus on neighbourhoods as the driver of integration.

Labour market institutions affecting employment opportunities of immigrants

Several labour market institutions appear to hamper the employment opportunities of outsiders on the Dutch labour market, of which migrants are an important group. In particular, high employment protection and minimum wages can make it more difficult to enter the labour market. The effects of these institutions are likely to be amplified because immigrants are probably facing some (statistical) discrimination on the labour market (Box 5.6).

Box 5.6. **Discriminating hiring practices could hamper labour market entry**

One reason for the observed difficulties of immigrants in getting employment may be discrimination, but evidence for it is not easy to obtain. Even in cases where immigrants have host-country qualifications, other factors such as lack of networks may also be present. This shortcoming is overcome in the ILO-sponsored and innovative large-scale experimental tests of hiring procedures carried out in a number of OECD countries over the last decade which suggest the existence of significant discriminatory behaviour on the part of employers (Simeone, 2005). Despite anti-discrimination laws, the tests for the Netherlands shows "net discrimination rates", defined as the net proportion of applications in which a person of immigrant background was eliminated from consideration in the application process, despite a *curriculum vitae* equivalent to that of a native-born applicant, to be nearly 50%. The measured discrimination could be partly "statistical": caused by employer's hiring decisions being based on average group characteristics when individual characteristics are not (easily) observable.

The impact of employment protection

An institution that could hamper labour market entry is employment protection legislation, which is strong in the Netherlands. Internationally, a weak positive correlation is found between the immigrants-to-native employment gap for low-skilled workers and the strictness of employment protection for regular contracts, which is weakly significant for low-skilled young men (Jean *et al.*, 2007). That employment protection seems to pose specific difficulties for immigrants can be seen in the fact that immigrants are more often working on temporary contracts than natives (Figure 5.7). Indeed, immigrants, especially those with a non-Western background, seem to function as a labour market buffer; the unemployment rate of this group went down from over 22% in 1996 to below 10% at the peak of the business cycle in 2001. During the economic downturn unemployment rose again rapidly, reaching 16.4% in 2005 (Figure 5.8). The authorities should therefore consider reducing employment protection for employees with regular contracts to share the economic risk more equally between native and immigrant workers.

Figure 5.7. **Share of temporary employment in total employment by birth status, 2005**

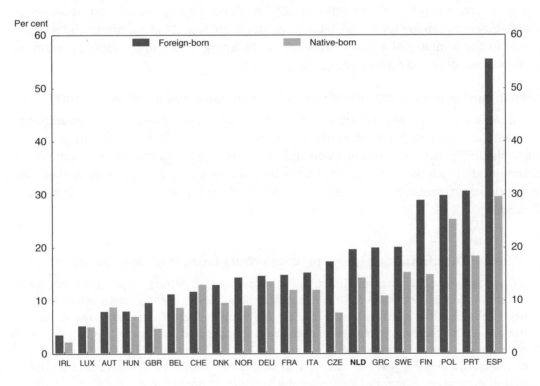

StatLink ⬛🔎 http://dx.doi.org/10.1787/186764543741

Source: OECD, *International Migration Outlook*, 2007.

The impact of minimum wages

High minimum wages are also likely to hamper an immigrant's employment opportunities (Causa and Jean, 2007). The minimum wage in relation to the average wage in the Netherlands is among the highest in OECD countries, while the relative participation rate of immigrants is among the lowest (Figure 5.9). Although empirical evidence of the

OECD ECONOMIC SURVEYS: NETHERLANDS – ISBN 978-92-64-04076-2 – © OECD 2008

Figure 5.8. **The unemployment rate of immigrants and natives over the cycle**

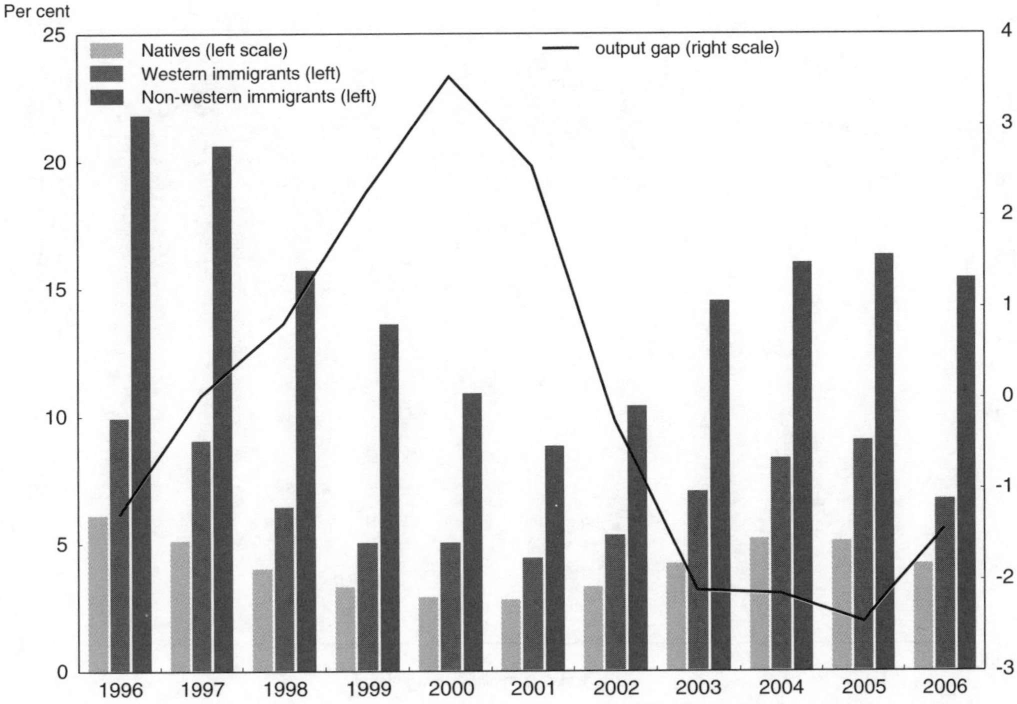

StatLink ⇒ http://dx.doi.org/10.1787/186812171177

Source: Statistics Netherlands and OECD Economic Outlook No. 82 database.

overall effects on employment is somewhat ambiguous, indications of an adverse effect for young workers and other vulnerable groups are stronger (OECD, 2006b; Neumark and Wascher, 2007). Indeed, minimum wages may function as a barrier to entry for low-productivity workers or workers suffering from (statistical) discrimination, as it limits their possibility to price themselves into the labour market. The latter is partly addressed through a lower minimum wage requirement for workers under the age of 23. The positive experience when the Netherlands lowered its youth minimum wages provides some indication of the adverse employment effects of minimum wages for the lower-skilled.[10] The government is planning to introduce targeted wage subsidies for people with a weak labour market attachment, which could help alleviate some of the barriers posed by the high minimum wage. However, reducing the overall level of minimum wages in the Netherlands would be a less costly and bureaucratic way to increase employment opportunities of (immigrant) workers with lower initial earning capacity.

Immigrant entrepreneurship

An alternative avenue into employment is provided by the possibility to become self-employed. The total number of self-employed immigrants with non-Western background more than doubled in the last ten years, a trend also observed in other OECD countries (OECD, 2007b). However, contrary to most other countries, the rate of entrepreneurship of immigrants in the Netherlands is still well below that of natives (Table 5.8). No formal obstacles to self-employment associated with the immigrant status are in place in the Netherlands, but immigrants face several specific difficulties. Firstly, access to credit can

Figure 5.9. **Minimum wage and immigrants' participation in OECD countries**[1]

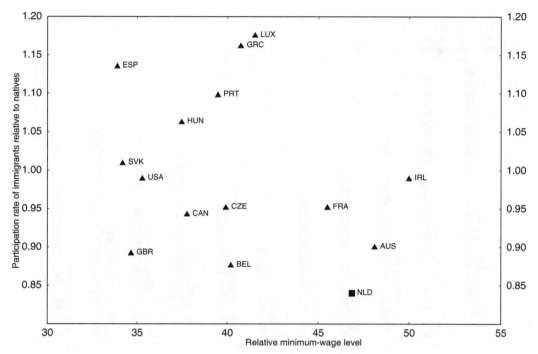

StatLink ⟨╦⟩ http://dx.doi.org/10.1787/186817114644

1. Relative minimum wage defined as gross earnings of full-time minimum-wage earners as per cent of gross average wages, 2004.

Source: OECD, *Taxing Wages* and OECD, *International Migration Outlook*.

Table 5.8. **Number of entrepreneurs relative to active labour force, 2005**

Natives	12.1%
Immigrants (first and second-generation)	10.4%
Western immigrants	11.8%
Non-Western immigrants	8.7%

Source: Statistics Netherlands and secretariat's calculations.

be problematic as the small size of the required loan and lack of collateral can make this market less interesting for private banks to serve. To address this problem, the government has allocated resources to create micro-credits for starting entrepreneurs. Another difficulty is that barriers to entrepreneurship are relatively high (Figure 5.10). This is related primarily to the high regulatory and administrative opacity, which can pose particular difficulties to entrepreneurs with weak language skills and smaller networks. Indeed, survey data shows that immigrants are twice more likely to experience (new) laws and government regulations as a bottleneck (EIM, 2007). The government has committed itself to further reduce the administrative and regulatory burden for companies; in doing this, the authorities should pay special attention to areas where immigrants in particular experience difficulties.

Figure 5.10. **Barriers to entrepreneurship in OECD countries, 2003**[1]

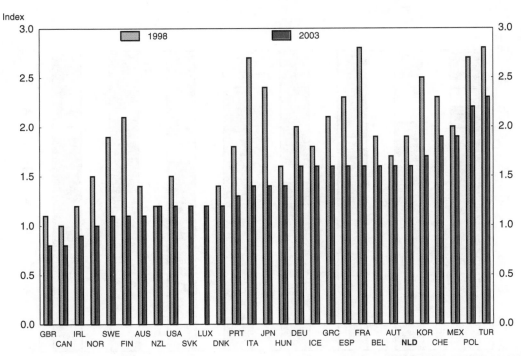

StatLink http://dx.doi.org/10.1787/187146163305

1. Includes regulatory and administrative opacity, administrative burdens on start-ups and barriers to competition.
Source: The OECD Product Market Regulation database.

The importance of early entry

Early entry into the labour market is important for successful labour market integration. Immigrants arriving during adverse economic conditions tend to take longer to find work and this weakens their longer term integration prospects (OECD, 2007b). Indeed, immigrants who arrived in the Netherlands during the economic slowdown in 2001 or 2002 are shown to have had a significantly lower probability of finding a job than those who arrived in 1999 when the economy was booming (WODC, 2007). This raises policy concerns for two specific groups where early entry should be promoted to improve labour market integration: female migrants entering for family formation or reunification and (former) asylum seekers. Employment rates for these groups are significantly lower than for other immigrants (Figure 5.11).

Non-Western migrants entering for family formation are obliged to take a language and culture test before obtaining a visa and are subsequently encouraged to follow language and integration courses upon arrival. However, employment rates of this group are low, especially for females. Analyses for Sweden have indicated that language courses shortly after arrival significantly enhance later employment prospects. However, there appear to be upper limits to the optimal number of hours; the disadvantage of prolonged learning is that it keeps the immigrants away from the labour market (OECD, 2007b). Although job-finding skills (*e.g.* job interviews) are a part of the integration exam in the Netherlands, the authorities should consider putting more emphasis on labour market participation through earlier entry. An option is to improve financial incentives for

Figure 5.11. **Source of income for the 1993 immigration cohort in 2003**

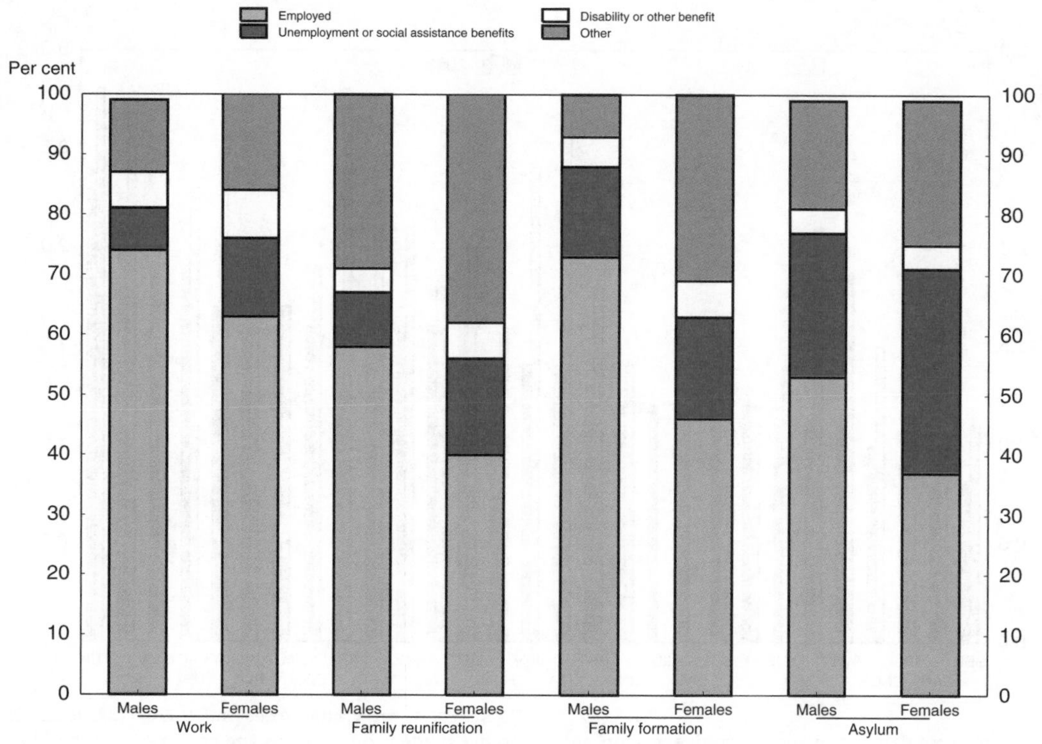

StatLink ⬛🔗 http://dx.doi.org/10.1787/187175287638

Source: Statistics Netherlands.

municipalities; as these migrants often do not receive benefits, the direct financial gains for municipalities when they find employment are currently limited.

Former asylum-seekers exhibit the worst labour market performance of all groups of immigrants, which could be related to their migration motivation. However, strict limitations to work are in place during the asylum procedures which, in combination with long procedures, have in the past led to lost economic potential, more so because asylum-seekers are often highly educated (Regioplan, 2007). In the Netherlands, asylum-seekers are not allowed to work during the first 6 months of the procedure so as to provide disincentives for economic migrants to use the asylum procedure as an entry route. After this period, the maximum number of weeks they can work per year was recently announced to be extended from 12 to 24. Although the asylum procedures have been sped up with the introduction of the new asylum policy, 9% of the asylum requests were not dealt with within the legal period of 6 months in 2006. Employment and schooling opportunities for asylum-seekers should be improved to allow for more rapid labour market integration. Full access to the labour market should be granted if no decision is made within 6 months and possibilities for (voluntary) work and schooling during the procedure should be improved.

Improving educational attainment

Education is an important determinant for labour market performance of immigrants. However, the level of educational attainment of non-Western immigrants in the Netherlands is low; this group is on average nearly three times more likely to have, at most, a primary education (Table 5.5). The Dutch educational system has an emphasis on supporting weaker pupils by calculating school funding in part based on pupils' socio-economic background. The educational attainment of new cohorts of second-generation immigrants has vastly improved over the last decade. However, when pupils with a Moroccan, Turkish or Surinamese background leave primary school they are on average still six months behind the average native student. Drop-out rates among immigrants are also higher than for natives (Box 5.7).

Box 5.7. **Reducing drop-outs**

A major concern in the Netherlands is the high drop-out rate of non-Western immigrants. In particular, first generation male immigrants from non-Western countries are over three times more likely to leave high-school without sufficient qualification (Table 5.9).* However, research based on a micro-database of 19 000 pupils that were followed since 1989 shows that the non-Western immigrants do not drop out more often than natives once other variables are controlled. Individual characteristics as well as educational and social characteristics of the family are important. Also, the probability to become a drop-out, increases if the school is situated in a more urbanised area and decreases when pupils attend mixed schools, where higher-level streams are also taught (Traag and van der Velden, 2007). The government has formulated extra measures to reduce the number of premature drop-outs. It has set targets to reduce the number of drop-outs in the 14 regions with the largest number of drop-outs by 10%. Furthermore, a law regarding "compulsory qualification" for everyone below the age of 18 is being drafted and a legal framework which will enable municipalities to apply more compulsion to bring youths between 18 and 23 back to work or training is being created.

Table 5.9. **Percentage of drop-outs for secondary education for natives, foreign-born and second generation**

	Male	Female	Total
Natives	2.5	2.2	2.4
Non-Western (first and second generation)	5.1	3.9	4.5
First generation	8.5	6.6	7.6
Second generation	3.6	2.8	3.2

Source: CBS integration monitor, 2006.

* A drop-out is defined here as a 23-year-old who left the educational system without a diploma of MBO level 2, Havo or VWO (considered as a starting qualification).

The importance of early education to combat language deficits

For immigrant workers in the 1960s and 1970s, learning the Dutch language was not encouraged and mother tongue teaching was widespread. The government now sees language attainment as a fundamental part of social and economic integration. However, language attainment remains a problem for many non-Western first and second-generation immigrants. Scores for language attainment at age 12 show a substantial gap, while language attainment of children of Western immigrants is comparable to that of natives (Table 5.10). The OECD PISA scores for reading indicate that language attainment among second-generation immigrants in the Netherlands is still significantly lacking at

Table 5.10. **Language proficiency scores at age 12**

Number of correct answers at final test primary school

	Male	Female	Total
Native	70	72	71
Western immigrants (first and second generation)	70	72	71
Non-Western immigrants (first and second generation)	62	65	63

Source: Statistics Netherlands and CITO.

the age of 15, but the gap is not larger than in neighbouring countries (Figure 5.12). Early education can be an effective way to prevent language problems at a later stage. Primary education, which includes kindergarten, is attended by practically everyone from the age of 4 and education is compulsory from age 5. However, attendance at educational pre-schools is voluntary and currently only 50% of the children within the target group attend, where the latter is mainly based on the educational attainment of the parents (Sardes, 2007). It is likely that non-attendance is disproportionally high among children of immigrants as the authorities have more difficulties in reaching the immigrant groups. The government has stated that it wants to reach 100% of the target group. Given the negative educational and economic consequences of language deficits, more actively promoting early education is indeed commendable. Making pre-school mandatory for all children with language deficits should be considered.

Figure 5.12. **Differences between the PISA reading scores[1] of natives[2]**

And those of children of immigrants, youth aged 15 years, 2003

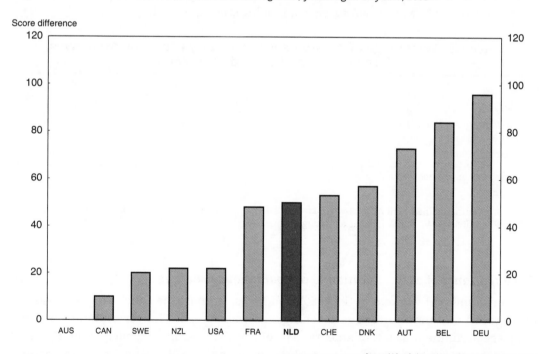

StatLink http://dx.doi.org/10.1787/187183102718

1. The mean score across all OECD countries was set at 500 points, with a standard deviation of 100 points.
2. "Natives" here refers to children with native-born parents.

Source: OECD *Employment Outlook*, 2006, calculations based on the OECD PISA database.

The adverse effects of early tracking

The achievement deficits with which immigrants and their children leave primary school also affect their further educational careers, as only just over 20% progress to education in the higher ranks of the general educational streams (*Havo and VWO*) during the third year of high school, compared to 46% for natives (SCP *et al.*, 2005). An important characteristic of the Dutch educational system is the tracking of pupils at the age of 12 based on the results of a comprehensive test. Although the advice given by the teacher on the bases of this test is not binding, in practice deviations from it are rare. Forms of early streaming are not uncommon, but many countries, like Canada, Japan, Norway, Sweden, the United Kingdom and the United States, do not track students at all during lower secondary education. Cross-country empirical research shows early selection generally leads to increased educational inequality and could even reduce average performance (see *e.g.* Hanushek and Wößmann, 2006). Analysis using the PISA-2003 data has shown that both early streaming and a high degree of stratification in the educational system decreases the ability to offset social inequalities. Given the weaker socio-economic position of immigrants, these aspects of the school system would negatively influence pupils from families with a migration background. In systems with a high degree of educational differentiation, parents from higher socio-economic backgrounds are in a better position to promote their children's chances than in a system in which such decisions are taken at a later age, and students themselves play a bigger role (OECD, 2005). Even though immigrants and their children in the Netherlands are initially more often streamed into low or middle-level learning programmes, they are more likely to continue their education at a higher stream afterwards. However, the share that eventually flows into tertiary education is still significantly below that of natives.[11] The Dutch educational system offers some flexibility to undo negative effects of early streaming at a later stage, but it is still likely to negatively impact both first and second-generation immigrant's educational performance. The authorities should take action to mitigate these potential negative effects of early streaming on the performance of pupils with a non-native backgrounds by postponing the age at which children are placed in different streams, encouraging schools to introduce or extend mixed-level education during the first phase of secondary education and by creating more flexibility to change streams at a later stage.

Clustering and housing policy

Another factor influencing social and economic integration of immigrants is geographical clustering, which potentially reduces the ability for creating social and work-related networks. Immigrants in the Netherlands are concentrated in the bigger cities; 39% of the non-Western immigrant population lives in one of the four biggest cities in the Netherlands compared to 13% for natives. Within cities, concentration is also visible on the level of the neighbourhood; in 2004, 20% of non-Western immigrants lived in a neighbourhood where over 50% of the population had a non-Western background (Table 5.11), often reflecting the availability of affordable (social) housing. Although on the national level no housing policy is aimed particularly at immigrants, many big cities strive to achieve a balanced neighbourhood. As around 30% of the total Dutch housing stock belongs to housing associations, with a concentration in the bigger cities, their assignation and (historical) building policies influence the neighbourhood mix. A large part of the social housing stock is only accessible to low-income earners and the awareness of the benefits of building for diverse income groups within the same neighbourhood is relatively

Table 5.11. **Percentage of natives and immigrants living in a neighbourhood with over 50% immigrants**

	1999	2004
Natives	1	1
Western immigrants	2	3
Non-Western immigrants	16	20

Source: WODC 2007, "Ontwikkelingen in de maatschappelijke participatie van allochtonen".

recent. The problem of deprived neighbourhoods is high on the political agenda. Upon taking office, the Dutch government created a new minister for "Housing, communities and integration", which has taken the initiative to work together with municipalities and housing associations to invest in the rehabilitation of the 40 most deprived neighbourhoods.

Indeed, the housing market is an important vehicle for integration, also by accommodating geographical and social mobility.[12] Although overall mobility on the Dutch housing market is close to the European average, mobility in the rental sector is far below, with waiting times for social housing equaling 3.4 years on average in 2004 and much longer in the bigger cities. These long waiting lists are caused by the large gap between actual rents paid and hypothetical market rents, as 85% of the rental market is subject to a price ceiling set by the central government (Ommeren, 2006). The marginal role played by the private rental market[13] is caused by the strict rent control, which makes it economically unrewarding for private investors to offer rental houses in medium and lower segments of the rental market. Also the interest deductibility on owner-occupied housing marginalises the private rental market in the Netherlands, since interest payments can only be deducted for owner-occupied housing. The government should consider scaling down housing policies that hamper mobility in order to improve the social and geographical mobility of migrants.

Box 5.8. Recommendations on migration and integration policy

Improving immigration policy to meet labour market needs

Improve selective migration policy by introducing supply-led scheme for employees

Although several selective migration policies have been introduced in recent years, the immigration system is generally demand-driven. To further enhance the pool of skilled workers in the country the authorities should introduce a scheme to facilitate supply-led migration, under which workers with desired characteristics would be granted a work permit without the *ex-ante* requirement of holding a job contract. Moreover, the tax incentive scheme for highly skilled foreign workers should be made more transparent and more targeted.

Consider introducing a transition scheme for workers from Bulgaria and Romania for sectors facing shortages

Restrictions on workers from the ten new EU member states were lifted recently. If shortages in specific sectors persist, the government could consider abolishing the labour market test in these sectors for workers from Bulgaria and Romania.

> Box 5.8. **Recommendations on migration and integration policy** (cont.)
>
> *Reduce bureaucracy in the labour market test required for work permits from outside EU*
>
> The labour market test should be simplified and shortened to increase the flexibility of the system. This can be done by abolishing the five-week search period for employers and reducing the processing time for the Center for Work and Income.
>
> **Improve labour market integration of immigrants**
>
> *Reform labour market institutions that hamper employment opportunities of immigrants*
>
> The authorities should consider reducing employment protection for regular contracts to share economic risks more evenly across the population. Minimum wages could be reduced to provide opportunities for immigrants with low (initial) earning capacity to price themselves into the labour market. When further reducing administrative and regulatory burdens for entrepreneurs, the authorities should give special attention to areas where immigrants experience difficulties.
>
> *Stimulate early labour market entry for groups with poor labour market performance*
>
> Asylum-seekers should be granted full access to the labour market if the asylum procedure takes longer than six months. Possibilities for (voluntary) work and schooling during the first six months should be improved.
>
> Consider more actively guiding women entering for family formation into employment at an early stage, for example, by increasing financial incentives for municipalities to activate this group.
>
> *Improve educational performance of immigrants*
>
> As early streaming in the Dutch educational system is likely to hamper the immigrant's educational career, the government should consider postponing the age a which children are placed into different streams, stimulating more mixed-level education during the first phase of secondary education and creating greater second-chance options for changing streams in later stages.
>
> *Reduce housing policies that lower geographical and social mobility*
>
> Reduce barriers to mobility in the housing market, most notably, rental regulation and transfer taxation, as they hamper the social and geographical mobility of immigrants.

Notes

1. When referred to Western immigrants in this chapter, the definition of Statistics Netherlands is used. This definition includes immigrants from Europe, North-America, Oceania, Indonesia and Japan (which are included because of the socio-economic and socio-cultural positions). Non-Western refers to other immigrants.

2. In 2006, the largest group of immigrants from former asylum countries was from the former Yugoslavia, constituting 3.4% of the total foreign-born population.

3. The unemployment rate has a significant negative impact on net migration. In fact, Jennissen (2003) shows that for the Netherlands, 76% of the fluctuation in the net migration rates in the 1960-1998 period can be explained by unemployment, GDP per capita and four dummy variables for specific events.

4. Popular countries for emigration of the Dutch-born are Belgium, Germany, the United Kingdom, the Dutch Antilles, Spain and the United States.

5. The long-term estimates for Spain and Italy are more tentative given the recent nature of mass migration into these countries.

6. With the exception of the labour participation of males coming in for family formation who work as often as native males.

7. These tiers are: I) exchange and temporary workers, II) Students and (low) skilled workers, III) Highly-skilled migrants, IV) Family and V) Humanitarian reasons.

8. The ICT, industry and higher education sectors were the biggest users of the scheme.

9. Besides tax rates many other factors influence the attractiveness of an economy for highly-skilled workers, like labour market opportunities, wage levels, language, certain public goods particularly valued by immigrants, etc.

10. Dolado *et al.* (1996) show that when the Netherlands lowered youth minimum wages in 1981 and 1984, the youth share in employment in low-skilled occupations rose relative to the overall youth share.

11. Of the non-Western immigrants, 19% eventually flow into higher vocational training (bachelor's degree) compared to 32% for natives. The inflow into university (bachelor's and master's degree) education is 9%, compared to 18% (SCP, WODC and CBS, 2005).

12. Given the presence of short-term benefits and longer-term cost, an immigrant's optimal strategy may be to locate in an enclave community initially, and then move out once a certain amount of assimilation has taken place (Cutler *et al.*, 2007), making mobility on the housing market an important requirement for social integration.

13. In total, the privately owned rental market comprises 11% of the total housing stock.

Bibliography

Blanchflower, D.G., J. Saleheen and C. Shadforth (2007), "The impact of the recent migration from Eastern Europe on the UK economy", *IZA discussion paper series*, No. 2615, Bonn.

Borjas, G.J. (1995), "The economic benefits from migration", The Journal of Economic Perspectives, Vol. 9, No. 2, pp. 3-22.

Borjas, G.J. (2001), "Does immigration Grease the Wheels of the Labour Market?", Brooking paper on Economic Activity, Vol. 1, pp.69-119.

Causa, O. and S. Jean (2007), "Integration of immigrants in OECD countries: do policies matter?", *OECD Economics Department Working Paper No. 564*, OECD, Paris.

CPB (2003), Immigration and the Dutch Economy, special publication 47, The Hague.

Dolado, J. *et al.* (1996), "The Economic Impact of Minimum Wages in Europe", Economic Policy, Vol. 11, No. 23, pp. 317-372.

EIM (2007), "Monitor nieuw ondernemerschap 2006", EIM, Zoetermeer.

Hanushek, E.A. and L. Wößmann (2006), "Does educational tracking affect performance and inequality? Differences-in-differences evidence across countries", The Economic journal, 116, pp. 63-76, Blackwell Publishing, Oxford.

Hartog, J. and A. Zorlu (2005), "The effect of immigration on wages in three European countries", Journal of population economics, 18, Bonn, pp. 113-151.

Iakova, D. (2007), "The macroeconomic effects of migration from the new European Union members states to the United Kingdom", *IMF working paper 2007/61*.

Jean, S., O. Causa, M. Jiminez and I. Wanner *et al.* (2007), "Migration in OECD countries: labour market impact and integration issues", *OECD Economics Department Working Paper No. 562*, OECD, Paris.

Jean, S. and M. Jimenez (2007), "The unemployment impact of immigration in OECD countries", *OECD Economics Department Working Paper No. 563*, OECD, Paris.

Jennissen, R. (2003), "Economic determinants of net international migration in Western Europe", European Journal of Population, Vol. 19, pp. 171-198.

Longhi, S., P. Nijkamp and J. Poot (2005), "A meta-analytic assessment of the effect of immigration on wages", Journal of economic surveys, Vol. 19, No. 3, Oxford.

Longhi, S., P. Nijkamp and J. Poot (2006), "The Fallacy of 'Job Robbing': A Meta-Analysis of Estimates of the Effect of Immigration on Employment", Tinbergen Institute Discussion Paper, No. 06-050/3.

Ministry of Justice (2006), "Towards a modern migration policy", policy note, The Hague.

Neumark, D. and W. Wascher (2007), "Minimum Wages and Employment: A Review of Evidence from the New Minimum Wage Research", NBER *Working Paper* No. 12663.

OECD (2005), "Education at a Glance", Paris.

OECD (2006a), "International Migration Outlook 2006", Paris.

OECD (2006b), "OECD Employment Outlook 2006", Paris.

OECD (2007a), "Economic Outlook", Vol. 2007/1, No. 81, Paris.

OECD (2007b), "Key findings on the labour market integration of immigrants", Jobs for immigrants, OECD, Paris.

Ommeren, J. van (2006), "Verhuissmobiliteit: een literatuurstudie naar belemmeringen tot verhuizen", Vrije Universiteit, Amsterdam.

PWC (2006), "Internationaal vergelijkend onderzoek naar systemen voor arbeidsmigratie", PricewaterhouseCoopers Advisory N.V., Rotterdam.

Regioplan (2007), "Vluchelingenwerk integratiebarometer 2006", Amsterdam.

Sardes (2007), "Landelijke Monitor Voor- en Vroegschoolse Educatie 2007", Utrecht.

SCP, WODC en CBS (2005). "Jaarrapport Integratie 2005", Den Haag/Voorburg.

Snel, E., J. de Boom, G. Engbersen and A Weltevrede (2007), Migration and migration policies in The Netherlands 2005, Dutch SOPEMI-report 2005, Rotterdam Institute of Social Policy Research, Rotterdam.

Social Economic Council (SER) (2007), "Advies arbeidsmigratiebeleid", Den Haag.

Simeone, L. (2005), "Discrimination testing based on ILO Methodology", mimeo, International Labour Office, Geneva.

Traag, T. and R. van der Velden (2007), "Voortijdig schoolverlaten in het vmbo", Sociaaleconomische trends, Issue 2, Statistics Netherlands, Heerlen.

WODC (2007), "Ontwikkelingen in de maatschappelijke participatie van allochtonen", WODC, The Hague.

OECD PUBLICATIONS, 2, rue André-Pascal, 75775 PARIS CEDEX 16
PRINTED IN FRANCE
(10 2008 01 1 P) ISBN 978-92-64-04076-2 – No. 55917 2008